THE ROMAN STOICS

Gretchen Reydams-Schils

THE ROMAN

STOICS

SELF, RESPONSIBILITY, AND AFFECTION

The University of Chicago Press   CHICAGO & LONDON

Gretchen Reydams-Schils is an associate professor in the Program of Liberal Studies and in the Department of Philosophy at the University of Notre Dame.

The University of Chicago Press, Chicago 60637
The University of Chicago Press, Ltd., London

24 23 22 21 20 19 18 17 16 15   3 4 5 6 7

ISBN-10: 0-226-30837-5 (cloth)
ISBN-13: 978-0-226-71026-6 (paper)

Publication of this book was made possible in part by a subvention from the Institute of Scholarship in the Liberal Arts, University of Notre Dame.

Library of Congress Cataloging-in-Publication Data

Reydams-Schils, Gretchen J.
The Roman Stoics : self, responsibility, and affection / Gretchen Reydams-Schils.
p. cm.
Includes bibliographical references and index.
ISBN 0-226-30837-5 (alk. paper)
1. Stoics. I. Title.
B528.R49 2005
188—dc22
2004014640

∞ The paper used in this publication meets the minimum requirements of the American National Standard for Information Sciences—Permanence of Paper for Printed Library Materials, ANSI Z39.48-1992.

TO LUC

Contents

Acknowledgments

The idea for this project first arose in a memorable seminar, "Roman Identity and the Coming of the Greeks," directed jointly by Anthony A. Long and Thomas N. Habinek in the Classics Department at the University of California, Berkeley, in the spring of 1990. The next phase involved a presentation of a broader sketch of the initial ideas at the Notre Dame Philosophy Colloquium in the fall of 1995. Publication of this outline of the project followed in the journal *Dionysius* 16, in December 1998, after a research stay at the Fondation Hardt in Geneva, Switzerland, in the spring of 1996, which was made possible by a grant from the Institute of Scholarship in the Liberal Arts of the University of Notre Dame. The final push came in a third wave, which included a presentation at Richard Sorabji's London seminar in the spring of 2000; a fellowship at the Center for Hellenic Studies in Washington, D.C., in 2000–2001, with leave support also granted by the University of Notre Dame; another presentation at the Notre Dame Philosophy Colloquium in the spring of 2002; and the publication of an earlier version of the second chapter of this study in *Oxford Studies in Ancient Philosophy* 22, in the summer of 2002. The manuscript was submitted for review to the University of Chicago Press in June 2003 and approved for publication that same year. Publication was made possible in part by a subvention from the Institute of Scholarship in the Liberal Arts, University of Notre Dame.

Given that this project has been under way for fourteen years, more people need to be thanked than I can remember. The published articles and the notes in each chapter mention the colleagues and friends who were helpful for particular aspects. But in addition to those mentioned already, Elizabeth Asmis, Christopher Gill, Carlos Lévy, and David Sedley deserve special thanks because they provided helpful insights and support throughout the entire process. In an act of spontaneous and remarkable generosity, Kenneth Reckford offered to read the entire manuscript in its penultimate version, and his expertise in Roman literature and poetry of the imperial era was a welcome complement to the interests pursued here. Most recently Julia Annas and Brad Inwood gave feedback on some of the arguments, and both readers for the University of Chicago Press provided very detailed and helpful reports.

I benefited from superb assistance by the librarians of the Fondation Hardt, the University of Notre Dame Libraries, the Center for Hellenic Studies, and the École Normale Supérieure in Paris. Freelance editor Lisa Harteker was indefatigable in pushing me toward spelling out the connections in my writing and arguments, and Michael Siebert, graduate student in the Notre Dame M.A. Program in Early Christianity Studies, provided assistance with proofreading and checking references. Finally, I would also like to express my gratitude to Senior Editor Susan Bielstein, her assistant Anthony Burton, and their team at the University of Chicago Press for seeing this project through to publication.

The book is dedicated to my spouse, together with whom, every day anew, I try to put theory into practice.

Abbreviations

ANRW: Aufstieg und Niedergang der römischen Welt. Edited by H. Temporini. Berlin: de Gruyter, 1972–.

D.L.: Diogenes Laertius. *Lives of Eminent Philosophers.*

LS: A. A. Long and D. N. Sedley. *The Hellenistic Philosophers.* 2 vols. Cambridge: Cambridge University Press, 1987.

RE: Paulys Real-Encyclopädie der classischen Altertumswissenschaft. Stuttgart: Metzler, 1864–.

SVF: Stoicorum Veterum Fragmenta. Edited by H. von Arnim. 3 vols. Leipzig: Teubner, 1903–5.

The names and works of ancient authors have been abbreviated according to standard lists, such as in The Oxford Classical Dictionary.

Introduction

"Take care that you are not turned into a Caesar." This is a concern that most of us would have no occasion to worry about (unless our mental health was seriously impaired). But it is odd even for the person who did raise it, Marcus Aurelius (*Meditations* 6.30). Why would a Roman emperor resist "being turned into a Caesar" and refuse to identify himself with his sociopolitical role? And why is Marcus Aurelius talking to himself? Apparently his *Meditations* served no other purpose, initially, than this soliloquy: they acquired the title "To Himself" in the tradition and display his self-assessment by monitoring his progress and strengthening his resolve to do the right thing.[1] But what kind of progress could the man who was supposed to be the symbol of supreme power have had in mind?

Through Roman adaptations of Stoic doctrine, a model of the self emerged in which the self functions as a mediator between philosophical and traditional values. The Roman Stoics, one of whom was Marcus Aurelius, successfully established a connection between a philosophical ideal and ordinary, everyday-life circumstances, and between a community shaped by Stoic wisdom and society as it is. How did they do this? Many scholarly accounts of the Stoic self focus on a limited range of doctrine, mostly psychology and the theory of "roles" (*personae*). But in order to

1. Brunt 1974.

understand how the Stoic self could function as a mediator between different value systems, we need, on the one hand, to adopt a broader perspective, paying attention not only to more aspects of Stoic theory, such as physics and the function of time and memory, but also to the literary modes of writing, as the embodiment and expression of a specific self unfolding. On the other hand, this study has a more circumscribed focus than others that provide excellent treatments of notions such as personhood and personality,[2] will,[3] and subjectivity.[4] The aim here is twofold: to let the Roman Stoics' self arise out of a comprehensive analysis of their extant philosophical work and to conduct that analysis from the vantage point of the specific question of social embeddedness. Such an approach yields a Stoic self that is constituted by the encounter between challenges and normative expectations.

Taken together, the Roman Stoics Seneca, Musonius Rufus, Epictetus, and Marcus Aurelius provide this picture of the self.[5] The more elusive Hierocles, about whom little else besides his fragmentary writings survives, and who is likely to have been a contemporary of the Roman Stoics, to a large extent corroborates and sometimes complements the information the others provide. Cicero, a hinge figure between Republic and Empire in Rome, also plays a crucial role. Admittedly, he would not have described himself as a Stoic. But he has some clear sympathies with this school of thought, and in cases in which he does not, he remains a valuable catalyst for the stances that Roman Stoics developed. Even if his rendering of Stoic doctrine was not entirely correct in all instances, his wording itself did influence later authors, because what Cicero presented as Stoic material came to be accepted as such. In particular his *Tusculanae Disputationes, De Finibus,* and *De Officiis* are very important sources, not only for the views that they recorded but also for the manner in which they framed the questions.

For my purpose, the common traits of the Roman Stoics matter more than their individual differences, though there will be occasions to point out divergences. I use the designation "Roman Stoics" or "later Stoics" not in the traditional sense, which would place them in the last phase of a three-part

2. For an excellent study on personality and self, see Gill 1996. See also Gill 1991.

3. See Dihle 1982; Inwood 2000; Kahn 1988; Voelke 1973. For up-to-date analyses of Stoic themes that are relevant to this study and for bibliography, see Inwood 2003, esp. ch. 2, "The School in the Roman Imperial Period," by Christopher Gill; ch. 9, "Stoic Ethics," by Malcolm Schofield; and ch. 10, "Stoic Moral Psychology," by Tad Brennan.

4. On this, see Gill, forthcoming. See also Sorabji 1999.

5. See also Reydams-Schils 1998.

development of Early, Middle, and Late Stoicism, but rather in a more limited, pragmatic sense that covers a group of Stoic thinkers who, in one way or another, all had to come to terms with the sociopolitical challenges of imperial Rome. To ask what they have in common is a methodological approach that explores what one can learn about general trends in Roman Stoicism by taking these thinkers together as a group. It is to claim, not that the differences are not significant or meaningful, but that the present inquiry does not focus on those differences.

I will argue that the Roman adaptation of originally Greek Stoic doctrine shows a distinctive pattern of emphasizing social responsibility. Not only do the later Stoics tend to emphasize ethics over logic and physics (though Seneca, of course, did write his *Naturales Quaestiones*), but they also devote most of their attention to an ethics *in* action. Although we do not have as much evidence for this emphasis in the early Hellenistic period, this lack does not necessarily imply a radical break within Stoicism, much less a betrayal of original intentions. If there is a shift within Stoicism—and that is a matter that our fragmentary early evidence may never allow us to settle—it is one that continues to operate within distinctive Stoic parameters.

The parameters are distinctive enough to allow us to determine what Roman Stoicism could accomplish that other, competing philosophical models could not. Scholars such as Pierre Hadot, Michel Foucault, and Anthony A. Long have eloquently highlighted the common thread of the care for the self in the Socratic project and in subsequent ancient thought.[6] Against the backdrop of this common theme, I want to bring out the features that are specific to the Stoic approach. Hence Plato and his Socrates are important to my argument for three reasons. The first is that I want to modify Hadot's claim that the full notion of the care of the self (as that notion is envisaged in this study) is already present in Plato's works. Second, the Roman Stoics rely heavily on *their version* of Socrates' behavior as a moral exemplum that is meant to underscore their claims about the good life. Finally, the Platonism that is contemporary to Roman Stoicism is its main antagonist and rival. Discovering how these Stoics transform the Socratic paradigm and constitute an alternative to Plato and the Platonists is as important as acknowledging the continuity.

As leitmotif for the questions pursued here we could use Hierocles' famous image of concentric circles (Stobaeus 4.671.7–673.11 Hense = LS57G).

6. See P. Hadot 1993b, c; also I. Hadot 1969, 179–90; Long 2000, 2002; Rabbow 1954. For other works on the importance of Socrates for the Stoics, see Alesse 2000; Döring 1979, 1974. For Michel Foucault's work, see ch. 1 of this study. See also Vander Waerdt 1994; Gourinat 2003.

At the center we find an individual, who could be any one of us—or more precisely, we find the mind (διάνοια). Around this core or center are drawn ever widening circles, starting with one's body and the things that serve its needs, ranging over one's immediate family, extended family, neighbors, tribe, city, country, and culminating in the widest circle of universal humanity. Hierocles enjoins his readers to draw the circles that are further removed from the center ever closer. If we keep "reducing the distance of the relationship with each person," ideally we would come to feel as close to every other human being as we are to ourselves or to the people who traditionally are closest to us.

What does this image imply? First, we need to get a better sense of this core that finds itself situated at the center of the concentric circles. In order to do that, in the first chapter I seek to understand the relationship between a human being's ruling principle and the divine principle that governs the universe as a whole. The main reason for this step in the argument is that the Roman Stoics posit an even broader community beyond universal humanity, one that includes both gods and humans and has the cosmos as its setting. Second, the image of concentric circles implies that the self for the Roman Stoics is fundamentally embedded: a Stoic turns inward only to surrender herself to a higher, divine principle that transcends the individual, and, even more surprisingly perhaps, given our notion of "being Stoic," a Stoic also turns inward for the sake of reaching out to others.

Upon closer scrutiny Hierocles' image also implies a tension between what ideally should happen, namely, the drawing closer of circles that are further removed and an ever increased harmonization, and what ordinarily happens in human society. In ordinary circumstances, all these different relationships create considerable conflicts and normative tensions. How then is one supposed to handle these conflicts without giving up on the relationships altogether? What kind of self would be best equipped to handle such a challenge? These questions provide the framework in which the notion of the self as a mediator arises.

Hierocles does not intend his readers to skip the more intimate relationships in favor of a common good as shared by all human beings, nor to replace traditional relationships with philosophically anchored friendships. This stance is motivated by the Roman Stoic view of the importance of sociability in all of its manifestations for the life of virtue. In the second chapter of this study I draw out the theoretical underpinnings and implications of sociability as the Roman Stoics construe it. The third chapter focuses on the political dimension of this sociability, whereas the two closing chapters take a closer look at traditional relationships that the Roman Stoics managed to retrieve for the life of virtue, with the fourth chapter focusing on parenthood and the fifth on marriage. This study thus reverses the Stoic progression from self to god and universe in order to devote more attention to the inner circles of relationships than has been customary in much of the scholarship on Stoic social ethics.

The results of this inquiry run counter to at least two currently circulating representations of the Stoics, one as evasive and the other as conformist. The Roman Stoics are often charged with leading a double life, with lacking empathy and involvement,[7] because they withdraw psychologically into the inner fortress constituted by the philosophical mode of existence while outwardly continuing to live like other people. If this were the case, Stoics would never be fully present or fully committed. But the Stoic self can answer the charge of evasiveness. The notion that self-reflection is not an end in itself is brought home by the emphasis on the practical application of philosophical doctrine. Epictetus captures this emphasis in the characteristically energetic tone that underlies all of his discourses:

> A builder does not step forward and say, "Listen to me give a speech about building," but takes on a contract for a house, completes it, and thus demonstrates that he has the skill. You too should act in this manner: eat like a human being, drink like one, take care of your appearance, marry, beget children, fulfill your political duties. Endure abuse: bear with an unreasonable brother, bear with a father, a son, a neighbor, a travel companion. Show us these things, so that we may see whether you have truly learned something from the philosophers. (*Diss.* 3.21.4–6)

As Epictetus describes it in this passage, a Stoic can prove her mettle only by participating in life's ordinary activities.

The charge of conformism finds extreme expression in the work of the French historian Paul Veyne. "Such a philosophy [Stoicism]," he writes,

> could easily have led to a critique of the institutions of politics and the family, and originally Stoicism did lead to such a critique. But it became the victim of its success with a clique of rich and powerful men of letters and was reduced to little more than a sophisticated version of prevailing morality: a man's duties to himself and others were identified with institutions, which this bastard doctrine ingeniously sought to internalize as moral precepts.[8]

This accusation, with a range of nuances, is a recurrent theme in the literature: after an initial, more radical phase, Stoicism supposedly lost its critical

7. For a good analysis of the different components of this critique, see Irwin 1998.

8. Veyne 1987, 45.

edge as it adjusted to the Roman context and settled for a compromise with the prevailing power structures.

In a subsequent study of Seneca (French version, 1993; English, 2003), Paul Veyne refines his judgment, but his assessment remains problematic. Once one accepts, as he does, that the distinction between a middle-of-the-road, commonsense morality and a maximalist, idealized one constitutes a dichotomy, the best any Stoic can do is to construct an uneasy juxtaposition of these two value systems, an attempt that is doomed to fail.[9] But this dichotomy will not allow us to see how in the Roman Stoics' image of the good life both ideal and so-called ordinary morality are transformed as a result of their encounter. We will not be able to detect how far-reaching and demanding this double transformation is. In Veyne's picture of Seneca, the concern for personal happiness falls in the crack between the two sides of the dichotomy. As a result, a Stoic's motivations to act in ordinary circumstances become unintelligible and the inner fortress becomes devoid of all content. Nothing could be further from the truth.

But how can one and the same philosophical stance be interpreted as both evasive and conformist? One could argue that if the Stoics were conformist, their conformism was a cover for philosophical activity. According to this line of reasoning, the Roman Stoics preferred not to marginalize themselves as rebels, which would have attracted unwanted attention. Left in peace, they could more easily hold on to inner freedom. As we will see, there are indeed indications that in the last stage of his life Seneca resorted to techniques of camouflage. But on the whole this answer does not match the evidence. In reality the Stoic stance, as this study lays it out, is far more complex and, for this very reason, philosophically interesting.

The sophistication of the Stoic view explains, in part at least, why Stoicism was so prevalent at the end of the Republic in Rome and in the imperial period. Sociocultural analyses taken by themselves cannot provide the full answer. To understand notorious Roman encounters between philosophy and politics, such as Cicero's predicament at the end of his life, Seneca's oscillation between distance and participation in politics[10] (and his political interpretation of noninvolvement),[11] or the so-called senatorial

9. Veyne 2003, 13, 127–30.

10. See Grimal 1989, 1976–77.

11. See, e.g., *Tranq.* 5.2–4, with reference to Socrates' attitude under the Thirty Tyrants; or *Ep.* 14.14, about Stoics who, when shut out from public life, devoted their time to "framing laws for the human race without incurring the displeasure of those in power."

opposition to the emperor's rule, it helps to place them in the larger context of ongoing philosophical debates about involvement. And to address the issue of involvement that Hierocles' image of concentric circles raises, it is fruitful to take a wider perspective than the strictly political and include less commonly discussed types of more intimate relationships.[12] For the Stoics, whether a philosopher should marry and have children is the invariable corollary to whether he should participate in public life and politics. The two questions should be treated together because they point to one and the same issue: the choice between detachment and involvement. It is striking, however, that in the literature the two questions have largely gone separate ways: topics such as the Stoics' involvement in the alleged senatorial opposition to the Roman emperors have led to one line of research, and Stoic views on women, marriage, and children to another.

To detect the philosophical importance of Stoic views about the traditional social fabric, we should question several assumptions. We cannot reduce the Stoic accounts to mirrors of sociocultural factors or ideology. Nor can we automatically assume a certain naïveté on the part of authors such as Seneca, Musonius Rufus, or Marcus Aurelius, with their views representing a system of transactions of economic resources and power that is unaware of itself or, worse, that either deludes itself into posing as something more noble or that is downright hypocritical. But refraining from such assumptions involves more than applying the principle of charity to our reading of texts. If, for instance, we claim a priori that Musonius's views on women reflect the prevailing social customs and norms of his times, a political platform such as Augustus's marriage legislation, or the conventions of a genre, then we are bound to miss potential innovations. We will also be at a loss to say why Stoicism in particular, as opposed to any other system of thought, could respond to Roman sociocultural realities.

Peter Brown assumes that because Roman Stoic views of marriage give us a "miniature of *civic* order," they were a vehicle for imperial ideology in the age of the Antonines, and that philosophy served merely to bring about

12. For an excellent discussion of the wider issues involved, see Griffin 1989. See also her book on Seneca (1976), where she states that she finds the prevalence of Stoicism in the Roman Empire a phenomenon that is difficult to explain. See also Nussbaum 1994, ch. 9, "Stoic Tonics: Philosophy and the Self-Government of the Soul," esp. 326–29, and ch. 11, "Seneca on Anger in Public Life." Miriam Griffin rightly points out (1989, 36) that "the *doctrines* of the dogmatic sects were too complex to provide definite directives on particular occasions, but they provided the moral *vocabulary* for weighing alternatives and justifying decisions." Martha Nussbaum focuses not so much on doctrines but on "certain procedural guidelines" for self-monitoring (1994, 338). My study centers on the problem of involvement specifically, and on the features of Stoic doctrine that bear on this issue.

a counterculture among an elite fully intent on maintaining its status.[13] If we go along with this view, we risk overlooking the challenges that these texts present to the slave-philosopher and the emperor-philosopher, to the powerful and ordinary citizen alike. For his part, S. G. Pembroke brings up the "bourgeois family" out of the blue, in the midst of his discussion of the Stoic notion of *oikeiōsis,* an anachronism that surely tells us more about our preconceptions than about the Stoics.[14] Paul Veyne too, as we have seen, considers the Roman Stoic texts to reflect uncritically prevailing social practices. In contrast, Charles Favez likes what he perceives to be the Roman Stoics' conservative caution. Favez praises them for their positive views of marriage and the family and for the lessons Musonius Rufus could teach "modern feminists."[15] This is the other side of the coin of the charge of conformism: an endorsement of the Roman Stoics' alleged "family values," as opposed to an a priori distrust of marriage as an institution that is maintained by a repressive ideology or political agenda.

The charge of conformism, however, meets with a challenge in the very mode of Roman Stoic discourse. The way in which the Roman Stoics write reflects the recommendation that we *mediate* with social norms from the vantage point of the good as defined by philosophy. Once we understand that they write in such a mode, we can expect them not to make a radical break with the usual way of doing things, while not engaging in hypocritical conformism either. For instance, it is probably true that Marcus Aurelius sought to legitimize his power by viewing and portraying himself as a philosophical ruler. Yet it is also the case that he strongly questioned traditional notions of power. Similarly, it is not unlikely that his use of alternative criteria in the selection of spouses for his daughters justified choosing men from the senatorial rank and thus helped promote the image of an imperial power striving to respect the Senate and freedom. At the same time, however, by preferring nobility of soul to nobility of birth and wealth,[16] he stepped outside the boundaries of established practices, much to the dislike of his spouse and his daughter Lucilla. In many instances, we will indeed find connections between Roman Stoic injunctions and broader social concerns. But that is not what these texts are about.

13. P. Brown 1987, 248.

14. Pembroke 1971, 126.

15. Favez 1933, 1938. At the time he wrote the second article, Favez was teaching at a gymnasium for girls.

16. Herodian 1.2.2. See also *HA* 20.6–7. After Verus's death, Lucilla was married to Claudius Pompeianus, the son of a Roman knight and hence a *homo novus,* a first-generation member of the Senate.

To consider the Roman Stoics naive and unaware of underlying sociocultural systems of transaction is to overlook or mask a salient feature of the Stoic approach: that a deeply probing diagnosis is the prerequisite for doing philosophy. This diagnosis involves a brutally honest assessment of sociocultural and economic realities. In essence, candidates for the right way of life have to realize what a sorry state they are in and reassess everything they consider important and valuable. Only then will philosophical teachings have a chance to bring about a cure. And only if pupils have made sufficient progress can they reenter the fray of society and face its responsibilities. As a telling example of diagnosis of wrong practices, Musonius Rufus and other Stoics are all too aware of the role that wealth, social status, and physical beauty usually played in the selection of marriage partners, and that this selection was indeed a transaction. After unmasking such motivations in a blunt and direct manner, they recommend a "transaction" of virtue instead, with virtue being philosophically defined. Roman Stoic accounts do contain residual sociocultural assumptions, but these thinkers nevertheless show an awareness of the tension between what they propose and society as it ordinarily functions. The Stoic project of transformation and reintegration of tradition and social norms has its dangers and limitations, but it is neither a mirror nor naive.

If one wants to probe more deeply the philosophical value of Roman Stoic accounts, one has not only to examine their views against the background of prevailing practices but also to pay close attention to the literary form in which these accounts were written. As pointed out already, the Roman Stoic mode of discourse and writing serves the exercise of self-assessment and embodies a mediation with prevailing normative frameworks. These claims can be unfolded further. A cluster of practices would go under the heading of self-assessment. There is the recurrent theme that philosophy in words and thought is useless when not matched by deeds and interiorization.[17] The Roman Stoics are interested not merely in what one can know but rather in how one is doing in terms of general moral progress. This interest accounts for the topoi of the so-called *meditatio,* the examination of conscience,[18] in which one's firm adherence to philosophical principles is

17. Sen. *Ep.* 20, 33.7ff., 45.5, 48.7, 82.9, 85, 111, 117; Marcus Aurelius 1.7, 1.16 (with reference to Socrates), 1.17, 7.67; Epict. *Diss.* 2.13.21ff. (some very stark examples, with reference to Socrates); Epict. *Ench.* 46 (with reference to Socrates), also 51. See also Aulus Gellius 17.19. It is also a recurrent theme in Philo of Alexandria, e.g., *Mos.* 1.29. Diogenes Laertius attributes it to Polemo, 4.18. For an excellent discussion, see Döring 1974.

18. According to Cic. *Senect.* 38, the Pythagoreans engaged in the practice in order to train their memory; on this topic see also ch. 1.

tested against reflection on concrete, practical challenges.[19] Did one in fact hold up in certain moments of crisis? In this context, writing becomes an exercise in self-assessment—and this is a kind of writing Epictetus is even willing to attribute to Socrates![20] The Stoics were not the first to recommend such techniques; we find many of these elsewhere as well, such as with the Pythagoreans and with the Epicureans.[21] But the approach did culminate with the Stoics.

As to the philosophical value of the mode of discourse used in these texts, changes in the assessment of Hierocles are an excellent case in point. In 1901 Karl Praechter had access only to the applied "How to . . ." passages preserved in Stobaeus: how to deal with one's parents, what the right attitude in exile would be, and so on.[22] On the basis of this evidence, which he deemed relatively trivial and insignificant, he did not place Hierocles higher than the rank of "ordinary soldier in the army of Stoicism."[23] Five years later, in 1906, von Arnim and Schubart published an edition of the papyrus that contains the theoretical counterpart to the Stobaeus excerpts, the *Elements of Ethics* (Ἠθικὴ Στοιχείωσις).[24] Because of this edition, Hierocles was up for a promotion, becoming considerably more important than Praechter had thought. Margareta Isnardi Parente has demonstrated how the aspects of Stoicism that are central to my study converge in and coalesce around the remaining texts of Hierocles.[25]

19. See Newman 1989. He also discusses (1477–78) Cicero's attribution to the Cyrenaics of a technique of anticipating future evils in thought in order to be better prepared, the *praemeditatio mali* (*Tusc.* 3.28–54).

20. Epict. *Diss.* 2.1.32–33, 2.6.26–27, on Socrates writing paeans in prison (cf. *Phd.* 60D); 1.1.25, on writing as an exercise. On writing for one's own use, see Sen. *Tranq.* 1.13–14. Epictetus is projecting a common practice of *his* circle on Socrates; see Döring 1974, 218 n. 2.

21. See, e.g., the beginning and end of Epicurus *Ep. ad Menoec.* 122, 135 = LS25A, 23J. Seneca does not mind "crossing over to the enemy camp," to borrow a saying from Epicurus, when it suits him (*Ep.* 2.5–6). For an evaluation of the Democritean/Epicurean strand in Panaetius's, Seneca's, and Plutarch's approaches to peace of mind, see Gill 1994.

22. Isnardi Parente 1989. She claims that the Stobaeus fragments point to a work Περὶ τῶν καθηκόντων, which she places in the tradition of πῶς χρηστέον treatises or, in Seneca's terms, *quomodo sit utendum* (*Ep.* 95.45–67). It is a matter of controversy how much of the Seneca passage goes back to Posidonius; cf. F452 Theiler and F176 Edelstein and Kidd.

23. Praechter 1901, preface, v.

24. H. von Arnim and W. Schubart, *Hierokles: "Ethische Elementarlehre,"* Berliner Klassikertexte, vol. 4 (Berlin: Weidmannsche Buchhandlung, 1906), papyrus 9780 and Stobaeus fragments; recent edition: G. Bastianini and A. Long, *Hierocles, "Elementa Moralia,"* Corpus dei papiri filosofici Greci e Latini, 1.1.2 (Florence: Olschki, 1992), papyrus only.

25. Isnardi Parente 1989.

So even if the Roman Stoics' contributions were limited by the mode of writing in which their accounts are preserved, as some have argued, it would be a mistake to conclude from these limitations that their reflections were dilutions and mere popularizations of genuine Stoic thought. In the second book of Xenophon's *Memorabilia* Socrates, much like Hierocles in the Stobaeus fragments, goes through a list of recommendations for different types of relationships. Imagine trying to assess Socrates' impact as a teacher exclusively on the basis of this evidence. It would be nearly impossible to understand Socrates' importance.

For Hierocles, we now at least have both practical recommendations and theoretical insights (even if we cannot necessarily figure out all the connections between the two). In Musonius's case too, the eleven shorter fragments transmitted by Arrian and Stobaeus reveal a more theoretical bent than do the longer passages. And as Seneca's *Letters* indicate, meditating on wisdom also involves reading the great works of the past, including those of the founders of the Stoic school. Thus it would be fair to conclude that even though Seneca did not write in the same manner as a Chrysippus, he still had a sufficient knowledge of central doctrines.

These central doctrines would not have been limited to ethics either but would have included logic and physics (in the ancients' sense of the study of nature) as well, to complete the three-part division of philosophy that was common in antiquity. As to logic, Jonathan Barnes has already established that Stoic authors in the imperial period did continue to show an interest in this field of inquiry.[26] Epictetus, for one, tells us flat out that logic is directly relevant for the proper functions (*Diss.* 1.7.1), that is, the duties. The least one can say about physics, the third branch of philosophy, is that doxographical accounts, the writings of opponents of the Stoics (such as Plutarch), and Seneca's *Naturales Quaestiones* demonstrate that the knowledge was still available.

Seneca assesses the value of studying physics as follows:

> First, we will remove ourselves from sordid things. Second, we will separate the mind from the body—and we need minds that are great and sound. In addition, subtlety of thought trained in hidden matters will be none the worse for matters that are out in the open. For nothing is more in the open than these salutary lessons we learn in order to counter our flawed disposition and madness, which we condemn but do not give up. (*QN* 3, Pref. 18)

The connection between the study of nature and ethics is explicit here. Nature is literally the larger context that allows us to put human folly into

26. Barnes 1997.

perspective, and parts of this treatise, the ones addressed directly to Lucilius, read very much like the *Letters*. The Roman Stoics could not write on applied ethics without taking into account a broader theoretical framework that would have included physics.

If Pierre Hadot's rendering is right, Marcus Aurelius, like other Stoics, does not reject theory out of hand.[27] The qualms he has about theory for the sake of theory are balanced by concerns about those who would like to dismiss theory altogether:

> All your fine sacred dogmas, which you think without founding them on a science of nature [in the reading φυσιολογήτως, instead of φυσιολογητός], and then abandon: they will disappear rapidly. From now on, you must see and practice everything, so that that which is required by the present circumstances is accomplished, but, at the same time, the theoretical foundation [τὸ θεωρητικόν] of your actions is always present in an efficacious way, and that you always maintain within yourself—latent, but not buried—that self-confidence which is procured by science [ἐπιστήμης], applied to each particular case. (10.9, trans. Chase)

This passage clearly demonstrates that Marcus Aurelius did have a genuine interest in the theoretical aspects of Stoicism. Writings such as his *Meditations* do not have to be theoretical, which they are not, to be anchored in doctrine, and conversely theory is displayed not only in passages that have formally structured arguments but also in literary modes and rhetorical devices.

This book, then, is about philosophy as the Roman Stoics see it, and it focuses on the Roman Stoic accounts in and of themselves. The reader will not find contemporary philosophical counterpoints to the ancient views here. This is not to say that no counterparts and connections are to be found. On the contrary, much of the current literature by scholars such as Julia Annas, Christopher Gill, Martha Nussbaum, and Richard Sorabji does this very successfully. There is no need to duplicate efforts. But the choice to refrain from such comparisons is motivated by another reason as well: connections with contemporary thinking carry with them the danger of "presentism." A philosophical stance is not necessarily more interesting, relevant, valid, or true insofar as it happens to connect with current concerns, methodologies, and answers.

It is a sound hermeneutical principle that we cannot acquire an absolutely neutral perspective (a "view from nowhere"), and that interpreters of texts are always to some extent shaped by their own sociocultural and historical contexts. And so this study is in part inspired by two contemporary interests:

27. P. Hadot 1998, 42–43.

the one in philosophy's role and responsibility in public life; the other in the conditions for women's admission into the circle of philosophical discourse as fully rational beings. It would not be hard to discover how and why a woman academic of the beginning of the twenty-first century is drawn to these interests. But to be aware of one's perspective is still a different matter from giving it uncritical priority. Like all real philosophers, the Roman Stoics can tease us out of intellectual self-complacency and lead us to question our assumptions, just as they challenged the values and opinions of their contemporaries.

Of all ancient schools of thought, the Roman Stoics are the most entitled to a strong notion of selfhood. But this self is in essence a mediator, and not its own final end: it adjudicates between different demands in different circumstances and weighs business-as-usual against a philosophical ideal of living according to the rational order that shapes all of reality, including human beings. The Stoics found a way to anchor the life according to reason in a fundamental commitment to community. This commitment entails not merely opposition to existing power structures, but more importantly, it advocates political responsibility in general. It also entails involvement in close, affective human relationships, of which not only friendship but also parenthood and marriage are paradigmatic cases. Of the latter two, it is the Stoic view of marriage in particular that allows the rapport between women and men to rise to the same level as friendship among men. Thus marriage becomes a partnership in the richest sense, promoting a shared pursuit of the philosophical life.

CHAPTER ONE

The Self as a Mediator

> **Space is not something that faces man. It is neither an external object nor an inner experience . . . . When I go toward the door of the lecture hall, I am already there, and I could not go to it at all if I were not such that I am there . . . . Even when mortals turn "inward," taking stock of themselves, they do not leave behind their belonging to the fourfold [earth, sky, divinities, and mortals].**
>
> Heidegger, *Building Dwelling Thinking*

Which current English term would best capture the Roman Stoic "core" of a human being? Both the terms "self" and "individual" have connotations in contemporary parlance that are anachronistic and misleading if applied to Roman Stoic ideas. But in spite of this obvious problem, the advantage of using one term for the notion of a "core" is that it allows us to bring together scattered components of Stoic doctrine and writings that reinforce one another and that together present a highly innovative approach. Thus we do need a clearly circumscribed and pragmatic working concept of the "self" for the purpose of this study. On the level of *language*, the "self" is evident in the Roman Stoics' extensive use of reflexive pronouns. But this linguistic feature would hardly be sufficient for a robust and philosophically interesting notion of "self." So, we have to ask ourselves, of what is this reflexive language a sign, and why do the Roman Stoics like to use it so frequently? Both the Stoics' theory and their mode of writing provide answers to these questions.

The Self: A Working Definition

On the level of Stoic *theory*, the "self" is the ruling principle in a human soul, the so-called *hēgemonikon*, or the mind, which represents a rational and unified consciousness. Whereas it is true that the Stoic self is not consciousness in the strong, and debated, (post-)Cartesian sense, it is the most unified soul model in ancient thought. For this reason, I will talk, not about a series of distinct but related selves, but about the Roman Stoic notion of *the* self. The apparent duality implied in self-reflexive language does not fundamentally undermine the unity of this self. Though moot points and controversies certainly remain, for my purpose the technical aspects of Stoic psychology are clear enough.[1] The issue here is not exactly how all the aspects of the soul's ruling principle work together but what they tell us about a Stoic's involvement in the world around her. The generation of a full-fledged Stoic notion of selfhood proves more than a matter of shifting doctrine[2] or of adopting new terminology to describe the workings of the inner self. This is why one needs to pay at least as much attention to the mode of Roman Stoic discourse as to its technical content.

Stoic doctrine, both early and later, claims that all human beings are endowed with a *hēgemonikon* capable of reason which one can analyze from a third-person and objective normative perspective. This normative perspective posits that virtue determines how any human being's *hēgemonikon* ought to function and that, vice versa, the proper functioning of *hēgemonikon* is virtue. Such a perspective appears to leave little room for individuality among people. But this *hēgemonikon* is also a "self" in the sense that we can claim it as our own, from a first-person perspective. In concrete situations and choices we are the ones who have to decide what the right course of action would be, in the light of how virtue would require us to act. Granted, according to the Stoics virtue is unified and does not admit of gradations, which is in line with the objective perspective. But virtue's unity does not prevent Seneca from stating that "there are many kinds of virtue. These unfold according to different life situations and actions" (*Ep.* 66.7).[3] By Seneca's reasoning, then, individual differences do matter. So the question that arises is how the Roman Stoics succeeded in endowing a universal notion of the "core" of a human being such as the *hēgemonikon* with traits that would be entirely specific to an individual.

Given that Stoic theory does appear to leave room for individuality, one could make a case that "the/an individual" would do as a working concept. But at this point, at least two reasons emerge why "individual" would be

1. See Inwood 1985.

2. For a similar methodology, see Citroni Marchetti 1994, 4546.

3. Unless indicated otherwise, the translations are mine. When I opt for existing translations, these can provide a common ground for discussion.

less suitable for this inquiry. First, individuality is but one aspect of the Roman Stoic notion of a human being's core. It is highly significant that the Roman Stoics make as much room for this aspect as they do, but it still remains the case that the term "individual" will yield only a partial perspective. More importantly, the contemporary concept of the individual as holding on to his uniqueness against all odds, who instead of conforming to norms holds himself to be the norm, a "rebel without a cause," is truly alien to the Stoic concept, which presupposes a normative framework with doctrines, teachers, and moral exempla.

This latter realization brings out another crucial dimension of the Roman Stoic self, namely, that it is fundamentally embedded. On the ontological level, this embeddedness indicates that the self is anchored both in a body and in a rational order that, Stoics would claim, structures all of reality as ultimately proceeding from an immanent divine principle. The social counterpart to this ontological aspect indicates that the self is intrinsically connected to others in a network of relationships that each has its specific claims and standards of behavior. The ontological and social aspects of embeddedness are meant to reinforce each other.

Last but not least, the Roman Stoics pay so much attention to the self because its very embeddedness presents it with the formidable challenge of having to mediate constantly between different and often conflicting normative structures and value systems. What a Stoic is supposed to consider good and right is fundamentally at odds with expectations that ordinarily tend to dominate social life, not unlike the ethical ideals of other ancient schools of thought, but a Stoic cannot simply exempt herself from social obligations and discard such challenges.

So, which working definition of the Roman Stoic self emerges from the above considerations? The reflexive language is a signifier for a unified and rational consciousness that can be considered both a general principle common to all adult human beings and something specific to each individual, in concrete life situations. This self is fundamentally embedded in physical reality and social relationships, and it mediates between ideal and ordinary, unreflective practices. Taken together, these components of the working definition not only indicate that the Stoics have a robust notion of self but also, I would argue, justify the claim that of all ancient models, Stoic theory has the strongest sense of selfhood.

In trying to establish a working definition of the self, so far I have focused on Stoic theory. The reflexive language that the Roman Stoics like to use, however, is not merely a signifier for a philosophical *concept*. In Roman Stoic texts, it also reveals a very distinctive *mode* of philosophical discourse and a meditative *practice*. In this respect the Roman Stoics took many cues from Socrates. But Socrates was also a foil and counterpoint for the Roman Stoics. Plato's Socrates would claim that most of us cannot arrive at understanding without sustained shared inquiry—that is, without skillfully directed dialogue. For the Stoics, by contrast, the conversation with oneself, which the exceptional Socrates could manage,[4] increasingly becomes the model. It is to this mode and practice of self-mentoring that I will now turn before examining more closely the Stoic concept of self.

In spite of their emphasis on self-examination and internal dialogue, Stoics do not do away with teachers. They freely admit that both initially and at recurring moments of weakness, one needs teachers to provide assistance, to pull one out of the bog mire of mistaken priorities, and to undermine one's deceptive self-complacency.[5] If would-be Stoics needed no guidance from others, whether in lecture or in dialogue, then Epictetus's and Musonius Rufus's impressive reputations as teachers would have been irrelevant to their philosophical status. But while it is true that Stoic philosophers teach, they primarily teach us how to stand on our own feet by examining ourselves and monitoring our own progress when no one is physically around to guide us. As much as Epictetus may complain about the emotional hold mothers have on their sons (*Diss.* 3.24.22; see also 78–79), in the long run most of his pupils must and will return to their mothers and families. They also return to politics and public life, contexts in which their teacher will no longer be around to advise, exhort, scold, or shame them. But by then, the former pupil should have interiorized the teacher's voice, so that the teacher's image is always present in his mind and memory.[6]

If a Stoic is expected to hone the skill of talking to herself, it is not then surprising that Seneca's letters to Lucilius are addressed as much to himself (*Ep.* 87.5) as they are to Lucilius, serving to encourage Seneca too even as they provide guidance to Lucilius. Seneca emphasizes that the letters are a substitute for a dialogue in conversation, and this emphasis has ramifications: even if one has received a letter to which to respond and the other person is present to the mind's eye, a letter is initially a conversation with oneself, especially when it is being dictated. This observation would hold all the more strongly to the extent that the correspondence is fictitious, and

4. See the ending of the *Hp. Ma.*; see also *Tht.* 189E; Olson 2000.

5. See Sen. *Ep.* 22.1–3, 22.52; opening of *Tranq.*, as in 1.17; opening of *Vit. Beat.*, as in 1.2.

6. See Sen. *Ep.* 2, 11.8–10, 25.5–6, 39.1–2, 55.8–11, 62.2–3, 72.1 (comparison between memory and a book), 78.18–19, 104.21–22; *De Matrimonio* 57 Haase, attributed to Theophrastus.

Lucilius is as much a literary character engaged in an ideal process of philosophical growth as a real person.[7] In their shared quest for moral excellence, the character Lucilius becomes a reflection of Seneca's conversation with and assessment of himself.[8] Self-reliance is essential to Stoic therapy because even if other people can help us along, our progress is ultimately a matter that cannot be entrusted to someone else (27.4–5).[9]

Because of this focus on moral progress, Seneca's letters to Lucilius are strikingly different from Cicero's correspondence, as Seneca himself points out (*Ep.* 118.2).[10] The letters are not meant to convey gossip about who did what and where, nor are they discussions about plans or ambitions. If they do focus on how the writer and recipient are doing, in the ordinary sense of the expression, it is because this information is relevant for the assessment of moral and philosophical proficiency. The loss of a dear friend, ill health, political temptations, or the burning down of one's hometown can all be occasions for examining how well one is handling life's challenges.

In order to maintain the right hierarchy of values, Seneca and other Roman Stoics recommend withdrawing into and examining oneself in daily exercises, preferably at night before falling asleep or in the morning before starting one's activities. Sometimes others even stay respectfully out of the way altogether when such an assessment is going on. As Seneca tells us, his wife knows to be silent so as not to interrupt his daily examinations of conscience: "I use this prerogative and daily plead my own cause to myself. When the light has been removed from sight and my spouse has fallen silent, because she is long since familiar with my habit, I examine my entire day, and review my deeds and words. I hide nothing from myself, I omit nothing. For why should I recoil from any of my mistakes . . . ?" (*De Ira* 3.36.3).[11]

Marcus Aurelius prefers fortifying morning exercises to help us face challenges: "Say to yourself at break of day, I shall meet with meddling, ungrateful, violent, treacherous, envious, and asocial men" (2.1; see also Sen. *De Ira* 2.10.7). If we experience difficulties getting up and leaving the comfort of our beds, such exercises can also cure morning temper: "Early in

7. On this, see Griffin 1976, 346–55.

8. See Sen. *Ep.* 27.1–2; see also 3.3.

9. For other relevant references, see *Ep.* 3.2–3, 10.2–3, 11.10, 25.5–6, 32.1, 62, 87.5, 105.6, 118.2, 119.1; and, letters as dialogue, 38.1, 40.1, 67.2, 75.1–2.

10. Edwards 1997.

11. Such a scene is satirized in Persius *Sat.* 3.41–43, discussed in Reckford 1998.

the morning, when you find it so hard to get up, have these thoughts ready at hand: 'I am rising to do the work of a human being. Why, then, am I so irritable if I am going out to do what I was born to do and what I was brought into this world for?'" (5.1, trans. Hard; see also 8.12, 10.13).

In sum, we are never less alone than when we are by ourselves.[12] This condition is a matter, not of suffering from a split personality, but of living with the constant presence of community, both human and divine, and having continuously to balance between different sets of values that carry with them the potential for considerable conflicts.

The Roman Stoic Self in Context

In his *Tusculanae Disputationes* Cicero provides an ideal glimpse of the context in which the Roman Stoic notion of the self arose. The work is full of illustrations taken from Greek culture, from the tragedians, from other poets, philosophers, and historians. Cicero's mode of writing justifies taking a look at well-known examples of Greek literature that testify to unstable situations in which the "self" starts to assert itself: Achilles' dilemma in the *Iliad*, Medea's predicament as rendered in tragedy, and Alcibiades' concerns in the *Alcibiades I*, attributed to Plato. Because such examples were part of the Roman cultural background and because they are directly relevant for the Roman Stoic viewpoint, they are a rich source for a better understanding of the "mediating" self.[13]

In the cases that illuminate this study, we are dealing with normative frameworks that regulate the lives of members of a community in terms of group identity. Tensions occur when the normative frame of reference that is supposed to guarantee the well-being of the individual within a given group for some reason turns itself against him or her—that is, when the previous ideal, or illusion, of a harmonized world and common standard shatters, leaving one torn between competing claims. In such situations the individual begins to question the framework's validity and, with the "self" as ally, opposes it. This metaphor of a strategic alliance refers to the very basic, gut level on which this opposition occurs.

12. Cic. *Off.* 3.1: a claim attributed by Cato to Scipio Africanus; see also Sen. *De Matrimonio* 57 Haase. See also the claim, for ch. 3 in this study, *numquam se minus otiosum quam cum otiosus esset*; see Cic. *Rep.* 1.17.27; Plut. *Reg. Imp. Apopht.*, *Scipio the Elder* 1 (196 B).

13. Scholars writing on the self have, in fact, taken the approach of interpreting philosophical claims in a broader context that includes literary models; see Gill 1996. Gill juxtaposes Achilles and Medea (ch. 2). See also notes 14–15 below and Williams 1993.

The notion of a strategic alliance points to war, and to Homer. In moments of extreme crisis[14] and danger we find Homeric heroes deciding whether to remain faithful to the warrior code or to run so that they might save themselves. On a grander scale, Homer's *Iliad* opens with the conflict that drives the entire narrative: the wrath of Achilles. The clash of power between Agamemnon and Achilles unhinges the code that regulates the distribution of spoils and leads Achilles to withdraw. Achilles chooses solitude and detachment over company and involvement (1.348–49) and thus is literally absent from the action. In addition to literal distance, Achilles' course of action also involves psychological detachment: Achilles turns to "himself," however the epic defines that "self" (1.428–29).

In the embassy scene of book 9 (308–429), Achilles weighs two different frameworks one against the other: the glory of war, with the premature death it entails, and the secure prestige of a long life lived in peace. Achilles does not merely rebel against the warrior code because he has not done well by it (316–22); he does not limit himself to a negative transgression but provides a positive alternative: the advantages a life at home could offer him. One could argue that in reality Achilles has little say in this matter because the course of his actions is already included in the plans of the gods. But the fact that the two alternatives and the final outcome are inscribed in his fate gives him (if not in reality then at least in appearance) a measure of freedom to choose. Hence the tension Achilles experiences leads him to weigh two sociopolitical alternatives: there is a trade-off between the world of war and the world of peace in which war does not necessarily come out on top.

As Euripides rendered it, Medea's complex and far-reaching psychological conflict was a favorite case study of the Stoics and served to build up the case against the passions.[15] Medea rebels against the "fate" of women (to which, ironically, Medea had seemed an exception) when the norms that regulate a woman's status turn against her. The code of conduct for marriage alliances allows Jason to abandon her because she is a foreigner and no longer fits into his plans and his newly found society. At this point of crisis Medea turns toward herself and, with lengthy, drawn-out psychological oscillations, agonizes over which course of action to take. In the end, she opts for the most radical transgression possible and kills the children born out of her union with Jason.

14. See also MacIntyre 1977.

15. See Gill 1983. See also the analysis of Hecuba in Nussbaum 1986, ch. 13; N. White 2002.

What is this self of which we can catch glimpses in epic and in such tragedies as Euripides' *Medea?* The self of Homeric figures is represented by an array of psychophysiological entities; there is no single term or locus for what in the later tradition comes to be called the soul or its central faculty, and it is not even clear how much of human agency is internally motivated as opposed to directed by the gods.[16] Nor is the self in tragedies fully unified and unambiguously located either. Instead of letting concepts and terminology do all the work, the stories provide their characters with unity and identity primarily through rich and complex narrative devices. Thus it might be a mistake to look for a clear conceptualization of the "self" in such narratives. In epic poems and tragedies, we see this "self," whatever it is, in action. For better or worse, these stories do not yield theories of the self, even though many a theoretical construct appears to have culled inspiration and support from them. Furthermore, in epic and tragedy the "self" has a limited role because the normative conflicts in the examples examined above are supposed to be the exception rather than the rule and occur primarily in crises. For these reasons, there may be no need for a theoretical articulation of a strong, opposing self to make the stories work as poetry.

Matters are quite different with Plato and his Socrates because, rather than present exceptional and tragic cases in which normative frameworks and expectations clash, Plato fundamentally calls the prevailing social norms into question. Sustained, philosophically motivated opposition calls for a stronger, conceptually defined sense of self. Plato's account of human souls, and of soul in general, is an impressive attempt at constructing a theoretical notion of the self. But Plato does not move beyond a mere typology—and a very rudimentary one at that—for distinguishing between souls;[17] and his notion of a soul with different parts leaves unanswered many questions about free will and human agency.[18]

One of the reasons for these lacunae may well be that according to Plato the "core" of ourselves—that is, the reasoning part of our souls—does not belong to the embodied environment of the senses; although our souls are here with "us," they belong to a different level of reality, to which they

16. For the state of the discussion on this issue, see A. Lesky 1968. For a critique of the Snell view of a "scattered self," see Halliwell 1990.

17. As, e.g., in the charioteer myth of the *Phaedrus*, where souls are distinguished according to the gods of whose train they are part (250B); or in the *Republic*, where Plato describes the one good type and the four bad ones into which a soul can degenerate (544D ff.). See also Sorabji 2000b.

18. See Kahn 1988.

connect us. Thus these cores are, if anything, a general principle rather than something we possess as individuals. How people lead their lives determines the duration of the reincarnation processes through which souls have to go; the more virtuous a person is, the sooner the soul gets released from this cycle, but individual existence does not affect the reasoning faculty as such. Souls go through different lives but in any given life do not carry with them memory traces of previous lives. As in the myth of Er at the end of the *Republic*, "existential" memories do not last beyond the choice of a new life in the underworld; on the other hand, Platonic "remembering" (*anamnēsis*) primarily recalls our knowledge of the Forms and knowledge acquired outside a human body.

One could argue that the soul as Plato describes it does mediate between two realms[19] and, in this sense, also between alternative normative frameworks. Yet because this soul is so disconnected from individual existence in the plenary sense of the word (according to which idiosyncrasies matter), one could hardly call it a "self" in the richest sense of that term, as circumscribed in the working definition at the start of this chapter. Still, it remains true that, according to Plato, we reach the ideal as opposed to the defective reality by turning inward, that is, through our souls. "I tried to persuade each one of you not to take care of any of the things that belong to you before taking care of your self, how that could become as good and as wise as possible," Socrates claims in the *Apology* (36C; see also 30A7–B1).[20]

In antiquity the authenticity of the *Alcibiades I* as part of the Platonic corpus was never questioned. And what matters here are the interpretations of this text in the ancient tradition. Thus we do not have to worry about the problem of later interpolations in the text either. That the *Alcibiades I* could be fruitfully related to Roman Stoic accounts is nowhere better attested than in the Platonist Simplicius's commentary on Epictetus's *Encheiridion*, dating from the sixth century AD. At the outset of this commentary, Simplicius ranks Epictetus's account on the level of ethical and political virtues, which Simplicius defines in terms borrowed from the Platonic dialogue.[21]

19. P. Hadot 1993b. He stresses that Plato's Socrates himself is the mediator between the two.

20. Rappe 1995.

21. See I. Hadot, *Simplicius, commentaire sur le "Manuel" d'Épictète: Introduction et édition du texte grec*, Philosophia Antiqua 66 (Leiden: Brill, 1996); translation, with introduction and notes, in the Budé series (Paris: Les Belles Lettres, 2001), first volume, up to ch. 29. For an English translation with introduction and notes, see T. Brennan and C. Brittain, *Simplicius, on Epictetus "Handbook,"* 2 vols., Ancient Commentators on Aristotle (London: Duckworth, 2002). For an assessment of the importance of the *Alcibiades I*, see Pépin 1971, 71–126, but see also the entire part (55–203), which includes reflections on Cicero and on the Stoics.

In the *Alcibiades I*, Socrates puts to the self-confident and ambitious Alcibiades a slightly different and thinly disguised version of Achilles' dilemma. Achilles had to choose between more glory, followed by an early death, and a long, peaceful life lived in relative obscurity. If Alcibiades could not progress beyond the social status he already possessed, would he prefer to die rather than live a long life? "Suppose that at this moment some god came to you and said: 'Alcibiades, do you want to live with what you have now, or die in an instant if you will not be allowed to gain greater things?'" (105A3–6). Socrates believes that Alcibiades would choose death rather than have his ambitions checked because ambition is what keeps Alcibiades going: he wants to increase his power as much as possible, beyond Athens, Greece, or even the European continent.

But Alcibiades needs help—Socrates' help, to be precise. In a move that is analogous to one he makes in the *Apology* (36C, 30A7–B1), Socrates avers that one really cannot do a good job of taking care of one's affairs, both private and public, if one does not first take care of oneself. Taking good care of oneself (τὸ ἑαυτοῦ ἐπιμελεῖσθαι) amounts to making oneself better, to improving oneself (128B). But in order to do this, one needs to know what this "self" is, as opposed to what merely belongs to it (128D, 129A). And in this dialogue, the discovery of the self lies in a crucial distinction between the user and the thing he uses, a distinction that aligns the self not with the thing used but with the user (129C). Given that a man merely uses his body, his identity cannot be reduced to his corporeal aspect (129E). That which uses the body and rules over it is the soul (130B–C). If the self is identified with the user, then, when "Socrates" and "Alcibiades" talk to each other, what actually occurs is a conversation between souls (130D). But, as Jacques Brunschwig shows, this is not the end of the story: the best mirror to discover "oneself" is not the soul of another human being, located in the horizontal plane of human interaction, but god, who draws out the best in us, "the part of our souls that has to do with wisdom and knowledge" (133C1–2), along the vertical axis of transcendence.[22]

Cicero also appears to have liked the idea of a conversation between souls and applies it to the dialogue of his *Tusculanae Disputationes* (1.52): "we are not bodies, nor am I who say this to you addressing your body." But even if we leave aside (for the time being) the question of the Platonist vertical relation with the divine, how much of a self can a soul without any specifications be? We are left with the puzzle that surely there must be more

22. Brunschwig 1996, esp. 71ff. The passage in question is 133C8–16 and could be a later interpolation in the text; see also 133C3–6.

to Socrates and Alcibiades besides their souls that can account for their being who they are. What could this be? And how can we account philosophically for a stronger sense of individual identity that does not do away with the notion of a common, shared human nature?

Alcibiades too makes an appearance in Cicero's account (*Tusc.* 3.78), but as the prototype of a character who is dissatisfied with his lack of virtue and moral progress. This situation provides for a peculiar possibility. In the lack of virtue and wisdom, we do have a case of a genuine, as opposed to a merely apparent, evil, even by the strict Stoic standard, which would recognize this deficiency as the only evil. So would the Stoics in this case allow for some form of distress that would be a legitimate and appropriate response? As Cicero explains it, the answer is that the Stoics would not deem even this kind of reaction acceptable because the passion distress is altogether beyond redemption.[23] The sage would have no need for Alcibiades' type of distress, because an accomplished Stoic would already be beyond the condition that could trigger the response in the first place. In Plato's *Symposium*, both Apollodorus (173D) and Alcibiades (215E–216C) are likely candidates for a case study of distress over lack of moral progress. In the tradition, the *Alcibiades I* and its focus on the care for the self appear to have justified turning the enfant terrible Alcibiades into the focal point for such questions.

The Roman Stoic Self

Moving on from tradition and context to the Stoics themselves, we encounter the Roman Stoic self in innumerable passages that contain reflexive language. We even find such language in the title that Marcus Aurelius's meditations were given in the process of transmission: *To Himself*. The Roman Stoics emphatically set this self apart from the body and external things. What is the self that is said to be at work here?

In Stoic psychology, there is one, and only one, center of awareness: the "ruling" *hēgemonikon*, or mind, which controls the seven subordinate, instrumental faculties—the five senses, speech, and reproduction.[24] Both rational and irrational behavior are explained in terms of reason, which either works properly or malfunctions. This view, with its strengths and limitations for explaining the passions,[25] gave rise to one of the most

23. See also Augustine *CD* 14.8.

24. On this see Voelke 1973, esp. part 1, chs. 2–3, 20–49; part 2, chs. 2–3, 131–89. But as stated in the introduction, I leave the notion of the will aside.

25. For a recent assessment, see Sorabji 2000a.

continuous debates in antiquity, of which the main antagonists were the Stoic unitary model and the Platonic tripartite soul, which explains passions on the basis of a conflict between reason and the two lower soul parts: spirit and appetite. According to the Stoics, four aspects of the rational principle work together: "reason" is the key function; it works with "impressions" through an act of "assent," thereby shaping "impulses." These four aspects are indistinguishable from the commanding faculty as a whole, and in each, the *hēgemonikon* in its entirety is at work, as this Stoic analogy underscores: "Just as an apple possesses in the same body sweetness and fragrance, so too the commanding-faculty combines in the same body impression, assent, impulse, reason" (*SVF* 2.826 = LS53K, trans. Long). Stoic psychology thus provides us with the most unified model available in antiquity.

The first aspect of the ruling principle, "impression" or "representation" (*phantasia*), carries *all* kinds of thought-content, sensory and nonsensory (thus the notion is much more unitary than in Aristotle's *De Anima*).[26] But for human beings, the representations based on sense perception are both chronologically and logically primary. The most fundamental of all "representations" is our self-perception and -awareness that we are hearing, seeing, and thinking subjects. This self-perception is the starting point for "appropriation" (οἰκείωσις), the awareness that our nature shapes our needs and our responses to the world, in terms of both self-preservation and reaching out to others. "Appropriation" is the Stoic version of the self's reflexive relationship with itself. It is not limited to reason, and it anchors the self firmly in the world with which it interacts. In the second chapter of this study we will take a closer look at "appropriation."

In animals, who do not have reason according to the Stoics, representations can create the urge (*hormē*, or "impulse") to do something—to act upon the representation of food, for instance. But rational human adults are not limited to stimulus-and-response behavior; in adult humans, "reason intervenes as the craftsman of impulse" (D.L. 7.86). So, in addition to representation and impulse, a third aspect operates upon the connection between these two, namely, the assent. If a representation rendered in a proposition with concepts and words yields something like "going for a walk now is appropriate," the assent given or withheld will yield the belief that "it is appropriate" or "it is not" and trigger action accordingly. In other words, adult humans have the opportunity to weigh and evaluate their representations. The conundrum remains, of course, that how one deals with

26. See Long 1991.

representation *x* is the result of beliefs and preconditioning that themselves result from previous representations.

In spite of the problem of preconditioning, however, one can work on representations, as Epictetus elaborates and emphasizes. All humans, not just a few exceptionally gifted ones, can and should learn to give assent cautiously, and for this Epictetus recommends a range of techniques. One can tell a representation to "wait," so that it may be examined more closely to see whether it is what it purports to be. One can juxtapose contrasting representations, playing them out against each other and thereby testing their worth. One can examine how consistent one's behavior is and whether it aims at ultimate happiness instead of immediate gratification. One can teach oneself to accept calmly the inevitable by anticipating potentially painful and upsetting incidents. If a pupil does all this, then, according to Epictetus, he "makes correct use of his representations." The Stoic process of "using representations" not only provides a counterpart to Plato's claim in the *Alcibiades I* about the soul using the body but also gives a human being a much more specific content for what it is she needs to work on and take care of.

It is precisely the belief structure connected to representations that leaves room for individual traits in the concept of the "core" of a human being. Stoicism can reconcile the general functioning of the ruling principle with individual variation by taking individual dispositions into account. The second-century AD Stoic Panaetius in particular developed a four-*personae* theory that can account for uniqueness.[27] As Cicero testifies in his *De Officiis* (1.107–17), Panaetius posits four factors that shape the identity of each individual human being: (1) the nature all human beings have in common, which is characterized by rationality; (2) each person's individual disposition, bodily, temperamental, and mental; (3) the circumstances that govern one's position in life; and (4) individual choices having to do with how to lead one's life. All these factors taken together can amount to a unique perspective on a commonly grounded virtue.[28]

Within the governing rational faculty of humans, then, representations constitute the core of a particular individual's consciousness and her moral character. In fully developed human beings, the function of assent is the still point for the self's mediation—that is, of its "correct use of representations."

27. Gill 1988; Long 1983. See also Taylor 1989, 27–51. Gill (1994, 4602) distinguishes between *two selves* in this framework: one consisting of our "individual capacities and inclinations" and the other, the "deeper" or "more essential self," of our "shared human nature." I posit only one self.

28. See Foucault 1988b, 16–49; 2001.

Other scholars have noticed that later Stoics like Seneca express a stronger voluntarism than do their predecessors.[29] Based on his analysis of the second book of *On Anger*, Brad Inwood claims that Seneca has an "interest in consciously controllable [as opposed to *implicit*] assent" and a "reduced interest in overall character."[30] The findings of these scholars point to the Roman Stoics' increased interest in psychological self-control. The thesis of a mediating self would help account for this increase: it is precisely if one is engaged in a very delicate, complicated, and sometimes even dangerous weighing of alternative normative frameworks that control matters.

Closely related to both functions of assent and impulse is the Stoic notion of "reservation" (ὑπεξαίρεσις, *exceptio*). For our purposes, reservation is best described as a margin of detachment: for instance, if we have arrived at the judgment "it is appropriate to go for a walk" and we act on this judgment through impulse, we have to take into account that because we do not have full foreknowledge of all relevant circumstances, something could always intervene and hinder the outcome. How fundamental this notion is to Stoic psychology is still a matter of controversy.[31] But the participants in this debate generally do accept that the notion is important for Stoicism in general. It is very striking, however, that almost all our evidence for "reservation," with the exception of a passage in Stobaeus (*SVF* 3.564 = Stob. 2.115.5 Wachsmuth, henceforth W.), comes from the later, Roman Stoics, in this case from Seneca, Epictetus, and Marcus Aurelius. One could argue that the notion is prominent in these later Stoic authors precisely because they give so much weight to involvement in society.

Whereas a passage that could hint at Chrysippus's use of "reservation" mentions the cases of a person accepting ill health or a foot becoming muddy (Epict. *Diss.* 2.6.9ff.), the other examples the Roman Stoics themselves give of the practical applications of "reservation" have to do with matters of greater social importance than going for a walk. Seneca mentions attending a dinner party, going to a wedding, or providing bail for someone

29. See Rist 1980, 224–32. He claims, contra Pohlenz, that this is merely a matter of changing terminology; but see important nuance in Rist 1989.

30. Inwood 1993, n. 60.

31. See Inwood 1985, 119–24. He sees it as central, and as giving the judgments involved in assent a fundamentally hypothetical nature, e.g., "it is appropriate to go for a walk *if* nothing intervenes." See also Brennan 2000. Brennan challenges the thesis of "reservation" involving hypothetical judgment. He claims that it is meant not to prevent frustration so much as error (162ff.) and to help us adjust our judgments to changing circumstances, being cast in the form of future-tensed beliefs that are not impulses. But he does not challenge the importance of this notion for Stoic doctrine in general, and the jury in this debate is still out (see Brunschwig, forthcoming).

(*Ben.* 4.39). Marcus Aurelius emphasizes the importance of generally being good and tolerant toward others (5.20) and of attempting to teach others how to follow a better course of action (6.50). The Roman Stoic examples, in fact, cover the whole range of social relationships, from the more intimate to the more inclusive. This emphasis on social responsibility indicates that for Seneca, Epictetus, and Marcus Aurelius "reservation" is a psychological factor that creates detachment not as an end in itself but as a means toward meaningful and consistent engagement.

We now have several key components of the working definition for the Roman Stoic notion of self. It is the governing principle of the soul. In its core of representations and the way in which it uses the faculty of assent, this principle is not merely generic but is an individual self as well because it creates a specific moral identity for each person. Other aspects of how the soul works for the Stoics help to underscore this identity claim. It is to these we now turn.

Time and Memory

Memory as such is not among the main aspects of the Stoic *hēgemonikon.* Whether or not someone has a good memory can even be ranked among the "indifferents" (Arius Didymus ap. Stob. 2.81 W.), things that in themselves are neither good nor evil. Yet memory and its relation to time do tell us much about the Roman Stoic view of the self. For the Early Stoics, time does not "exist"; it ranks among the incorporeals even though it is a real feature of the world: it falls under the heading of a "something" (τι) but cannot claim the status of a "being" (ὄν). In addition, the present as a duration of time is a specious notion because, in the continuum of time, the present is a mere limit between past and future. The present, however, does "belong" when we are truly predicating an attribute of a subject, as, for instance, in "I *am* walking," if that happens to be a true proposition. By contrast, the past and the future merely subsist (LS51). Yet in case the relatively weak ontological status of time should tempt us to underestimate the importance of time in the Stoic sage's life project, Seneca (*Ep.* 124.17) cautions: "How then can the nature of those people seem perfect who do not have a notion of the perfection of time?" Because memory is ranked among the indifferents, and time is one of the incorporeals in the Stoic system, the importance of these two notions has been overlooked in assessments of the Stoic idea of selfhood. But they are, in fact, very revealing and crucial to the question.

It is possible, of course, that Seneca attaches such great importance to time because something is happening with the Roman Stoics that gives a different twist to the original account outlined above. Marcus Aurelius, for one thing, admits the "present" as a duration of time in a manner for which the Early Stoa could not have allowed. He enjoins us to draw a circle around the present; the present is sufficient unto itself, past and future are indifferent:

> I consist of a body and a soul. Now to the body all things are indifferent; for it is unable to differentiate between them. And to the mind, all that forms no part of its own activity is indifferent, and all that belongs to its own activity is within its own control. But even in relation to that, it is concerned only with the present; for its future and past activities are themselves indifferent at that moment. (6.32, trans. Hard)

Part of the exercise of "retiring into oneself" is precisely that one not get lost either in anticipation of the future or in grief over the past.[32]

Hence Marcus Aurelius literally gives the self a clearing in time to take a stance. But this focus on the present conjures up another problem: if the present is all one has, how does one build bridges between different instants and maintain one's identity over the course of time?[33] In response to this version of the identity problem, Seneca at first appears to suggest that a human life is merely a succession of a series of distinct selves. He often emphasizes that we die many deaths in the course of our lives: "None of us is the same in old age as he was in youth; none of us is the same in the morning as he was the day before. Our bodies rush along like rivers. Everything you see runs along with time. Nothing of those things we observe remains. I myself, while I am enouncing that these things change, change" (Sen. *Ep.* 58.22–23; see also 24.19–21). Yet, the same Seneca also claims that though our constitution (*constitutio*) changes with our age, the dynamic of appropriation and the self always remain constant: "Different periods belong to the infant, the child, the youth, the old man; yet I am the same who was the infant and the boy and the youth. Thus, in spite of the fact that each age has a different constitution, the appropriation to its constitution is the same. For nature does not commend a boy to me or a youth or an old man; it is me it commends to myself" (*Ep.* 121.16).

For Seneca, the answer to this paradox of flux and identity lies in his use of the connection between time and memory. As the first passage quoted above explicitly points out, that which goes through a series of deaths is the

32. Marcus Aurelius 7.27–29, see also Marcus Aurelius 2.14, 3.12, 8.36, 9.6, 12.1, 12.3; Sen. *Ep.* 1.3, 32.4, 32.49. On this topic, see also Engberg-Pedersen 1998.

33. See as counterpoint the discussion in Sorabji 2000a, ch. 16, 228–52.

body. And for Seneca the self is not the body but the soul, or, even more specifically, the mind as ruling principle. The body may go through changes in the same manner as in the course of time the planks of Theseus's ship are replaced—and because children are not born with reason, even the *hēgemonikon* goes through some type of development—but memory and its relation to the past provide psychological continuity and guarantee identity.

In one key passage of Seneca's letters, time is not linear, circular, or spiral. Rather, time is a reversed cone, as strange as that may seem at first glance.[34] Seneca connects time to the concentric circles that the Stoics adopted to describe the web of social relationships by adding the notion of linear progress to the image. These relationships, as we have seen in the introduction, range from the more intimate, such as the relationship to oneself and to one's family unit, to those that embrace all of humanity and even the city of gods and men, the *cosmopolis.* Of time, Seneca says: "Our entire lifespan is made up of parts and has larger circles going around smaller ones. There is one circle that encircles and bounds all of them; this one reaches from our day of birth to our last day. Another encloses the years of youth. There is one that confines our entire childhood within its circumference" (*Ep.* 12.6; see also 49.3). Seneca continues this analysis all the way down to the year and the "smallest circle of all," the day.

What could the implications be of mapping a conical structure of time onto social relationships? If we did some creative thinking, we could say that an infant starts out with a relationship to his mother or nurse. That relationship then widens to include his father and the other members of his household, other relatives, schoolmates, the city, and finally—in circles ever widening *over the course of time* and with the advent of reason—humanity in general and the gods. Self, society, and time would then be inextricably interwoven. And as the span of time widens, so, ideally, would our social horizon. According to this perspective of time, memory would serve the human being who is intent on moral progress. Rather than the epistemological function that memory has for Aristotle, memory would have a primarily existential function. In its existential dimension, memory would also imply more than the record of friends, past pleasures, and a founding father's sayings, as it does for the Epicureans.[35] In its existential dimension, memory would contain the lived experiences from which we could learn, the doctrine, precepts, and general sayings that we should always have ready

34. On this point, see Laurand 2003, 103–4; Lévy 2002, 2003; Habinek 1982.

35. D.L. 10.22; Cic. *Tusc.* 3.33, 3.76, 5.74, 5.88, 5.95–96; Cic. *Fin.* 1.60, 2.96; Plut. *Non Posse* 1099E, F437 Usener.

at hand as aids, and the reminiscences of all the people (moral exempla) who matter to us and from whom we have learned.[36] In spite of some points of similarity between them, then, the Stoic use of memory is radically different from its Epicurean counterpart. First, Stoic memory has the broadest existential range conceivable. Second, memory of people is not limited to memory of one's friends but includes the entire social fabric of relationships. Third, memory does not dwell on pleasure (*voluptas,* ἡδονή), as the Epicureans would have it, but is a vehicle for the good emotion (*eupatheia*) joy (*gaudium,* χαρά; Sen. *Ep.* 99.23ff.), to which we shall return below.

Hence in addition to the present, the past can acquire an importance that goes beyond original Stoic doctrine. Seneca considers the past to be the only part of life of which we can be certain: "Life is divided into three kinds of time: that which has been, that which is, and that which shall be. Of these the one we spend now is short; the one we will spend is doubtful; the one we have spent is certain. For this [the last one] is the kind of time over which fortune has lost its jurisdiction and which cannot be brought back under anybody's control" (*Brev. Vit.* 10.2).[37] To be sure, only the person striving toward virtue and, a fortiori, the sage can take advantage of the past; others are too engrossed in their daily lives and dread looking back: "It is a mark of a stable and calm mind to be able to go through all parts of its life; the minds of people who are preoccupied, as if they are bearing a yoke, cannot turn and look back" (*Brev. Vit.* 10.5).[38] Ultimately, the truly sovereign person can own not only her own past but also the collective past of history (14.1–2), because she will know what to look for and value in that past, namely, the moral exempla. And because she will be able to face life's vicissitudes calmly (15.5), she will also be able to embrace the future. A wise person thus has all of time at her fingertips, or "time in its perfection," to put it in Seneca's words (*Ep.* 124.17).

In spite of his emphasis on the present, existential memory is also at work in the first book of Marcus Aurelius's *Meditations,* in which he goes one by one through a list of the people who helped make him what he is. His list amply demonstrates how memory can hold on to things and peo-

36. For passages on memory, see Sen. *Ep.* 5.9, 33.7, 40.1, 49.1–4, 72.1 (memory like a book roll), 75.7–8, 78.14, 78.18, 81.25, 83.2, 94.21ff., 94.29.

37. See also *Ep.* 63.5–7, 98.10–11, 99.4–6; *Ben.* 3.4.1–2.

38. Plutarch uses a similar approach: see *De E* 392C–E with *Tranq.* 473B–474B, and the ending of his *Life of Marius*, quoted below. See also Martial 10.23.

ple when they are no longer physically present. At the end of his *Life of Marius,* Plutarch attributes this use of memory to Antipater of Tarsus, contrasting him to the anxiety-ridden Marius and to "forgetful and mindless persons" in general, for whom "all that happens slips away as time goes on":

Indeed, they say that Antipater of Tarsus too, in a similar manner, at the end of his life enumerated the blessings that he had received and did not even forget to mention his smooth crossing from home to Athens, as if to show that he was deeply grateful *for every gift* of a favorable fortune and that he had preserved them in his memory to the very end, which is the most secure storehouse of goods a human being has. (*Life of Marius* 46, emphasis mine)

Right before this passage, we are told that Plato gave thanks to fortune and to his guardian spirit for having been born a human being, a Greek, and at the time of Socrates' activity, and not an irrational animal or a foreigner. In other words, he appears to have been relieved that his type of incarnation was, in his eyes, of the least damaging kind; Plato's gratitude is very different from Antipater's attitude of looking at his life as though in its entirety it had been guided by Providence, up to even the smallest details.

As the Stoics construe it, memory is a counterpoint both to more traditional notions of fame (Marcus Aurelius 8.37; Sen. *Ep.* 79.17) and to Platonic *anamnēsis.* On Plato's terms, recollection is supposed to concentrate on the Forms, which the soul in any case can grasp more fully when it has been separated from the body.[39] If anything, the myth of Er at the end of the *Republic* indicates that a soul's memories of its bodily existence and lived experiences get in the way of a correct choice of life: because they have no knowledge of the Forms, most souls just keep exchanging good lives for bad ones, and vice versa (619B–E). On the one hand, a good previous life that was not based on philosophical knowledge but instead on habit makes the one who has to choose a new life unaware of the risks of a bad life; a bad former life, on the other hand, does incline the soul toward a better life, but not for the right reasons. Rather, souls of this type still register the pain of having been burnt. Beyond the interval between two lives in Plato's reincarnation narratives, as I have already indicated, all traces of previous lives are erased from memory (cf. Sen. *Ep.* 88.33–34).

For Plato, existential memories are not reliable guides to the moral life,

39. See Plut. *Cons. Uxor.* 611E to end. This creates a major tension with Plutarch's endorsement of the use of "existential" memory, in the consolation itself and elsewhere, as in *Tranq.* 473B–474B. A similar tension runs through Plutarch's *Cons. Apoll.* See also Aristotle *EN* 9.4, 1166a10–30.

as Porphyry's *Life of Plotinus* also demonstrates. Porphyry skips most of the biographical details about Plotinus as irrelevant for an understanding of the Platonist philosopher: Plotinus gave the impression of feeling shame at being in a body, we are told, and for that reason refused to reveal information about his origins, his parents, or his fatherland (1). By contrast, according to the Roman Stoics, life as we know it is what we have to work with, even if one leaves open the possibility that we may be granted a better view of the universe right after death (Sen. *Cons. Marc.* 25ff.). There is an irony in the fact that Plato's accounts of Socrates contributed greatly to the collective and individual memory of moral exempla that plays such an important role for the Roman Stoics. For Epictetus, Socrates' life has become an exemplar par excellence (*Diss.* 4.5.2: παράδειγμα). But whatever purpose Plato may have had in writing the dialogues, his Socrates is not a self-subsistent Form; he is not the message but the messenger (or in Plato's terms, the midwife). A Stoic sage, on the other hand, if any exist, is not only a signpost, though he is that too, but the living embodiment of the philosophical ideal of human reason in tune with divine order.

The *Hēgemonikon* as an Embedded Self

How the sage can be said to be the living embodiment of the ideal requires further explanation. The starting point for this inquiry is the interaction between soul and body. In Stoic doctrine, the soul is itself a corporeal entity, albeit one that is distinct from the body, strictly speaking. The corporeal nature of the soul entails continuity between body and soul. And this continuity is described as one existing between the lower, instrumental soul functions (namely, the five senses, speech, and the reproductive faculty) and the aspects of the commanding principle, discussed above (reason, representation, assent, and impulse). A corporeal soul that is intertwined with the body implies that individual immortality is at best a moot issue or, as Seneca puts it, a dream (*Ep.* 102.1–2).[40]

The Stoic notion of "appropriation" (*oikeiōsis*) also indicates that self-awareness—as in the awareness of one's needs and what would be beneficial to oneself—requires a close synergy between soul and body, which is in fact the way in which Hierocles sees it:

> Since an animal is a composite of body and soul, and both of these are tangible and impressible and of course subject to resistance, and also blended through and through, and one of them is a sensory faculty which itself undergoes movement in

40. See Hoven 1971.

the way we have indicated, it is evident that an animal perceives itself continuously. For by stretching out and relaxing, the soul has an impact on all the body's parts, since it is blended with them all, and in making an impact it receives an impact in response. (4.38–48 Bastianini and Long = LS53B5–6, trans. Long, slightly modified)[41]

Given the Stoic claim that a human animal consists of a soul and body that are closely interwoven, one would have good reasons to expect that, contrary to the Platonic notion, the Stoic "self" would consist of the organism as a whole, that is, of *both* body and soul. As Seneca succinctly puts it: "one's constitution [*constitutio*] consists of a ruling power in the soul which has a certain relation toward the body" (*Ep.* 121.10).[42] Yet, in the Roman Stoics, the emphasis on interiority is striking. Strictly speaking, not even the soul qualifies as the "self," but rather the commanding principle, mind (*nous*), or moral purpose (*prohairesis*, "choice")[43] does.

This Stoic emphasis on the soul and reason can in fact lead to very Platonic-sounding language about the soul being purified and freed from the burden of the body, as in Plato's *Phaedo, Phaedrus,* and *Timaeus.* Such echoes are unmistakable in this passage from Seneca's *Letters:*

Then our mind will have reason to rejoice in itself, when sent forth from this darkness in which it is dragged; it will not merely have glanced at the brightness with weak vision but will have admitted the full light of day and will be restored to its part of heaven, when it will have regained the place that it occupied when it drew the lot of its birth. Its origin is calling it back. But it will arrive there even before it is released from this prison when it will have discarded its vices and will have leapt forth, pure and light, toward divine thoughts. (79.12)[44]

We can find the same theme of the soul's liberation at the end of Seneca's consolation to Marcia (25ff.), in which, echoing Cicero's *Dream of Scipio* (*Rep.* 6.9ff.), he describes how the soul of her deceased son has found a place of greater vision and clarity in the heavens. On closer examination, however, we still find ourselves within a Stoic universe and within the parameters of Stoic doctrine. One could make a claim analogous to what was said at the end of the previous section about how the Stoic

41. See also D.L. 7.85; Sext. Emp. *M.* 11.46.

42. See also Lee 2002.

43. See Asmis 2001; Dobbin 1991; Long 2002, 211–20. Long calls it "volition."

44. On the issue of a Platonic influence, see also Veyne 2003, 119–23.

sage compares to Socrates: the celestial realm in Seneca's accounts may be a place where souls can have more insight, but it is still the abode of the Stoic immanent active divine principle and not a window onto the radically transcendent Platonic Forms.[45] The order and higher state of being are *in* the cosmos, which, as in the *Ad Marciam* (26.6), is still subject to periodic world conflagrations. For the Stoics, our "origin upward" is the divine breath (*pneuma*) that permeates everything, and of which the human mind is a fragment. Within these limits, Seneca apparently feels free to co-opt Platonic phrases in order to denigrate the body.

The instances in which Seneca and Epictetus mention the opposition between soul and body are indeed numerous. Epictetus often designates the body with the scornful diminutive *sōmation,* "this little body of (y)ours." Marcus Aurelius (4.41) quotes Epictetus on the subject: "You are a little soul carrying a corpse around, as Epictetus used to say." Marcus Aurelius's own contempt for the body (along with the externals) makes for a good read:

> When you have savories and fine dishes set before you, you will gain an idea of their nature if you tell yourself that this is the corpse of a fish, and that the corpse of a bird or a pig; or again, that wine is merely grape-juice, and this purple robe some sheep's wool dipped in the blood of a shellfish; and as for sexual intercourse, it is the friction of a piece of gut and, following a sort of convulsion, the expulsion of some mucus. (6.13, trans. Hard)

As he explains in the context of this passage, it takes a lifetime of practice to reduce matters such as these to the proper dimension of trifles.

Marcus Aurelius pushes the point of interiority to the very edge of Stoic orthodoxy by distinguishing among the "three things of which we are composed: body, breath, and mind" (σωμάτιον, πνευμάτιον, νοῦς, 12.3; note the diminutives). A little further down in the same passage is the line "body . . . or the breath conjoined with it." Together with the disparaging diminutives, this distinction leaves open the possibility that the mind itself is not *pneuma,* and that it could be incorporeal (see 2.2, 3.16, 4.41), a claim Marcus Aurelius stops short of explicitly stating.[46] "Of these, the first two [body and breath] are your own in so far as it is your duty to take care of them (ἐπιμελεῖσθαι); but only the third is your own in the full sense"

45. Even in a passage such as *De Ot.* 5.6, in which Seneca suggests that our "thoughts can break through the ramparts of the sky," what he appears to have in mind are questions such as what the conditions of space are and what physical things could look like outside our universe.

46. On this, see Asmis 1989; P. Hadot 1998, 112ff. See also Epict. *Diss.* 4.11.4ff., 4.11.27.

(κυρίως σόν, 12.3, trans. Hard). Nevertheless, even an incorporeal mind would not amount to the Platonic position; Marcus Aurelius still equates *soul* with *pneuma* (2.2, 12.3), thus making soul corporeal.[47]

In addition to these indications of an increased interest in interiority, I have already pointed out that the Roman Stoics emphasized conscious control of the emotions. Seneca enjoins that reason "ought to turn back upon itself" (*in se revertatur*). This emphasis on self-reliance could well have been Seneca's main motivation for further developing the notion of pre-emotions. Pre-emotions are involuntary reactions that as such do not involve value judgments and for which we cannot be held accountable.[48] Because reason's sovereignty matters so much to Seneca, one could argue that he sees a need to elaborate more fully than his predecessors what it is one can and cannot control and therefore pays special attention to involuntary reactions.

Would favoring reason and interiority to such an extent then constitute a Platonizing move on the part of Seneca, Epictetus, and Marcus Aurelius? The answer is again in the negative because, in the process of acquiring knowledge and in taking action, the Roman Stoic "self" remains fundamentally relational or embedded rather than detached in the Platonist sense. In Christopher's Gill terminology,[49] the Stoic self is "objective-participant": "objective" because it presents a view of human nature as part of the nature of the universe that holds independently of subjective dispositions or individual preferences; "participant" because it locates the self in a network of relationships. Moreover, the Roman Stoics developed the connection between the two sides of this formula, the objective and the participant, to its fullest extent. Let us first take a look at the claim of objectivity and approach it via a fragment of Epictetus that would seem to go against my thesis.[50]

Echoing Aristo,[51] Epictetus responds to someone questioning him about "being" (περὶ οὐσίας):[52]

47. Compare this with Seneca's explicit claims about the soul being corporeal at *Ep.* 50.6 and 106.5.

48. See Inwood 2000; Sorabji 2000a.

49. Gill 1996, 10. See also Gill, forthcoming.

50. See also Reydams-Schils, forthcoming-b.

51. D.L. 7.160; Cic. *Acad.* 2.123, with a comparison to Socrates.

52. The full title in the Loeb edition is Ἀρριανοῦ Ἐπικτητείου πρὸς τὸν περὶ οὐσίας πολυπραγμονοῦντα; but the last word was suggested by Wachsmuth, who himself added διαλεγόμενον in his edition of Stobaeus, in an attempt to make sense of the passage.

"Why [Epictetus says] should I care whether existing things are compounded from atomic or incomposite elements, or from fire and earth? Isn't it enough to learn the essence of good and bad and the measures of desires and aversions and also of positive and negative impulses, to run our lives using these as rules; and not to bother about those things that are beyond us? Perhaps they cannot be known by the human mind, and even if one were to suppose that they are perfectly knowable, what is the advantage of such knowledge? Shouldn't we say that people who make this essential to a philosopher's discourse are wasting their time?"

"So, is the Delphic precept, 'Know yourself,' superfluous?"

"Certainly not."

"Then what does it mean?"

"If someone told a member of a chorus to know himself, wouldn't he attend to the instruction by concentrating on his fellow singers and with being in tune with them?"

"Yes."

"And so with a sailor or a soldier. Do you think that human beings have been made to live alone or in community?"

"In a community" [supplied by Heeren].

"By whom?"

"By Nature."

"Is there no longer any need to busy oneself over Nature, what it is, how it governs the world, and whether it exists or not?" (F1 = 175 Schweighäuser, trans. Long, last line modified)

What matters, Epictetus tells us, is that we "know ourselves," know good and evil, desire, aversion, choice, and refusal, and that we apply this knowledge to the proper ordering of our lives. Questions about nature as a whole are beyond our grasp. Even if they are not, they are of use only to the extent to which they help us realize that Nature also made humans intrinsically social beings. This sounds strikingly "Socratic."[53] Yet can we really expect a Stoic not to care about whether Nature exists or not, or how it administers the universe? Even more importantly, this passage contradicts other recorded statements by Epictetus, in which he claims that our judgments, desires, and actions ought to conform to the will of the divine principle that administers the universe as a whole.[54] And elsewhere in the *Discourses,*

53. Long 2002, 149–50. My reading here differs from his, which requires an emendation in the text that is not adopted by Schenkl but is in his critical apparatus: "whether or not it [Nature] is <know-able>" πότερον <καταληπτοῦ> οὔσης ἢ μή; it differs also from Jonathan Barnes's interpretation (1997, 25–27).

54. All human beings have in their rational faculty a kinship with the divine principle (*Diss.*

Epictetus also appears not to follow Aristo's dismissal of the value of logic and physics—if that is indeed what the latter did.[55]

How can one explain this contradictory information, assuming, that is, that Epictetus was not being downright incoherent? Possibly there is something wrong with the fragment, and it does not represent vintage Epictetus. Or, because Epictetus addresses a student who is overly concerned with natural philosophy (to the detriment of taking care of his own life and affairs?), perhaps he got carried away with his own rhetoric. The answer could lie in a combination of factors, but the problem may also be that this is a fragment, and that we have only half of a dialectical argument in which a position gets discarded only to be reintroduced in a fundamentally modified version. Seneca can help us see why the opposition between ethics and physics would merely be the first half of the argument. Two passages in particular come to mind: one attributed to the Cynic Demetrius in book 7 of *De Beneficiis* (1), the other in the preface of book 3 of the *Quaestiones Naturales.*

The similarities between the passage from Demetrius the Cynic in Seneca[56] and the Epictetus fragment could lead us to posit another possibility: that the latter gives us an Epictetus who shows certain sympathies with Cynicism. But how the "Cynic" elements fit into Epictetus's own outlook is also a moot issue; it is very hard to draw a sharp line between Stoics and Cynics in the imperial period, and it is also not entirely clear to what extent Epictetus would embrace and recommend the Cynic's attitude to life. More importantly, there are crucial differences between the two passages. At first glance Demetrius too gives us a stark opposition between physics and ethics. It is better, he says, to have a few maxims of philosophy at hand for practical use—precepts that can make us "better and happier" (7.1.6)—than to have a vast storehouse of recondite and useless knowledge. The "few maxims of philosophy" (3) contrast with the vast but useless knowledge of physics: it will not do us much good to be able to explain ocean tides, optical illusions, the seven-year intervals in a human life, or the intricacies of the conception, birth, and destiny of twins (5).

1.14.6–7, of souls); humans should be grateful for the gifts received, align their will with the divine will, reason to *understand* divine governance, sing hymns of praise, and join in the pageant and celebration (4.1.104, 3.5.10).

55. D.L. 7.160; Sen. *Ep.* 89.13, 94.2.

56. See also *Ep.* 20.9–10.

Yet as Michel Foucault has astutely observed,[57] Demetrius has in mind neither a fundamental incompatibility between ethics and physics nor an insurmountable tension between self and world. At least some of the facts of nature Demetrius mentions do affect human life; he is merely telling us not to delve too deeply into them. In addition to physics having implications for human life, ethics properly construed locates us not merely in society with other human beings but in the community of men *and gods,* adding the essential divine element lacking in the Epictetus fragment (*Ben.* 7.1.7). Also, Demetrius refers more explicitly than does the Epictetus fragment to Nature's design: it is Nature that has hidden the things that will not help us much, and Nature that has, on the other hand, put the foundational precepts "either in plain sight or nearby" (6). Demetrius emphasizes more strongly than Epictetus that Nature means well (see also Sen. *Ep.* 94.56ff.). And so, because he keeps the gods in the picture and has a stronger sense of Providence, the Cynic Demetrius here paradoxically turns out to be more of a Stoic than Epictetus.

The *Preface* to book 3 of the *Quaestiones Naturales* sheds yet more light on the matter of the relation between ethics and physics.[58] In his old age, Seneca is starting on the vast project of "surveying the universe, to uncover its causes and secrets, and to pass them on to the knowledge of others" (1). "Uncovering secrets and causes" falls under the heading of physics. Now, given the cautions cited above about useless knowledge, one could expect him to have some qualms about the validity of the undertaking, especially given that he is regretting "years spent in idle pursuits" (2) and a "misspent life" (2). After all, here as elsewhere he recommends that the mind should fall back on itself: "The mind should be entirely free for itself. Toward the very end, at least, it should look backward in contemplation of itself." With the repeated question "What is important?" (11ff.), he goes through a list of things that do matter:

1. "What is important? To raise your mind above the threats and promises of fortune, to consider nothing worth hoping for" (11);
2. "To be able to endure adversity with a cheerful mind" (12);
3. "Not to admit evil plans into your thinking" (14);
4. "To lift your spirits high above chance occurrences" (15);
5. "To have your breath on your very lips" (16).

57. Foucault 2001, esp. 221–28, 250–73.

58. For a recent assessment of this passage in the context of the *Quaestiones Naturales,* see Inwood 2002.

Animum, spiritus, animam—these are all terms that underscore the principle that what matters is the right inner disposition.

But if Seneca is intent on reestablishing the proper hierarchy of priorities by putting the condition of his mind first, how can he establish a connection between self-contemplation and the study of the universe? Seneca's injunctions in the preface do not lead away from the study of nature, because "having a mind free for itself" (2) is an entirely different matter from being narcissistically engrossed in or enslaved to (17) oneself. Rather, his emphasis on the mind's freedom only serves to increase the value of this field of inquiry. This value becomes clearer when we contrast his assessment of physics with the low opinion he has of historical narratives about the "actions of foreign kings" (5–10) such as Philip, Alexander, or Hannibal and about "the misfortunes nations have suffered or inflicted on others in turn." Though elsewhere in his writings history does have a moral value (but that is a different type of dialectic than the one at hand), in Seneca's opinion these traditional historical narratives, much like individual memory gone awry, provide the wrong normative perspective. The study of nature, however, has the inverse effect: it leads us away "from sordid things," "separates the mind from the body," and trains the mind in subtle thinking (18).

The connection between the study of physics and the good life is even more fundamental than what we have seen so far: to study nature in the Stoic sense is to give absolute priority to the relation between the self and the immanent divine principle that orders both humans and nature in general.[59] We are part of nature. Seneca mentions in one breath "having seen the universe in your mind and . . . having subdued your vices" (*animo omne vidisse et . . . vitia domuisse,* 10) because the first goal, contemplation of the universal harmony, both implies and promotes the second one, the moral life. Plutarch's rendering of Chrysippus's view confirms Seneca's point: "There is no other or more appropriate way of approaching the theory of good and bad things or the virtues or happiness than from universal nature and from the administration of the world" (Plut. *Stoic. Rep.* 1035C = LS60A, trans. Long). "To draw *away* from an association with divine things and turn to human affairs" (11), Seneca continues, will not enhance self-knowledge; on the contrary, it will result in "blindness." One who has investigated the universe thoroughly will arrive at the conclusion "that all things happen in accordance with a decree of god" (12). "Raising pure hands to heaven" (14), she will have an attitude of deference toward the divine. Studying physics "makes a man free not by right of Roman citizenship

59. On this issue see also the debate between Annas (1993, 1995) and Cooper (1995).

but by right of nature" (16), and freedom that is the fruit of natural philosophy surpasses any kind of political freedom.

So, Seneca recommends the turn toward the self not merely for the self's sake, and the study of nature not merely for the sake of engaging in physics. Outside the context of the *Quaestiones Naturales,* he emphasizes that we will escape from Fortune's grip on us only when we apply "the knowledge of self and nature" (*sui naturaeque cognitio, Ep.* 82.6).[60] The true turn toward the self is simultaneously the true way of doing physics, and vice versa, because we are required to look at ourselves from the proper perspective, which, for the Roman Stoics, means from the perspective of the self's relation to a world that is the product of immanent divine agency. From this immanent perspective, the Roman Stoic notion of the subject, for all its emphasis on the soul's opposition to the body, remains fundamentally anti-Platonic.

The passages from Seneca's *De Beneficiis* and *Quaestiones Naturales* reveal the possibility that Epictetus, by going after someone who engages in physics in the wrong manner purely to straighten him out, may well have been having his cake and eating it too. The nonexistent "other half" of the argument—as revealed by the *Discourses* and the *Encheiridion*—would be that once this fellow has his "moral purpose" in order and understands the full implications of human sociability, he will also be open to the right view of nature and Providence. If one does not want to get lost in abstruse fact-finding missions and convoluted theoretical questions, one might do better to postpone the study of physics until one has one's priorities straight.

Not unlike Epictetus, Marcus Aurelius sometimes leaves the question open whether the world is governed by Providence or, as the Epicureans would have it, is made up of random configurations of atoms.[61] His rhetorical strategy appears, on the one hand, to aim for a common ground between different views that would strengthen his claim. For example, he points out that both Stoics and Epicureans would argue against the fear of death. In many of his letters, Seneca does the same. On the other hand, Marcus Aurelius uses an a fortiori argument: if reliance on one's own reason and social responsibility would hold even for someone who did not believe in Providence, a Stoic would have all the more reason to adhere to these ideals. And so, like Seneca and Epictetus, Marcus Aurelius too eloquently brings to the fore the themes of the self's relational nature and its cosmic dimension, saying that an ideal person, with "the mind of one who

60. See also *Ep.* 95.12, 65.15–16, 65.18ff.

61. His shorthand version of this question is "either Providence or atoms"; see, e.g., 4.3, 4.27, 6.24, 6.44, 8.17, 9.28, 10.6, 11.18, 12.14. See Annas, forthcoming.

has been chastened and thoroughly purified" (3.8), is "not dependent on others." So far, so good. This is the self-sufficiency we are accustomed to find in a Stoic author. But Marcus Aurelius immediately adds a nuance we have a tendency to overlook: "nor is he cut off from them." In order to bring the point home that all human beings are related to one another, Marcus posits a kinship of mind among humans: "mind is common to us all" (4.4) and "the soul of all rational beings is but one" (4.29). To substantiate the latter claim, he relies heavily on Stoic physics: the unity of human minds is ultimately anchored in the divine principle, which is the rational being par excellence and the point of origin in the order of the universe.

The unity of divine and human reason sheds light on how the Stoics apply the notion that a *daimōn* dwells in each human being. This notion derived much of its impetus from the ending of Plato's *Timaeus.*[62] In the *Timaeus,* the rational part of the soul is the divine element in us, the *daimōn* entrusted to us (90A). Through observation and contemplation of the heavenly revolutions, we can harmonize the order of the rational element with the order of the World Soul and thus lead a virtuous life because we are cultivating the best in us. Both Chrysippus and Posidonius[63] echo this passage, each according to his own soul model. The Chrysippus passage is worth quoting in full:

> Further, living in accordance with virtue is equivalent to living in accordance with experience of what happens by nature, as Chrysippus says in *On Ends,* book 1: for our own natures are parts of the nature of the whole. Therefore, living in agreement with nature comes to be the end, *which is in accordance with the nature of oneself and that of the whole,* engaging in no activity wont to be forbidden by the universal law, which is the right reason pervading everything and identical to Zeus, who is this director of the administration of existing things. And the virtue of the happy man and his good flow of life are just this: *always doing everything on the basis of the concordance of each man's guardian spirit with the will of the administrator of the whole.* (63C = *SVF* 3.4 = D.L. 7.87–88, trans. Long and Sedley, emphasis mine)

The formula of the end (*telos*) that Diogenes Laertius here attributes to Chrysippus interprets "living in agreement with nature" as implying an alignment between our own natures and the nature of the whole, and between each man's guardian spirit and the will of the divine principle.

62. See Reydams-Schils 1999.

63. F187 Edelstein and Kidd = Galen *Plac. Hipp. et Plat.* 5, 326.20–27 De Lacy; Marcus Aurelius 5.27 (see also 2.13, 3.12).

In light of this formulation, it should not come as a surprise that the guardian spirit in Stoic texts has a strangely ambivalent status: sometimes he is intrinsic to the human soul; sometimes he stands over and beyond the soul itself (as also in Plato's myth of Er, *Rep.* 620D–E).[64] As we have seen, the Stoics posit that human reason is literally a piece of divine reason. In other words, they posit the strongest possible *physical* connection between the divine principle and a human being's ruling principle. In the *Timaeus,* Plato too claims that the human reasoning faculty is a mixture of the same ingredients that constitute the World Soul, but the Platonic World Soul itself is not the highest divine entity in his universe. The mixture in the human soul is less pure, and in addition to the reasoning faculty, the human soul also gets saddled with the lower parts, spirit and appetite. In contrast to Plato's view, the Stoic guardian spirit is the liminal entity that embodies a much more radical continuity between human and divine reason and, as such, indicates the very fluidity of the boundary between the one and the other.[65]

Such a radical continuity implies that ideally the Stoic integrated self overcomes the oppositions between subjectivity and objectivity and between autonomy and heteronomy. The self is autonomous insofar as it carries the moral injunctions within itself, in its nature properly understood. Yet these injunctions are not merely subjective. Because of the unity between human and divine reason, they are related to and derive their validity from a universal order that holds objectively in nature in general. If we take the argument in the other direction, starting with natural order and objectivity, we arrive at the outcome that although natural law and right reason are embedded in physical reality, they do not create a problem of heteronomy: these regulative principles literally belong to each person's ruling principle, only there is nothing distinctively individual about them. Yet because the Stoics make room for the encounter between generally applicable regulative principles and concretely lived experiences, they are entitled to a notion of "self" to which the Platonist viewpoint cannot do justice.

Another important consequence of positing an integrated self is that, depending on the context, the Stoics can adopt more or less inclusive or exclusive perspectives on the self that are perfectly compatible with each other: whether they look at a human being's self from the perspective of

64. See Bonhöffer 1890, 81–86. See also Sen. *Ep.* 31.11, 31.41, 74.16, 78.1–2, 87.21, 110.1; Epict. *Diss.* 1.14.11–13, 2.8, 3.22.53.

65. Sen. *Ep.* 41.5, 66.12, 124.14; Epict. *Diss.* 1.14.6, 2.8.11; Marcus Aurelius 5.27.

mind and reason, of the soul in its entirety, of the composite of soul and body, of a person by herself or in community, or from the most inclusive perspective of them all, the universe, it is the connection between human and divine reason that anchors all of these.

Suicide and Others

That the Stoic self is not only "objective" because it is integrated in a natural order but also fully "participant" is brought home by Cicero's[66] and Seneca's emphasis on the weight that human relationships ought to have in one's decision whether to commit suicide.[67] Not for the last time, Plato's *Phaedo* is useful in framing the question. Unlike in the *Laws* (873C–D), in the *Phaedo* Plato emphatically rejects suicide: Socrates claims that the gods are our masters and they are in control of our lives; it is not up to us when to call it quits (59C–63E). But in some curious respects Socrates' attitude toward his death sentence could be interpreted as passive suicide: he does nothing to appease his judges and the assembly, to put it mildly, and he refuses every opportunity to escape from prison. In his old age, he does not let people hold him back but sends his spouse and children away and will not take any measures to save his life for his friends' sake either. One of the reasons his friends cannot undo his resolve is that, as he puts it, he is bound to find other, even better dialogue partners in the afterlife (*Phaedo* 69E, *Apology* 41A ff.). But one could argue that by taking his own death so calmly and philosophically Socrates bestows the ultimate benefit on those who are capable of appreciating it: a correct understanding of death that ought to rid us of fear once and for all,[68] namely, the understanding that, far from being a disaster, death frees our souls to a better purpose.

For the Stoics, however, the soul's existence apart from the body, as we have seen, is at best a matter of merely temporal survival. Yet Roman senators such as Thrasea and Seneca himself do clearly model their own suicides after Socrates' example. That at least is how Tacitus renders the scenes.[69] Even more baffling is Seneca's claim that Cato the Younger did not see a conflict between his reading of the *Phaedo* and his suicide: "on that last glorious night he read Plato's book with a sword laid next to his head"

66. See his letters *Att.* 3.4; *Q. Fr.* 1.3.5–6, 4.4.5; *Fam.* 14.4.5. For a broader discussion of Cicero's views on suicide, see Grisé 1982, 194–205.

67. For comparison, see Pliny the Younger *Ep.* 1.12, 1.22, 3.7, 6.24.

68. See also Sen. *Ep.* 13.14, 14.4–5, 24.4–5.

69. For Seneca, see Tac. *Ann.* 15.60–64, more on this in ch. 5; for Thrasea Paetus, see Tac. *Ann.* 16.34–35; Dio Cassius 61.15.4. See also the excellent tables by Grisé 1982, 34–53.

(*Ep.* 24.6).[70] Cato's reading must have been very selective if he could keep a sword at hand. How did he and the Stoics justify suicide, both in light of the *Phaedo* and in the context of received doctrine, and what are the limitations of their defense?

Epictetus appears to echo the *Phaedo* when he claims: "Men, wait upon god. Whenever he gives the sign and frees you from this service, then you are free to return to him. But for now be content to remain in the place where he has stationed you" (*Diss.* 1.9.16, trans. Dobbin). But contrary to Plato's explicit language, the phrase "giving a sign" is ambiguous enough to allow for suicide: external circumstances can be interpreted as the signal to exit from life (see D.L. 7.28, on Zeno's suicide). According to a doxographical passage in Olympiodorus,[71] five types of circumstances may be interpreted as a sign from god that suicide is advisable: (1) a major emergency (μεγάλην χρείαν) that demands the sacrifice of one's life for the sake of friends, kin, or community; (2) dishonor (αἰσχρορρημοσύνην), such as when tyrants try to force us to engage in shameful acts and speech; (3) the threat of insanity (λῆρον); (4) incurable illnesses or, presumably, other bodily conditions (τὸ σῶμα νόσοις ἀνιάτοις κατεχόμενον) that would prevent the soul from using the body as an instrument (with a clear echo of the reasoning in *Alcibiades I*); and (5) extreme poverty (πενίαν).

Different Stoics valorize these motivations differently. Epictetus, for instance, would push the poverty condition to its most extreme, allowing suicide only when one does not even have the absolutely bare minimum for sustaining life, which according to him is very little indeed. On the other hand, he does something quirky with the clause on personal honor when he claims that the threat to have his beard shaved could induce a philosopher to take his leave from life (*Diss.* 1.2.29). The motivation behind this stance is presumably that the beard is, after all, a divinely bestowed sign of masculinity (1.16.10) and, as such, a necessary, if not sufficient, condition for dignified manliness. The beard may not make the philosopher—nor may any other outer trappings, for that matter (as in 3.22, 4.8)—but insofar as he is a man, the philosopher does not do without.

Now if Olympiodorus's account is reliable, old age, with its increasingly debilitating symptoms, could well justify suicide in the Stoics' eyes.[72] This

70. Griffin 1986. See also Cic. *Tusc.* 1.74; Plut. *Cato Minor* 68.2, 70.1; and the analogous case of Cleombrotus of Ambracia, in Cic. *Pro Scauro* 4–5 and *Tusc.* 1.84.

71. *In Phd.* 1.8, *SVF* 3.768; D.L. 7.130.

72. Reydams-Schils 2003.

position, in fact, is attested in Seneca: "I won't abandon old age if it preserves me whole for myself, or at least whole in the better part; but if it starts to shatter my mind and tear down its parts, if it does not leave me life, but mere breath, I will sally forth from the decrepit and tottering building" (*Ep.* 58.35).[73] In this passage, old age is fundamentally ambivalent: on the one hand, it can bring us to the pinnacle of our intellectual power;[74] on the other, it can leave us decrepit and "tottering" like an old building (see also *Ep.* 12, 30.2). Xenophon (*Ap.* 6–9) claims that Socrates himself was motivated to act the way he did because he did not feel like holding off death until old age had gotten the better of him.

But mental acuity and minimal cooperation on the part of the body are not the only justifications the Stoics acknowledge for declining the option of suicide. Seneca highly values our commitments to other people. He postpones his suicide for the sake of his father and, at a later stage, for the sake of his wife, Paulina. Three main passages from his *Letters* bring the point across:

[An old man at the end of his life, Seneca claims,] has his fill of life. He does not want to add anything on his own behalf, but on behalf of those to whom he is of use. He deals generously because he continues to live. (*Ep.* 98.15–16)

[When Seneca himself was suffering from his bad health, he testifies:] Often I took the first step toward breaking off my life; the old age of my most tender father held me back. For I considered not how bravely I could face my death but how incapable he was to bear his loss bravely. And so I ordered myself to live. For there are circumstances in which remaining alive is a deed of courage. (*Ep.* 78.2)

[And when he is older he evokes the love of his spouse in these terms:] This is what I said to my Paulina [his reason for traveling in spite of his fever], who makes me take care of my health. For, because I know that her life breath hangs on mine, I begin, as I am concerned about her well-being, to be concerned about mine. For one ought to give in to honest emotions (*honestis adfectibus*). . . . because a good man should live not as long as he likes but as long as he ought. The man who does not value *his wife or his friend* highly enough to remain longer in life, who will insist on dying, is a weakling. . . . It is a sign of a great mind [*ingentis animi*] to return to life for the sake of another. But this too I consider to be a mark of utmost kindness [*summae humanitatis*]: to guard one's old age more diligently—old age, the greatest boon of which is a firmer charge over oneself and a bolder use of one's life—if you know this to be sweet, useful, desirable to any member of your circle. Besides, this

73. See also Sen. *Ep.* 98.16, 72.5ff., case of Tullius Marcellinus; Marcus Aurelius 3.1.

74. *Ep.* 26.2–4, 30.13ff., 58.33.

brings with it no mean joy [*gaudium*] and reward; for what could be more delightful than to be so dear to one's wife so as to become more dear to oneself. (*Ep.* 104.2–5, selection)[75]

It will take the remainder of this book to unfold all the implications of these rich passages; we will need to examine how relationships in general (ch. 2) and marriage specifically (ch. 5) fit into the project of the philosophical life.

Seneca is aware that his perspective here is not entirely in tune with Socrates' attitude toward his death and toward the people his execution affects. To get out of this bind, he draws from the tradition that represents Xanthippe and Socrates' children as difficult people (104.27), leading us to conclude that they were too much of a pain to deserve tender considerations on the part of Socrates. In another letter, Seneca attributes his recommended attitude to Socrates too, but shifts the focus toward his friends. Seneca avers that Socrates actually postponed his death for the sake of his friends: "Socrates could have ended his life through abstinence, and he could have died because of lack of food rather than poison. Yet he spent thirty days in prison awaiting death, not with the thought that everything is possible, or that such a long time span harbors many hopes, but in order to show himself submissive to the laws and in order to give his friends the benefit of Socrates until the end" (*Ep.* 70.9). Here we find Seneca explicitly spelling out how Socrates' death could have benefited his friends because—unlike Xanthippe and Socrates' children, we are meant to add—they were receptive to the message.

Musonius Rufus tries to deal with the problem of Socrates' death in a different manner. He attempts to reconcile Socrates' decision not to avert his execution with the injunction that we cannot die as long as we are useful to other people. One is allowed to disregard one's current obligations, Musonius says, if through one's death one would benefit even more people: "One who by living is of use to many has not the right to choose to die unless by dying he may be of use to more" (F29 Lutz). But then, whichever decision one makes, whether to live or to die, the concern for others ought to remain central.

For now, let us register two main points about the passages from Seneca quoted together above. First, social duties do not involve a merely general attitude toward humanity in its entirety. Rather, they are embedded in community relationships closer to home and in the close relationships of friendship, parenthood, and marriage, as well as other kinship relations. The Stoics often do talk, of course, about sociability in the community that

75. See Elorduy 1936, 172.

all human beings share as a function of their rationality. It is with reference to sociability that Epictetus tries to dissuade a friend of his from committing suicide: "Without any reason you are removing from life, and depriving us of, a human being who is a friend and companion, and a citizen of the same city, both great and small" (*Diss.* 2.15.10). The "great city" here is the famous notion of the *cosmopolis*, the community of gods and men on a universal scale. But notice that Epictetus does not rely exclusively on the argument of shared humanity; he also reminds his interlocutor of the bonds of friendship and citizenship in the ordinary political sense. Thus the Stoics do not ask us to abandon closer and localized ties for the sake of universal humanity.

Second, the terminology of duty—of moral imperatives clearly expressed in the language of obligations—does not preclude genuine affection. Seneca uses a wide range of terminology to express the affection that colors relationships: he talks about kindness (*humanitas*), honest emotions (*honesti adfectus*), and magnanimity (*ingentis animi*). The other person is "dear" (*carus*) to one, and accepting one's responsibility toward the other is "pleasing, useful, and desirable" (*dulce, utile, optabile*), as well as "sweet" (*iucundum*), and brings with it no mean joy (*non mediocre gaudium*). *Humanitas*, the shared condition of being human, is a form of *kindness*. It is not, for instance, a detached calculation of the greatest possible good for the greatest possible number of people. The Roman Stoics in particular take full advantage of the theoretical possibility of *eupatheiai*, the good "emotions" that not only are compatible with the life of reason, hence with virtue, but are also the very expression of the correct use of reason. "Above all," Seneca advises Lucilius, "make this your business: learn how to feel joy," even if a Stoic's joy is a rather stern matter (*Ep.* 23.3–4; see also 59.2, 14, 16).

For the Stoic doctrine of the *eupatheiai* and their role in ethics, Cicero once again is an important link in the transmission: in his *Tusculanae Disputationes*, he gives a key account of how the Stoics distinguished between passions and "good emotions" (*constantiae*, 4.14). As the doctrine of *apatheia* stipulates, passions are to be avoided. The four main types (3.24) are distress, fear, exuberance, and desire. Distress and exuberance have to do with beliefs about something evil or good being present. Fear and desire involve beliefs about future evils or goods. Fear, exuberance, and desire, however, have good counterparts (4.11ff.; D.L. 7.116)[76] in precaution (*cautio*, εὐλάβεια), joy (*gaudium*, χαρά), and wish (*voluntas*,

76. See also *SVF* 3.432.

βούλησις).[77] This stance is fundamentally different from that evolving out of Aristotle, of acceptable emotions being a mean between two extremes—the so-called *metriopatheia*. The Stoics would argue that a more moderate dose of something intrinsically problematic, such as anger, for instance, does not make it good, and hence they would posit a difference in kind between the passions (πάθη) and the good emotions (εὐπάθειαι).

The problematic nature of distress discussed already in the case of Alcibiades helps explain some of the features of the Stoic attitude toward suicide, such as the apparent lack of reciprocity in expressions of affection. Seneca's description of his affective rapport with Paulina appears curiously narcissistic: because she cares so much for him, he cares more for himself. But what about his affection for her? Likewise, when Seneca tries to console his mother about his exile, he addresses the issue of her missing him but does not dwell on how he himself copes with the absence of loved ones (*Cons. Helv.*). On one level, one could read such a one-sided account as exhibiting a reluctance on the part of a traditional Roman man to portray himself in public discourse as affectionate. It is fine for women to show their affection, and as Seneca states too, he could not "prevail upon her [Paulina] to love him more courageously" (*Ep.* 104.2). Yet this cannot be the whole answer, because other Roman Stoic texts do not refrain, albeit in a third-person perspective, from describing the affection between spouses in reciprocal terms.[78]

Whereas the explanation based on different gender roles may work at the surface level, something else could be going on here as well. To get at the deeper explanation, we need to keep in mind the first-(or second-) person perspective that Seneca uses when he talks about his relations with others. Given that distress is a passion to be avoided, a Stoic, even one of the merely would-be type, is supposed to be able to cope with absence and loss of loved ones; he has to come to terms with the fragility and vicissitudes of human life. But although he has to accept the death of others, he has no right to impose his own death through voluntary suicide on those who are living. The Stoic precepts that instruct one to cope with absence and death cannot serve as a pretext to walk away from the people to whom one has a responsibility; a Stoic has no right to demand that they brace themselves and just "deal with it." The burden of both fortitude and affective responsibility rests fully on the self in its rapport with others (see also *Ep.* 103.5). A Stoic can teach about this first-person attitude and communicate it to

77. For a good background discussion of the issues involved here, see Brennan 1998.

78. See ch. 5 on this.

others so that they in turn may choose to adopt it, but that matter would be, precisely, up to their own discretion.

We witness an analogous form of altruism in Seneca's (*Ep.* 9.8–12) and Epictetus's (*Diss.* 3.22.62-66) more traditional injunction, already well developed in books 8 and 9 of Aristotle's *Nicomachean Ethics*, that one ought to engage in friendships not for the sake of oneself but for the sake of the other person—not to get help in times of need but to give help (see also Sen. *Ep.* 95.48–49). So when we hear that Seneca got help from a friend when he was sick, the charitable interpretation would be that Seneca was fortunate enough to have a friend who himself respected the Stoic principle (*Ep.* 78.4). The analogy with friendship also matters because it helps address whether a Stoic has to be patient merely out of a condescending consideration for those who are not as advanced as he is: Seneca is concerned about his father's inability to deal with his death and about Paulina's lack of strength in the face of his absence.[79] But in his passage about Paulina, he puts a spouse on the same level as a friend (*Ep.* 104.3), and the passage from Epictetus quoted above attests that the patience is not merely a matter of condescension: Epictetus tries to dissuade a friend from committing suicide because even friends who are aiming to be Stoics are not allowed to walk out on each other, and Epictetus reproaches his friend for acting irresponsibly (*Diss.* 2.15.10). This attitude in itself already puts a meaningful constraint on the claim that for Stoic sages, one friend is as good as another, and physical presence is irrelevant for friendship.[80] For the Stoics, the importance of duties in the social web of relationships makes a deep commitment to specific persons not only possible but also morally required.

The Stoic self is a unitary, existentially informed, mediating psychological notion. It takes its cues from a philosophical ideal that connects it to a divine rational principle and that integrates it within a universe ordered by that principle. In its relation with fellow human beings, not all of whom endorse the same philosophical ideal, the Stoic self has, as the analysis of suicide here would already indicate, and contrary to common opinion, a profoundly altruistic outlook. In fact, most of the subtypes of the *eupatheia* "wish" are feelings of goodwill toward others of some form or other: well-wishing (εὔνοια), friendliness (εὐμένεια), respect (ἀσπασμός), and affection (ἀγάπησις). Even joy, as the outcome of the virtuous life, is the kind of

79. See Harich 1994.

80. See Inwood 1997; Lesses 1993. Inwood uses a technical term, "fungibles," to express this idea. For a good recent assessment of Epicurus's views on friendship, see E. Brown 2002.

disposition that can be shared by others and enhanced in common undertakings. The self is that inner realm in which both traditional values and experiences are constantly measured against a philosophical normative framework; it is a place of refuge, not for the sake of itself, but to make sustained commitments possible in the face of considerable challenges.

CHAPTER TWO

From Self-Sufficiency to Human Bonding

For he who is either fast bound in the love lures of his wife, or under the stress of nature makes his children his first care, ceases to be the same to others and unconsciously has become a different man, and has passed from freedom into slavery.

Philo of Alexandria *Hypothetica* 11.17 (on the community of the Essenes)

I am doing my country a favor. I don't need to go into office for power. I have houses all over the world, stupendous boats. . . . I have beautiful airplanes, a beautiful wife, a beautiful family.

Italian media magnate and prime minister Silvio Berlusconi in the *New York Times Magazine*, April 15, 2001

The previous chapter drew attention to the Stoic notion of appropriation, οἰκείωσις, that is, the ability to be aware of one's nature and needs and to adjust one's choices accordingly. But because sociability is part of animal and human nature, appropriation is also supposed to embrace care of others. And the Roman Stoic version of "appropriation" yields a striking appreciation for relationships with friends, parents, lovers, spouses, children, siblings, parents-in-law, and the like. But given that *oikeiōsis* implies a focus on one's own needs as dictated by one's nature, both ancient and contemporary critics of the Stoics have not failed to question how this dynamic could be reconciled with life in a community and the needs of others.

To tackle this challenge, the Roman Stoics make the most of a theoretical move that emphasizes the continuity between parts and whole. The previous chapter examined the connections between human and divine reason. Here we turn our attention to a related connection, that between individual people in local communities and universal humanity in the community of gods and men. The Roman Stoics carry out a radical shift from Plato's notions of interiority and self-sufficiency in the *Phaedo* to a notion of selfhood that fully embraces relations with others. In order to understand this shift, we have to examine more closely the place people occupy in the Roman Stoics' scale of values.

The Stoics inherited from Plato[1] and Aristotle (*EN* 1098b13–14) a threefold division of "goods" into "goods of the soul, goods of the body, and externals." In the *Phaedo* (63E–69E, esp. 68B–C), Plato emphasizes the opposition between soul and body and uses this threefold division to locate virtue and happiness in the soul. In the *Phaedo,* as we have already seen, Plato has Socrates send his spouse, "the women," and his children away (60A, 116B) to "avoid the unseemliness" of crying and emotional breakdowns (117D–E). The company of his friends, however, Socrates keeps until the end, even though they too cannot entirely control their emotions. He shows patience with Crito, who does not quite seem to have gotten the point of the philosophical exposition on death, given that he asks Socrates how he wants to be buried (115C; see also 116E). Socrates also shows respect for and indulges his weeping jailor (116D), who is trying to make the best of a lousy job. The differences in Socrates' treatment of these people could be interpreted in terms of a hierarchical scale, in which friends matter more than one's wife and children, and some pupils belong to the inner circle whereas others do not. Hence, out of the *Phaedo* emerges the question of how other people are supposed to fit into the classification of goods, and how this classification would affect one's assessment of the different types of human relationships.

The language of book 5 of Plato's *Republic,* particularly the phrase "holding women and children in common," suggests that spouses and offspring are ranked among external possessions. So too would Epictetus's notorious analogy between a wife or child and a jug that can break—at least at first glance.[2] Aristotle considers friends to be "the greatest of external goods" (*EN* 1169b10–11). And procreation seems to tie in not only with the external goods (e.g., in accounts that rank children among possessions) but also with the goods that are related to the body, insofar as procreation is the means of preservation for the species. An example of this point of view is Plato's claim in the *Symposium* that, like animals, humans can strive for immortality through procreation and "labor of the body" (207D; see also 208E). The examples drawn from Plato and other thinkers reveal that if we want to understand how Roman Stoics could give so much importance not only to friendship but also to more traditional relationships such as parent-

1. As, e.g., in *Lg.* 743E; *Phlb.* 48E; *Euthd.* 279A–C. An earlier version of this chapter appeared as Reydams-Schils 2002.

2. Epict. *Ench.* 3, 11, 14; Epict. *Diss.* 3.24.11, 27–28, 58–60, 84–88, 4.1.111–12; Marcus Aurelius 11.34.

hood and marriage, we have to examine the role that people play in their view of the good life.

Oikeiōsis, Sociability, and Cicero's *De Finibus*

According to the Stoics, as we have seen, animals and human children (in their prerational phase) are each born with a benevolent self-awareness that triggers the impulse to reach for what is necessary to their self-preservation, the so-called dynamic of "appropriation."[3] For human beings, however, appropriation evolves over time, as Seneca tells us: "Each period of life has its own constitution, one for the baby, and another for the boy, <another for the youth,> and another for the old man. They are all related appropriately to that constitution in which they exist" (*Ep.* 121.14–15, trans. Long and Sedley, LS57B).[4] *Oikeiōsis,* then, always has a history and in human beings changes in the course of their lives, because their "nature" evolves. A child activates the prerational type of *oikeiōsis* (D.L. 7.85). But in full-grown adults "reason intervenes as the craftsman of impulse" (D.L. 7.85–86), and so, in contrast to a child, an adult human being has subsumed the prerational type of *oikeiōsis* under the reason type. The most important transition in a human being's development is that from the prerational phase to the advent of reason.[5]

The third book of Cicero's *De Finibus* provides a good framework for analyzing how the doctrine of appropriation treats relationships. An earlier account in this text (3.20–21) focuses on the perspective of the child, who at birth appears to activate only the self-directed aspect of appropriation. This focus raises the question of how human beings learn to care about others. Both the development from the child's to the adult's perspective and the move away from self-centered behavior are issues that have received much scholarly attention. But in a later passage in that same book (*Fin.* 3.62ff.), Cicero uses the distinction between arational and rational behavior, not to highlight a tension between self-centered *oikeiōsis* and an other-directed or altruistic counterpart, but to develop *two perspectives on social oikeiōsis.* This

3. See LS57. For my purpose the following are, besides the works quoted in the notes below, the most useful works on *oikeiōsis*: Engberg-Pedersen 1986 (with an emphasis on Cic. *Fin.* 3.16–18, 3.20–21), 1990; Isnardi Parente 1989; Pembroke 1971; Philippson 1932; N. White 1979; Whitlock Blundell 1990; Voelke 1961. See also Bodson 1967; Brunschwig 1986.

4. See also Sen. *Ep.* 76.8–11; Cic. *Tusc.* 5.37–39. I do not include material from books 4 and 5 of Cicero's *De Finibus*, because of the complications of the Peripatetic influence and Antiochus's stance. The same holds for the Peripatetic section in Stobaeus's doxography.

5. See also Sen. *Ep.* 76.8ff., 118.14, 121.14ff., 124.8ff.

emphasis brings across the crucial point that both levels of *oikeiōsis* (the arational and the rational) have an impulse toward self-preservation, as well as a fundamentally community-oriented aspect.[6] In other words, according to this analysis it is not the case that arational appropriation is exclusively self-centered. Babies may start off with predominantly self-serving behavior, but there is no reason to deny that the Stoics believe that socialization is already well under way before the age of reason. In fact, there is good evidence to the contrary.

In order to explain human development, all the Stoics need to do is to posit that a child has the potential to become (1) a parent and (2) a human being gifted with reason (albeit without guarantee of its proper use), and that the latter (2) is the foundational requirement for a successful outcome. That does not seem to be a hugely mysterious move. Nor does it seem to require too much from the teleological thesis that Nature made us this way. It does not entail that in order to be wise one would have to be a parent, nor that one does not become social until one has become a parent, but merely that parenthood is a paradigmatic case in which we can see human bonding at work. The first point underlies Chrysippus's claim (which Plutarch ridiculed) "that we have an appropriate disposition relative to ourselves *as soon as we are born* and to our [body]parts and to our *own offspring*" (*Stoic. Rep.* 1038B = LS57E, trans. Long and Sedley, modified). Clearly we are not born parents, but what Chrysippus must have meant is that parenthood stands for a dynamic of socialization that is part of a human being's makeup *right from the start* of his or her life.

As Plutarch indicates, it is the adult's perspective that matters, and Cicero tells us that adults have two approaches[7] to human bonding: (1) one inherent in the nature and the kind of impulse we share with animals, which is based on the care for offspring; and (2) another inherent in our rationality (which distinguishes humans from animals) and anchored in the divine principle. The two approaches are related, because all of nature, from stones to human beings endowed with reason, owes its order to the divine

6. See also Plut. *Stoic. Rep.* 1038B. My starting point is different from that of Inwood (1983, 1984, 1996). It is more in line with that of Annas (1993, 262–76). The crucial issue of development is not one from personal *oikeiōsis* to a social type, or from egoism to altruism. See also Annas 1993, n. 89. This implies that I interpret Cicero's *De Finibus* 3, not as moving from personal *oikeiōsis* to the social kind, but that the later passage, discussed here, allows us to see both of these as connected because they go together in the different stages of the *oikeiōsis* dynamic.

7. See Schofield 1995. I emphasize here that Cicero *readily combines* the two perspectives in Cato's exposition.

principle permeating the universe and manifesting itself differently on different levels.

In the *De Finibus,* Cicero's Cato combines both approaches. According to the Stoics, we share with animals the urge not only toward self-preservation but also toward procreation and social bonding: "They [the Stoics] think it is important to understand that nature engenders parents' love for their children. That is the *starting* point from which we derive the general sociability of the human race" (*Fin.* 3.62 = LS57F, revised at the translator's suggestion). The relationship between parents and offspring is the starting point for the move from self to other: it is a form of self-preservation that also entails the care of another being. This point is borne out by a difference between Aristotle's viewpoint and a passage in Cicero. Aristotle sees children primarily as part of the parents' *selves* (*EN* 1161b18–20, "another self" that in this sense is different from the way in which a friend is "another self"; see below). By contrast, Cicero congratulates Atticus on the birth of his daughter, emphasizes the other-directed aspect of parenthood, and criticizes the Epicureans because they do not allow for *altruism* (*Att.* 125.4.6). Also, in spite of drawing on analogies with animal behavior in *De Finibus,* Cicero uses an a fortiori argument to emphasize that the "bond of mutual aid is far more intimate" in human beings (3.63).

The main reason that the bond among human beings is stronger than are the ties between animals is that, in humans, sociability is also directly anchored in reason and the divine will: "The Stoics hold that the world is governed by divine will: it is as it were a city and state shared by men and gods, and each one of us is a part of this world. From this it is a natural consequence that we prefer the common advantage to our own" (3.64 = LS57F).

Given that human beings are naturally inclined toward enhancing the common good, Cicero's Cato ends this section with a grand peroration about involvement:

> Furthermore, since we see that man is created with a view to protecting and preserving his fellows, it is in agreement with this nature that the wise man should want to play a part in governing the state and, in order to live the natural way, take a wife and want children by her. They [the Stoics] do not even consider pure emotions of love [*sancti amores*] incompatible with the sage. As to the way and life of the Cynics, some say they are applicable to the sage under certain circumstances; some say not at all. (3.68 = LS57F, trans. Long and Sedley; last lines my translation)

What is striking here is that the vantage point of reason does not leave behind the traditional relationships of marriage and parenthood; reason's perspective on universal humanity is always contextualized in specific communities and specific relationships. The "way and life of the Cynics" is a case in contrast, because Cynics rejected traditional commitments in order to serve (or pester, depending on one's perspective) a community in its entirety (see also Epict. *Diss.* 3.22). Cicero's account seems to indicate that Stoics debated among themselves how far to take traditional modes of sociability. But there is no doubt that the Stoics took very seriously questions of how sociability pertains to the philosophical way of life.

The two-level view of *oikeiōsis* that Cicero presents is related to the issue of the Stoic scale of values because it conjures up a potential conflict between our specifically human nature as rational beings and our bodily and material needs. In the prerational phase of our lives, taking care of needs and necessities is desirable and natural ("according to nature," κατὰ φύσιν), that is, our nature at that point in time, which has traits in common with all animal nature. The necessities constitute all that matters, but this is precisely why both self-sufficiency and genuine altruism seem to be unattainable: humans depend on others and their environment for sustenance, survival, and recognition, and this dependency can lead to exploiting others for the sake of one's own needs. But when human beings mature into reason, the priorities shift, and nature in this sense is superseded (Sen. *Ep.* 124).

For the Stoics, everything that matters stands or falls with reason. Unlike the Peripatetic viewpoint, Stoicism is notorious for equating virtue, the good, and happiness with wisdom only—that is, with the correct use of reason. Human virtue means living "according to nature" as a rational being, with a mind that "subjects other things to itself, and itself to nothing" (Sen. *Ep.* 124.12) and that "counts nothing of its own to be outside itself" (23). Epictetus posits that the only thing "up to us," that is, over which we have control, is the correct use of our impressions, which is his rendering of the injunction to use our reason correctly.[8] Like his analogy between a wife or child and a jug, this notion of radical self-reliance admittedly does not sound promising for the value of people and human relationships.

The higher-level *oikeiōsis,* however, does not cancel out the lower level. Nor do the two types of *oikeiōsis* merely coexist in an adult human being. If they did, this coexistence would immediately raise the specter of a dualist, "two-nature" claim. Instead, reason is supposed to subsume and transform the earlier mode, so that even if, let's say, a sage, a greedy adult, and a two-year-old child have a meal together, and all three reach for a piece of

8. *Diss.* 1.1.7ff., and *Ench.* 1, so that we would not miss the point.

bread on the table, they would not be engaging in the same action, because of the radically different underlying motivational structures. The sage would be rationally selecting nourishment that his body needs and that circumstances allow him to take. The non-sage carried away by gluttony would be using his reasoning faculty incorrectly, and his behavior would be a case of passion. The two-year-old would merely be satisfying the call of a grumbling stomach. But if the two modes of appropriation do not alternate or merely coexist, what, then, is a human being's perspective on these two modes (the one we share with animals and the one according to reason) once she has reached maturity? For the Roman Stoics, traditional intimate relationships such as parenthood and marriage are not relegated to a lower level sociability in deference to friendship and the bond of universal humanity that would embody the sociability of reason.

People and the "Preferred Indifferents"

Compared to the strict notion of the "good" in Stoic theory, all other things that humans value are "indifferents." These indifferents include psychological features beyond the proper use of reason; they also include the body and most externals—with the possible exception of the sage's friends, to which we shall return below (LS60M). Yet, leaving aside for the moment Epictetus's radical emphasis on self-reliance and his analogy between people and ordinary breakable objects, Roman Stoic accounts either hesitate to list among the external indifferents the people with whom we have bonds or do so only under specific conditions. In this regard, the gaps and the silences are as revealing as explicit accounts and doctrine. For instance, when Seneca writes to his mother to console her about his banishment, he goes through the traditional list of things of which one is deprived, only to turn around in the Stoic manner by claiming that riches and honor do not really matter. People and relatives, however, are conspicuously absent from Seneca's list, and, in a manner not atypical, Seneca deals with his mother's longing for him without telling us how he himself copes with absence.

In more informal and less technical lists of "traditional goods," such as the ones we find in Seneca's writings rather than in expositions of doctrine, people show up among the items that make us vulnerable to fortune and loss.[9] Yet the notion that one's loved ones are among the things "merely borrowed" from fortune also leads to the realization that we should not take them for granted (Sen. *Cons. Marc.* 10.1ff.; see also *Cons. Pol.* 10.4), and that

9. Sen. *Prov.* 3.2, 4.5; *Const.* 5.6, 6.5, 8.3; *Vit. Beat.* 17.1; see also *Ben.* 1.11ff., where relationships are listed among the things without which we do not want to live; see also *Ben.* 5.13.1: goods of fortune instead of externals.

we should devote ourselves to the sacred duty of preserving what has been entrusted to us (Sen. *Tranq.* 11.1ff.).

In Roman Stoic accounts, relationships such as friendship, marriage, and other forms of kinship are different from externals such as fame and wealth because relationships are not prone to the pitfalls of acquisitiveness and insatiable desire—at least not directly. They can, however, become conduits for that desire. In common with "acquisitions" such as prostitutes or multiple partners, wealth and fame carry the risk of addictive behavior (Sen. *Const.* 6.3–4 contra 7), whereas children, spouses, or relatives do not. Another way in which Seneca (*Ep.* 120.1–3) tries to separate relationships from other externals is by distinguishing between the "useful," such as riches, horses, wine, and cheese, and the "honorable," under which heading would fall the dutiful care of one's aging father or the relieving of a friend's poverty.

The stance that marriage properly construed is the acceptable alternative to sexual passion is an outcome of the Roman Stoics' evaluation of sex and of their analysis of the structures of desire. In the eyes of a grumbling Seneca, women who pile up husbands through repeated divorce (*Ben.* 3.16.2) are the exception that proves that marriage is supposed to counter promiscuity. In line with Seneca, Epictetus complains that women of his era excuse their sexual excesses by purposely misapplying Plato's proposal in the *Republic* that women be held in common (F15 = 53 Schweighäuser; see also *Diss.* 2.4). Sex, it should be remembered, especially in the case of Seneca with his emphasis on *pudicitia,* is not central to Roman Stoic views of marriage. If the passage attributed to Seneca's lost treatise on marriage is authentic, he holds the view that a husband should love his wife with restraint, lest he love her as he would a mistress in an adulterous relationship (*De Matrimonio* 84–86 Haase). But even if created in the "proper" manner, the affective bond with spouses, relatives, children, and friends triggers problems at the time of loss and bereavement. In principle, grief and mourning, not the relationship as such, threaten the life of philosophy.

How can Stoic doctrine help us to understand these patterns? Arius Didymus's version of the theory of indifferents in Stobaeus (2.79–86 W.), or at least such as it is attributed to him, provides the best background in this context.[10] As we have already seen, because the Stoics strictly limit the

10. There are two other main accounts in addition to the one attributed to Arius Didymus: (1) D.L. 7.101–10; (2) Cic. *Fin.* 3.20, 3.50–61. I have given a more detailed and technical analysis of these sources in Reydams-Schils 2002, 228–30. Both Diogenes Laertius and Arius Didymus put the classification soul-body-externals to use. The Stoic Hierocles puts the distinction to use as well, as when

"good" and happiness to virtue, which is itself equated with the correct use of reason, they thereby relegate other traditional "goods" to the rank of indifferents (ἀδιάφορα). Yet indifferents of this type—as opposed to absolute indifferents, such as whether the number of hairs on one's head is odd or even—belong to the category of things that have the power to stir inclination or aversion. They stir inclination if they are according to nature (κατὰ φύσιν) qua prerational and fall under the heading of the things that have "selective value" (ἀξία ἐκλεκτική, terminology coined by Antipater, 2.83 W.) and hence can activate impulse (ὁρμῆς κινητικά). They stir aversion if they are "against nature" (παρὰ φύσιν), have disvalue (ἀπαξία ἀπλεκτική), and activate an impulse "away from" (ἀφορμῆς κινητικά). Arius Didymus calls for all the indifferents that have any value whatsoever "to be taken" (ληπτά) in a broad sense (Stob. 2.82.20 W.). The term "preferred" (προηγμένον) is to be limited to a stricter usage, designating only those indifferents that have *much* value (Stob. 2.80.14–15, 80.19, 84.14–15 W.; see also Cic. *Fin.* 3.51).[11] In other words, the articulation of Stoic ethics as Arius Didymus presents it contains a distinction among the indifferents that are according to nature, between those that are merely to be taken and those that are also preferred indifferents: all preferred indifferents would fall under the heading of "to be taken," but not all the items that are "to be taken" would automatically qualify for the status of being preferred.

The next issue to address is how Arius Didymus makes room in his categories of indifferents for people and the social fabric. His account invites us to align indifferents that have selective value in themselves with the "preferred indifferents." Indifferents that exist for the sake of other things—or "productive" (ποιητικά) indifferents, as he also calls them (Stob. 2.80.15–16, 83.1–7 W.)—do have value, and they fall under the broader category of "to be taken" (ληπτά, 82.20–83.9) but do not qualify for the status of "preferred indifferents" in his sense. Arius Didymus uses the distinction between soul, body, and externals as a subheading of "preferred indifferents." Thus he includes among the preferred indifferents a type of externals that can be selected for its own sake (in the qualified sense of being according to nature), and under this heading he includes certain types of people with

he discusses the care of one's parents from the perspective of both soul and body (*How to Treat One's Parents*, Stob. 4.642.5–6 Hense = 57.30–31 von Arnim). See also Sen. *Ep.* 5.4; *Ben.* 5.13.1; *Vit. Beat.* 8; and the testimony of Sextus Empiricus, with the claim that in the division of goods soul stands for the ruling principle, *M.* 7.234.2–235.4 = LS53F (part); more on this below; see also Epict. *Diss.* 3.7.4.

11. Diogenes Laertius, by contrast, uses the term "preferred" (προηγμένον) itself in the broader sense: 7.105, 7.106. Cic. *Fin.* 3.56 is parallel to D.L. 7.107, which reflects the structure of 7.106.

whom we have relationships—parents and children—as well as "property in due measure" (κτῆσιν σύμμετρον) and "recognition from others" (ἀποδοχὴν παρὰ ἀνθρώπων, 81.5–6). He does, however, stipulate that the "preferred indifferents" pertaining to soul have more value than those pertaining to the body and externals.

As a result of Arius Didymus's rendering of Stoic ethics, "recognition" and "property in due measure" fall under the heading of "preferred indifferents" (indifferents with much value), but "wealth" and "fame" fall under the ληπτά as having selective value merely in function of other goals one may have (83.4–7). Cicero gives us a valuable glimpse of what may be going on here. He claims that Chrysippus and Diogenes did not attach any value to good fame (*eudoxia, Fin.* 3.57) except insofar as it could be useful (*detracta utilitate*). Their successors, however, allegedly swaying under the attacks from Carneades, allowed it to be "preferred and to be taken for its own sake" (*propter se praepositam et sumendam*). It is not any kind of good fame, though, that switches categories here: it is the good opinion bestowed by one's parents and relatives and by good people in general, during life and beyond one's death, that gets promoted. In Arius Didymus's terms, glory as traditionally conceived would be merely of value for the sake of other things, whereas social recognition—our being enmeshed in the social fabric, that is—ranks higher in the value scale and belongs with the preferred indifferents, which have intrinsic value.

Arius Didymus's careful distinction between the preferred indifferents with intrinsic value and the merely useful indifferents that are to be taken, and his noticeable upgrading of the social fabric, is a double move that is reinforced by the doctrine of the "proper functions," by the "circumstances" and "reserve" clauses, and also by the way in which certain Stoics redefined the *telos.* "Proper functions" (καθήκοντα), as defined in the broadest sense, cover all actions that conform to a living being's nature. Hence there are proper functions for plants and animals as well as for humans. On the other end of the scale of nature, the functions that conform to human beings' rationality, the so-called κατορθώματα, are the "perfect" (τέλεια) proper functions (D.L. 7.107ff.; Arius Didymus ap. Stob. 2.85 W.), the actions performed by the Stoic sage. In this line of reasoning, there are human *kathēkonta* that correspond both to our lower-level nature and to our reason.

Two issues pertaining to the relationship between proper functions and right actions have significance for my argument here. First, it is clear from our sources that proper functions have a privileged application in the field of social relationships. In this context, the term is frequently translated as "duty." An important passage of Epictetus in which he talks about duty confirms the point that social relationships are prominent among human proper functions: "for I ought not to be unmoved like a statue, but I should maintain my natural and acquired relationships, as a dutiful man and as a son, brother, father, and citizen" (3.2.4, trans. Long).[12]

Second, social duties appear to have a privileged connection with reason. "Befitting acts are all those which *reason chooses to do*" (ὅσα λόγος αἱρεῖ ποιεῖν), such as "honoring one's parents, brothers, and country and conversing with friends" (D.L. 7.108–9). When Hierocles claims that "wanting to obey reason, we would fulfill our duty [toward our parents]" (Stob. 4.642.7–8 Hense = 57.31–32 von Arnim), we could interpret this to mean that even a sage would not neglect the "lower" proper functions, including her social duties. We could also pursue the stronger reading that these duties belong to the sage qua sage. Cicero puts the latter reading in an extreme and puzzling form: "That wisdom which I have called the most important is the knowledge of divine and human matters, which includes the community of gods and men, as well as the bond among men; if this is the highest knowledge, as it certainly is, it necessarily follows that the duty that is derived from this bond is the most important" (*Off.* 1.153).[13] To understand fully what is going on in this passage, we would need to explore the connection between reason and sociability, as I will do below.

But first, back to proper functions. Proper functions are context specific. What may be an appropriate action concerning a preferred indifferent in one situation, such as taking care of one's bodily well-being, may not do at all in a different context. Both the "reserve" clause and circumstances enter the picture here because indifferents, whether they are valuables of the preferred kind or not, are not, as their name indicates, good in an absolute sense. They merely give scope for the exercise of virtue and for the good strictly speaking. This idea is expressed in Diogenes of Babylon's version of the Stoic *telos* of human life as "reasoning well in the selection and avoidance of things in accordance with nature." Thus it is not the things themselves that matter but whether we use them in accord with reason or not.[14] Or, as Seneca puts it in his *De Beneficiis,* because we cannot guarantee the outcome of actions pertaining to the body or externals, it is our inten-

12. For an illuminating discussion of this passage, see P. Hadot 1998, ch. 8. See also Epict. F27 = 177 Schweighäuser = Marcus Aurelius 11.37.

13. See Dyck 1996, 340–42.

14. *SVF* 44 = LS58K; see also Hierocles ap. Stob. 4.502.20ff. Hense = 52–53 von Arnim; on this, and connections with Chrysippus's formulation of the *telos*, see Long 1967.

tions that matter. Thus we should always maintain a certain "reserve" (ὑπεξαίρεσις, *exceptio*), a certain inner distance that allows us to let go of the indifferents if we have to in order to keep our happiness intact.[15]

How exactly circumstances enter into play where indifferents are concerned can vary, however, as can the tone of the injunction behind duties. To say that one will engage in an action "if nothing prevents it" can reflect different attitudes. In the case of the indifferents that are merely productive of other things—the indifferents that have value but that are not preferred in Arius Didymus's strict sense—the predominant attitude appears to be one of taking and enjoying if the opportunity presents itself. These things are what we may call "the good things of life," such as abundance, riches, and fame. Marcus Aurelius gives us an example of the right attitude in his adoptive father Antoninus Pius: "the things that contribute to the comfort of life, of which fortune had granted him copious supply, he used without ostentation but also without apology, so as to enjoy them unaffectedly when they were at hand but to feel no need of them when they were not" (1.16.4).[16]

But in other instances the circumstances clause is used with a stronger injunction: for "necessities" such as taking care of one's health (D.L. 7.109) or fulfilling social obligations, the implication is that we had better have good reason for rejecting them. In this regard the Stoic position was the opposite of the Epicurean as recorded in the doxographic material: Seneca (*De Ot.* 3.2–3) tells us that the Epicurean sage will not participate in public life unless circumstances require it (for the parallel on marriage, see D.L. 10.119), whereas the Stoic needs a reason to abstain (see also D.L. 7.121).[17] Similarly, Arius Didymus tells us that in the case of the indifferents that have to do with the "intermediate" *kathēkon,* "we may fall short of happiness if we do not select them, or reject them without an attenuating circumstance" (ἀπεριστάτως, Stob. 2.86.15–16 W.), presumably because we would not be using our reason correctly in the selection process.

I have already mentioned Diogenes of Babylon's recasting of the Stoic *telos,* but a version attributed to Antipater of Tarsus is even more to the

15. See also Epict. *Ench.* 2; F27 at Marcus Aurelius 11.37; Marcus Aurelius 4.1, 5.20, 6.50; Arius Didymus ap. Stob. 2.115.1–5 W.; Sen. *Ben.* 4.34.4, 4.39.4. See also the current debate between Brennan 2000 and Brunschwig, forthcoming. See also Inwood 1985.

16. He compares his adoptive father to Socrates in this respect (1.16.9). See also Epict. *Ench.* 15; Sen. *Vit. Beat.* 25.5.

17. See also Cic. *Off.* 1.70ff., where noninvolvement in general would be the exception; see also Cic. *Fin.* 3.68; Epicurus ap. Plut. *Tranq.* 465F–466A.

point here: "to do everything in one's power continuously and undeviatingly with a view to obtaining the predominating things that accord with nature" (*SVF* 57 = LS58K). Gisela Striker interprets the phrase "the predominant things that accord with nature" (τῶν προηγουμένων κατὰ φύσιν) as the "primary natural things" (πρῶτα κατὰ φύσιν),[18] but I submit that it may refer to what we find recorded as the preferred indifferents in Arius Didymus's sense: things that have much selective value and that have this value in themselves. This would explain why in Antipater's formula the emphasis is not so much on rational selection as on the continuous effort (πᾶν τὸ καθ' αὑτὸν ποιεῖν διηνεκῶς καὶ ἀπαραβάτως) required in this process. Rather than looking at this formula from the perspective of the debate between the Stoics and their critics from the New Academy (and between Antipater and Carneades in particular), I would like to establish a connection with the social relationships as they are included in Arius Didymus's account of the preferred indifferents and with Cicero's testimony (*Fin.* 3.57) that, after Diogenes, a "good reputation" in the sense of recognition from one's fellow human beings was switched to the category of "preferred and desirable for its own sake." Based on the claim recorded in Arius Didymus that preferred indifferents have much value, it would make sense for Antipater to hold that these indifferents justify a greater effort on our part than things that are merely to be taken. And if a basic form of sociability belongs with the preferred indifferents, it would follow that the relationships Arius mentions under this heading are worthy of the "continuous effort" Antipater emphasizes in his *telos* formula.

In addition to the *telos* formula, Antipater (if it is the same person and not the later Antipater of Tyre) is also said to have written our earliest Stoic account in praise of marriage, with an injunction to marry that is clad in the strongest terms possible. For him, marriage is not a question of the sage being "willing" to marry (Cic. *Fin.* 3.68). Nor does he consider marriage to be merely compatible with philosophy. He does not use the future tense (D.L. 7.21) but instead uses an "ought" (δεῖ) clause that places marriage among "the most necessary and primary proper functions" (τῶν ἀναγκαιοτάτων καὶ πρώτων καθηκόντων). So it is entirely possible that by emphasizing the effort required of us in our handling of preferred indifferents, Antipater became a catalyst in the process of the upgrading of social

18. See Striker 1986, 187, with references to Hirzel and Bonhöffer. See Plut. *Comm. Not.* 1071A6; Galen *Plac. Hipp. et Plat.* 5, 328.9–10 De Lacy = *SVF* 3.12; Long 1967. Long reads the phrase as τὰ κατὰ φύσιν. I read the phrase as προηγμένα in Arius Didymus's sense. On the other hand, my hypothesis does not go as far as Görler's (1984), who posits that πρὸς τὸ τυγχάνειν τῶν προηγουμένων κατὰ φύσιν may aim at ἀγαθά as well. See also LS58 and 64.

relationships.[19] In any case, for Epictetus, Antipater ranks among the Stoics of primary importance (*Diss.* 3.2.13–14).

With this outline of the doctrine of (preferred) indifferents in place, we can now turn to why the Stoics would want to rank the people with whom we have relationships among the (preferred) indifferent externals to begin with. Epictetus makes this move with a bluntness worthy of a Cynic, but as we have noted already, other Roman Stoics are more hesitant in this regard.[20] There appear to be two main concerns at work: first, the problem that relationships can leave one vulnerable to pressures that would conflict with the life of reason; second, that the threat of absence and loss is a very real factor in any type of relationship. Concerning the first problem, the Stoics hold that the lower-level *oikeiōsis* in humans can be overruled if there is a conflict between necessities or social duties and the demands of reason. Under the right circumstances, bodily self-preservation, for instance, can be overruled by suicide, and Epictetus indicates that it could be appropriate to die for a friend (*Diss.* 2.7.3; D.L. 7.130). One's relationships too may have to make way for moral action and choices.

In the case of social relationships, Marcus Aurelius points out that "in so far as any of them [other human beings] stand in the way of our closest duties, a human being then comes to be one of the things that are indifferent to me, no less than the sun, or the wind, or a wild beast" (5.20, trans. Hard; see also 3.4.1; Epict. *Diss.* 4.1.100–102). Here human beings fall as low as the absolute indifferents, which would not even prompt inclination or aversion.[21] In the context of a discussion of the Stoic Hecato's views, Cicero hints that when a father has turned tyrant, a son who has exhausted all other possibilities may decide to "prefer the well-being of his

19. See Pohlenz 1948, 190.

20. See also *Diss.* 1.1.14–15 (includes brother, friend, child), 3.24.5 (human beings, on separation), 14–15 (wife, children, Hercules), 84ff. (comparison to a jar or crystal goblet, discussed above and below, life expectancy theme), 4.1.67 (child, wife, brother, friends, but explicit issue of life expectancy), 4.1.87 (child, brother, friend), 4.1.100–101 (child, wife), 4.1.107–8 (child, wife, issue of life expectancy), 4.1.111–12 (image of pot, discussed above and below), 4.1.153 (kindred, friend, country, Diogenes the Cynic mentioned as paradigm), 4.1.159 (Socrates' attitude toward wife, children, country, friends, kinsmen).

21. In this passage as a whole, either human beings are "very close to us," οἰκειότατον, which, as the context indicates, refers to our *inner* disposition (διάθεσις, more on this below)—insofar as it has to do with the injunction to do good and to bear with other people—or they fall under the absolute indifferents. Marcus Aurelius skips the category of preferred indifferents. In general, like Epictetus, he does not use προηγμένον, and he uses προηγούμενον in the nontechnical sense. For Epictetus, see Bonhöffer 1894, 43. In Marcus Aurelius's writings the classification body-externals-soul is predominant.

fatherland over that of his father," in which case parricide is legitimate (*Off.* 3.90).[22] Seneca, for his part, mentions a good man slaying his sons (*Prov.* 6.2) and praises Augustus's rejection of his daughter Julia (*Brev. Vit.* 4.5; *Clem.* 1.10.3–4). As Epictetus warns, the good takes precedence over all blood ties (*Diss.* 3.3.5–7).

Blood ties and social relationships in general can become the conduit for pressure to acquire material advantages and social status, which create conflicts with the life of reason. The classic instance is found in Plato's *Republic* (549C ff.): the son of a good man is corrupted by the slaves and his mother, who grumble that his father is a social failure. Seneca echoes the theme of corruption through relationships,[23] and Epictetus repeatedly gives examples of interference and pressure from the people around us, such as one's father-in-law or one's sweetheart (*Diss.* 3.22.70–71, 4.1.15–18). If one is not careful, one could end up like Aristotle, on all fours and with Alexander's concubine riding on his back, as medieval lore has it. The Early Stoics also cite the bad influences of other people as one of two factors of corruption (διαστροφή). The deceptiveness of external pursuits is the other, and both are opposed to "the starting points of nature," which supposedly are "never perverse" (D.L. 7.89).[24] In the passage I used as epigraph, Philo of Alexandria picks up the Platonic version of the theme that people who are too tied up in their intimate relationships are lost both to themselves and to the community at large.

The inherent potential for moral conflicts within relationships adds a new dimension to the Roman Stoic appropriation of a topos from stock discussions about the pros and cons of married life: the criteria for selecting a partner. The idea is that although we cannot choose our parents, children, or other relatives, we can, at least in principle, make an informed choice when selecting a partner (or, in the case of an arranged marriage, someone else can do so on our behalf). As Musonius tells us, we should transform the traditional selection criteria and aim, not for wealth, social status, or physical beauty, but rather for virtue and soundness of body.[25] If we use the wrong criteria, then we have only ourselves to blame for negative outcomes. But in the *Liber Aureolus de Nuptiis* attributed to Theophrastus and preserved in Jerome, this notion is turned on its head (F486, 310.7–11 For-

22. See also *Dig.* 11.7.35, quoted by Saller 1994, 116.

23. *Ep.* 31.2–3, 33.4, 60.1, 94.54, 95.3, 103, 115.11.

24. Cf. also Cic. *Tusc.* 3.2; Sen. *Ep.* 94.13, 123.8ff.

25. 13B Lutz; see also Antipater *SVF* 62, 63; Hierocles ap. Stob. 4.506.8–507.5 Hense = 55.3–20 von Arnim; *De Remediis Fortuitorum*, attributed to Seneca, 16.6–7, pp. 54–55 Haase.

tenbaugh). There, the conditions for a sage marrying are so stringent and so impossible that we might just as well conclude that the sage ought not to marry at all. The author of this text deems the marital relationship beyond redemption for the life of philosophy, but that is not the route the Roman Stoics took on this issue, as I will explain below.

In addition to the concern about social pressures that come with relationships, the Stoics are also worried about the potentially destabilizing effects of absence and loss. Even if the correct criteria have been applied, and the relationship does not create conflicts, we still need to practice a certain measure of detachment. If a marriage happens to be childless, we have to be able to let go of the desire for offspring. In the case of our blood relations, we must let go of the prospects for mutual aid and for advantage. Epictetus makes the point that nature has given us parents and siblings without guarantee that they will be good to us or that they will necessarily be our friends.[26] In addition to realizing that death is not an evil, we also need to have a realistic view of our spouse's and children's life expectancy, and this, I would argue, is the proper context for understanding Epictetus's terse comparison of one's spouse or child to a jug: "In the case of everything attractive or useful, or that you are fond of, remember to say just what sort of thing it is, beginning with the least little things. If you are fond of a jug, say "I am fond of a jug!" For when it is broken you will not be upset. If you kiss your child or your wife, say that you are kissing a human being; for when it dies you will not be upset" (*Ench.* 3, trans. N. P. White). The point is not to minimize and do away with human affection—Socrates did love his children, we are told, though in a free spirit (*Diss.* 3.24.60)—but to render us aware of human frailty and to enable us to cope with mortality. It is a blunt memento mori. As Seneca reminds us, "What is a human being" but "a vessel that the slightest shaking, the slightest toss will break?" (*Cons. Marc.* 11.3; see also *Ep.* 49.10–11). What is harsh in this picture is not the Stoic stance but the reality we have a tendency to overlook. Romans of all social classes had to face a very high infant mortality rate. For instance, of the thirteen children that Marcus Aurelius and Faustina had, only six survived into adulthood. Thus Marcus Aurelius had plenty of opportunity to train himself to remain "ever the same . . . at the loss of a child" (1.8, trans. Hard) while nevertheless "showing genuine love to his children" (1.13).

Contrary to what Epictetus's analogy between a human being and a vessel may at first glance suggest, the Roman Stoics, as I argue, consider

26. *Ench.* 30; *Diss.* 3.3.8–10, 3.21.4–6; see also Sen. *Ben.* 4.33.2.

human affection and the social affective bonds very important. The analysis of the doctrine of (preferred) indifferents and related matters has yielded the conclusion that social relationships are the most important sphere of action for proper functions and that, for the later Stoics at least, relationships fall under the strong version of the circumstances clause, requiring a special dispensation to be overruled. People fall under the category of preferred indifferents only in certain, delineated aspects—that is, only insofar as, in Marcus Aurelius's wording, relationships involve unpredictable outcomes and carry the potential for obstructing the exercise of virtue.

If we now turn from the indifferents to the heading of the "good" in the doxography attributed to Arius Didymus, we are in for a surprise: a certain category of people, namely, "friends," turns out to be a type of externals that even the Stoics would admit under the heading of the good rather than under the heading of the indifferents, and other sources confirm this inclusion.[27] In other words, friends occupy a *position between* the good in the strictest Stoic sense, namely, virtue as the correct use of reason, and the indifferents. In Cicero's rendering (*Fin.* 3.55), friends fall under the good not as "constitutive" of the goal of human life (*telika*) but as "productive" (*poiētika*) of the good, a distinction we have already encountered on the level of indifferents as well.[28] Arius Didymus includes "friendship," along with "honor, goodwill, and <harmony>," under the good, but as "being related in a certain way to something" (τὰ δὲ πρός τί πως ἔχειν; ap. Stob. 2.73.17–20 W.).[29] Posidonius and Hecato are reported to have posited that "a friend is worth having for his own sake and that it is a good thing to have many friends" (D.L. 7.124).[30] In all of this evidence, moral virtue, friendship, and reason are closely aligned.[31] How this is possible we need to examine next. But even in the most ideal form of philosophical friendship, loss and separation need to be addressed, and this is what "friends," as opposed to "friendship," have in common with other externals.

27. Arius Didymus ap. Stob. 2.70.8 W.; D.L. 7.95; Sext. Emp. *M.* 11.46. For an excellent analysis of the evidence that shows how "friends" are related to the good rather than being "indifferents," see Banateanu 2001.

28. See also D.L. 7.96–97; Arius Didymus ap. Stob. 2.71.15 W.; Sen. *Ep.* 109.1.

29. See also Arius Didymus ap. Stob. 72.3–6, 2.94.21 W.; Sext. Emp. *M.* 11.22–30; Sext. Emp. *PH* 3.169–72.

30. δι᾽ αὑτόν θ᾽ αἱρετὸν τὸν φίλον ἀποφαίνονται καὶ τὴν πολυφιλίαν ἀγαθόν. See also Cic. *Fin.* 3.70; Sen. *Ep.* 9, 20.5: definition of friendship as definition of wisdom.

31. See Fraisse 1974, 355ff.

Reason and Relationships

The Stoic tradition and Cicero (*Fin.* 3.64) define the "community of reason" as embracing all beings that partake of divine reason, including the divine principle itself. This stance implies that relationships are not limited to human beings. The divine and active principle too is "relational" as it unfolds itself in the ordering (*diakosmēsis*) of the universe. To express this relational mode, Epictetus describes Zeus as a father, thereby transferring the model of parenthood from humans to god himself.[32]

In Roman Stoicism, taking the "community of reason" beyond the bond among the sages—if any exist!—leads us both to the community of gods and men and to universal humanity, in the sense that every adult human being has a reasoning faculty that is directly related to the divine reason permeating the universe. As the Roman Stoics tell us time and again, we are to look at ourselves as parts of a whole. Human beings, as Marcus Aurelius indicates, have a common origin and a common point of return (4.14, 4.40) in divine reason (see also Epict. *Diss.* 1.9). If we take into account Stoic physics and its connection with ethics,[33] as we did in the first chapter, the implication is that this common origin is prior not only in the sense of being more fundamental but also in the history of the universe, even though human beings do not start out with reason at birth, and hence reason appears not to be prior with regard to us.

In the form of *oikeiōsis* that corresponds to our rational nature, not only can the distinction between objectivity and subjectivity be overcome, a point discussed in the first chapter, but also the potential conflict between self-interest and altruism: that which merits preserving is reason; though it is my or your reason that is at work, what matters is not *my* or *your* reason as such.[34] Perfection of human reason is perfection according to nature *as a whole* (Sen. *Ep.* 124.14–15). *Homo sacra res homini;* a human being is sacred to a human being precisely because of the reason they share (*Ep.* 95.33). One must live for one's neighbor, if one would live for oneself (*Ep.* 48.2–4),[35] says Seneca in a passage in which he explicitly links friendship and universal humanity. And "a sage considers nothing more truly his own than that which he shares in partnership with all mankind" (Sen. *Ep.* 73.7, 85.36).

32. See Sen. *Ep.* 110.10; Inwood 1996, 259ff.

33. See Cooper 1995, esp. 599–610 (in a debate with Julia Annas). See also Cooper 1996; Long 2002.

34. See Cic. *Leg.* 1.29; Epict. *Diss.* 1.19.11–15; Engberg-Pedersen 1986, 162ff.; Frede 1999, 85ff.; Voelke 1961; S. White 1995; Whitlock Blundell 1990, 231ff.

35. See also Marcus Aurelius 11.4; Epict. *Diss.* 1.19.11–15; Arius Didymus ap. Stob. 2.94.21 W.: τὴν δὲ περὶ αὐτὸν φιλίαν, καθ' ἣν φίλος ἐστὶ τῶν πέλας . . . .

Cicero, in turn, attributes to Antipater the claim that "you ought to be concerned with the well-being of [fellow] humans and to serve human society; you were born under this law and have these principles from nature, which you ought to obey and follow, so that your advantage should be the common advantage and that the common advantage, in turn, should be yours" (*Off.* 3.52).

Now that we have (1) reminded ourselves that divine reason is the common origin of all human rational beings and (2) taken note of the fact that the Stoics blur the distinction between self and other, we are in a better position to assess the criticism to which the anonymous Platonist commentary on the *Theaetetus* subjects the Stoics.[36] In an imaginary debate between Stoics, Academics, and Epicureans, the commentary (5.3–8.6 Bastianini and Sedley) uses a dilemma to tackle an alleged Stoic attempt to derive justice from the notion of *oikeiōsis* (appropriation): either (*a*) we say that there are no differences in degree for appropriation, whatever the closeness of the relationship, and then we can save the notion of justice; or (*b*) we admit that appropriation does come in different degrees, and that we do feel closer to ourselves than to other human beings. The commentary rejects the first alternative as wrong, for three reasons: (1) there is a disjunction between appropriation in relation to ourselves as "natural and arational" (φυσικὴ καὶ ἄλογος, 5.38–39) and appropriation in relation to one's neighbors as "natural but not independent of reason" (φυσικὴ . . . οὐ μέντοι ἄνευ λόγου, 5.40–42); (2) whereas we can fall out with other people, we can never become alienated from ourselves; and (3) even concerning our own bodies we have different degrees of appropriation in relation to different body parts.

If, on the other hand, a Stoic were to admit that there are different degrees of appropriation, she could in theory still safeguard philanthropy, the commentator claims, but two problems would present themselves here. First, crises—such as the notorious example of two shipwrecked sages struggling to hold on to a piece of driftwood that will carry only one of them (Cic. *Off.* 3.90)—show that the Stoic notion of philanthropy is impracticable. Second, the Stoic who admits different degrees of appropriation is not really in a better position than his Epicurean counterpart who denies appropriation in relation to one's neighbor altogether; the Stoic cannot guarantee that egoism will not prevail, and one instance of failure is enough to undermine the claim to virtue and art (*technē*). The last part of this exposition reveals

36. For the edition of and excellent commentary on this text by G. Bastianini and D. Sedley, see *Corpus dei papiri filosofici Greci et Latini*, vol. 3 (Florence: Olschki, 1995), 227–562, esp. 491–96. See also Lévy 1990; Opsomer 1998, 44–49.

the polemical tenor of the passage, which sets the Stoics up against the Epicureans, and the Academics against the Stoics in turn. That this setup is part of a polemic should put us on our guard.

Disjunctions are both the strength and the weakness of such arguments. If, in the passage from *De Finibus* (3.62ff.), Cicero is on to something genuinely Stoic, then the commentary's disjunction between arational appropriation as being self-centered and the rational kind as being other-directed does not hold.[37] It is not true that self-preservation corresponds to the lower-level *oikeiōsis* that we share with animals and that altruism corresponds to our *oikeiōsis* as rational beings. Both levels of *oikeiōsis* provide a grounding of community among adult human beings; other-directedness starts with the care for offspring, even while ultimately being anchored in divine reason. *Oikeiōsis* according to reason, in turn, may transcend the distinction between self and other, but it does not obliterate self-preservation; instead, the notion of the "self" that is worth preserving has shifted radically.

In addition to the problem with the disjunction between arational and rational appropriation, we can detect that something is wrong with the second horn of the commentary's dilemma as well, namely, the case in which a Stoic admits that there are different degrees of appropriation. A Stoic such as Hierocles does indeed allow for such a variable, which literally entails different degrees of *kinship*. With his image, however, of drawing the circles of relationships at the farthest remove closer to the center, he also enjoins us to work on those differences and to intensify the lower degrees of relationships. It would be one thing for the Platonist voice in the commentary to doubt that human nature is capable of such an exercise, which it does, but quite another to unmask inconsistencies in the Stoic account, which it does not.

A second crucial disjunction comes toward the end of the exposition in the anonymous commentary: rather than deriving his notion of justice from *oikeiōsis*—that is, from a potential embedded in human nature—Plato relies on the theme of "becoming like god" (τῆς πρὸς τὸν θεὸν ὁμοιώσεως 7.14–20; *Tht.* 176B1–2). Here, the commentary pits human nature against the divine but ignores the Stoic concept of god. This line of attack is typical of Platonists of the period. Because they can accept neither the radically "immanent" stance of a divine principle that constitutes and permeates the universe nor the Stoic notion of Providence, they proceed as if the Stoics had no notion of the divine at all, and as if their physics is irrelevant

37. On this see also Annas 1993, 270–74.

for ethics. But if one turns to the Stoic accounts themselves, one quickly discovers that these have their own equivalent of the theme of "becoming like god"; in the case of human rationality, "living according to nature" presupposes, and is anchored in, the fact that human and divine reason are connected. "Follow god," Seneca (*Vit. Beat.* 15; *Ep.* 16.5), Epictetus (*Diss.* 1.30), and Marcus (7.31) urge us. Through this connection the human "self" is transcended, but this self does not open up to a radically transcendent notion of the divine, as the Platonists would have it. "You have forgotten that the intellect of each of us is a god and has flowed from there," Marcus Aurelius says (12.26, trans. Hard). The "there" in this line, as we have seen in the first chapter, is still firmly within the cosmos.[38] For the Stoics, to take care of the common good is to follow the example of the Providence that administers the universe. One could turn the tables on both the Platonists and the commentary by saying that an assimilation to their notion of the divine entails a stronger risk that we end up treating our fellow human beings as merely instrumental, and that their notion cannot ground the claim that human beings are sacred to each other.

The commentary relies for its arguments on the famous test case of two shipwrecked sages with only one piece of driftwood. So what would happen to them according to the Stoics themselves, and can Stoics address the criticism that their theory would fall apart in a crisis? Let us assume that indeed it cannot be decided which of the two sages matters most for the common good and that neither are semi-unconscious or prone to involuntary reactions. A genuinely Stoic option would be that both sages—whether men, women, spouses, or friends—will be committed to not jeopardizing the rational self that truly merits preserving, and that they will in all likelihood prefer to perish together rather than fall prone to passion and fight each other for their lives.

The really difficult test case would be the scenario of a sage and a group of children in a shipwreck, with all or only some being her or his own. According to the Stoics, a child depends on its parents for its well-being and cannot be expected to make a rational choice on its own behalf. How would this Stoic decide whom to save? Should she save her own child? If so, which one? Or would saving one's own child be a type of self-centered act? But if she chooses to sacrifice her child for the sake of someone else's, she would betray the promise structure of her parental obligations (not to mention her affection for the child). The Stoic stance can do more than Platonist critics allow for, but it cannot resolve all moral dilemmas. But the Platonic,

38. See also Marcus Aurelius 10.11; Sen. Ep. 31.8ff., 48.11, 59.14, 90.34, 92.27–31.

Peripatetic, Epicurean, or Cynic views arguably fare no better in such a situation.

If one can, in fact, refute the charges of the Platonist commentator against Stoic sociability, what does the Stoic view look like when we examine it more closely? Many passages in the later Stoics, including the one from Antipater preserved in Cicero and quoted above (*Off.* 3.52), tell us that human beings are "born" social creatures and come equipped with the "innate faculties" required for fellowship. But this innate faculty in itself does not tell us much about the connection between reason and sociability. It is Marcus Aurelius who has preserved the most concise, and at the same time most radical, formula for this connection. For him, and he repeats this claim over and over again, to be rational is to be social.[39] "A property, too, of the rational soul, is love of one's neighbor, and truthfulness, and modesty, and to regard nothing of higher value than itself—which is also a property of law, and there is thus no difference between right reason and the reason that underlies justice" (11.1, trans. Hard; see also 7.55, 8.12, 8.26, 8.43).[40] Or again, in a passage in which Marcus Aurelius distinguishes between the lower aspects of our nature and our rationality: "Every rational being is, by virtue of its rationality, also a social being" (10.2, trans. Hard). As Pierre Hadot has demonstrated, the discipline of action (that is, the discipline of our impulses) aiming at the common good is one of three key exercises, together with the discipline of judgment and that of desire, that underlie the entire *Meditations*. Because of the intimate connection between action and justice, Marcus Aurelius emphasizes the importance of the discipline that controls our impulses over the other two disciplines.[41]

The Stoic correlation between reason and sociability goes much further than the stance Aristotle defended, that by nature human beings tend to form communities.[42] In fact, the Stoic correlation challenges yet another distinction, that between the contemplative life and practical wisdom: even when we appear the most withdrawn, whether in ourselves or on the remotest of islands, we are actually still involved in community and cannot be otherwise. Such a strong connection between reason and sociability could also explain Cicero's startling claim that even if his other needs were

39. See, e.g., Marcus Aurelius 3.7, 5.29, 6.44, 7.64, 7.68, 7.72, 8.2, 10.2; see also Cic. *Off.* 1.50, 1.153; Epict. *Diss.* 3.3.8, 4.6.35.

40. On this, see also Engberg-Pedersen 1998, 330–34.

41. P. Hadot 1998, 236.

42. *Pol.* 1253a2, 1253a30; *EN* 1097b8–15, 1169b16–22.

abundantly provided for, a sage who was entirely cut off from human society would die (*Off.* 1.153). Diogenes Laertius too takes the stance that "the wise man will not live in solitude; for he is naturally made for society and action" (7.123, trans. Hicks). If, as the Stoics claim, sociability belongs to reason itself, other people can never be *reduced* to mere preferred indifferents. Even if in *some respects* they do fall under this category, unlike other externals they are never *merely* the "material" for our exercise of virtue.[43]

One can look at relationships from two perspectives: people around us have features in common with external objects, but there is also an internal aspect to relationships, because of one's inner disposition toward others. Marcus Aurelius focuses on the importance of this second aspect, the internal one, by recommending a "loving and affectionate disposition" (τῆς φιλητικῆς καὶ στερκτικῆς διαθέσεως, 10.1). Along similar lines, Epictetus—after he has just told us that the good ranks above all kinship ties—goes on to claim that "if we situate the good in *correct volition* [προαίρεσις], the preservation of social relationships [σχέσεις] becomes a good [ἀγαθόν]" (*Diss.* 3.3.8, trans. Long).[44] But how would this inner disposition toward people be different from our inclination to accept external indifferent valuables when nothing prevents us from doing so or when physical self-preservation is at stake? In the latter case, reason's operation consists in a rational selection of valuables that answer to the inclinations and needs of our lower-level, prerational nature and *oikeiōsis;* in the case of social relationships, the affective disposition and inclination are intrinsic to reason itself. That makes all the difference. Hence we can understand that, in some of our Stoic sources, friends are allied to the life of virtue and the good because they are conducive to this life. Cicero, Arius Didymus, and Diogenes Laertius establish a connection between friendship and the good, and Seneca's letter "On the Fellowship of Wise Men" (109; see also Cic. *Off.* 1.55–56) highlights the friendship, affection, and joy that sages derive from one another's company, from shared inquiry and mutual prompting toward virtuous action. As we have seen, friends constitute a category between the indifferents that have value and things that are intrinsically good, in the strict Stoic sense.

The fundamental relational aspect of reason unlocks a different reading of Stoic passages on friendship, such as that found in Seneca's ninth letter. This letter is cited as evidence that the Stoics consider friends to be

43. Chrysippus cited in Plut. *Comm. Not.* 1069E ff.; Cic. *Fin.* 3.61.

44. See also Sen. *Ben.* 4.18.2; Bonhöffer 1894, 86–87.

replaceable.[45] In it, Seneca does compare the loss of a friend to the loss of external possessions and to the loss of bodily members, such as a hand. He also enjoins that if we happen to lose a friend, we should concentrate on finding a new one. Yet traditional readings of this letter make at least two mistakes. First, it is not because the *loss* of a friend is structurally analogous to the loss of indifferents that the *possession* of a friend has exactly the same value as the possession of external and bodily things. Second, upon careful reading, the letter shows that even the structural analogy in the case of a loss is limited: as I have indicated already in the first chapter, memory plays a crucial role in relationships.

What difference does memory make? Admittedly, one can imagine a musician cherishing the memories of the time when she had full use of her hands, or a Roman dwelling on childhood memories of his grandfather's country estate. For the Stoics, all the occurrences of one's life are worth remembering because they reflect divine forethought and are part of the ordering of the universe. But memory has a very special function in the case of human relationships, precisely because the latter have an essentially *internalist* aspect, a connection with the development and exercise of reason and virtue. Rather than give in to mourning, Seneca tells us, we should preserve in our memory what friends meant to us, as well as how they came to mean so much. And there is nothing that would prevent these portraits of the mind from preserving a unique character specific to the friends in question. The Stoic view of memory and the intrinsic connection between reason and relationships guarantee that one friend is not just the same as another. It does matter who your friend is.

Besides our attitude of affection and our memory, there is another crucial way in which the death of others is not merely an external event but affects our inner disposition. Others require that we make efforts on their behalf to help secure their well-being. So how does a Stoic deal with the loss of a friend whom he did his utmost best to save? In a restricted sense, a Stoic can say, "I would have preferred things to turn out otherwise." The past tense aspect of this phrase would be acceptable: the Stoic can justify having done her utmost best to rescue the other person before the outcome became fatal. But the counterfactual aspect of the expression would be problematic: once an event has happened, a Stoic must resign himself to the outcome.[46] So a Stoic could not say, "I wish this had never happened." Nor could she say, "It would have been better if this had not happened." A Stoic

45. As in Inwood 1997; Lesses 1993.

46. See Irwin 1998.

cannot be true to the teachings of his school and make such claims, because they would constitute not only a fruitless rebellion against the order of things but also an aphilosophical ignorance of what it is humans can and cannot control. With this realization and the revised reading of texts such as Seneca's ninth letter, we have a sense of both the possibilities and the limits of the Stoic view on human bonding. While focusing on the limitations, many assessments have in fact painted much too bleak a picture of the Stoic's attitude toward relationships.

So far I have focused on the connection between reason and sociability in universal humanity and in friendship. Roman Stoicism, however, also rather remarkably applies the correlation between reason and sociability to the traditional relationships of kinship and marriage. In so doing, Roman Stoicism extends the language of affection, as Cicero does when he mentions the *sancti amores* of a sage engaged in marrying and having children (*Fin.* 3.68).[47] The revalorization of traditional relationships is strikingly noticeable in a passage preserved in Sextus Empiricus (*M.* 11.46). In a classification not of the indifferents but of the good, we read that the Stoics included under the heading of external goods not only friends, as we see in our other evidence,[48] but also "good children and parents and the like" (τὰ σπουδαῖα τέκνα καὶ γονεῖς καὶ τὰ ὅμοια).[49] The trend can also be noticed in Seneca, who mentions friendship and the household together as spheres for virtuous action (*Ep.* 66.8).[50] Thus, the Stoics considerably upgrade both parenthood and marriage. A crucial point to be made about Hierocles' image of different degrees of affinity existing in concentric circles is that we cannot cut out the close and traditional kinship relationships for the sake of humanity at large. Even though we strive for the common good, the exercise of virtue is meant to be contextualized in specific, intimate relations. Aristotle (*Pol.* 1261a4ff.) had already criticized the notion that underlay book 5 of the *Republic:* that close social ties stand in the way of the common good. On this issue, the Roman Stoic stance is firm: there

47. Asmis 1996; Babut 1963; Foucault 1988a, esp. part 5; Stephens 1996.

48. Arius Didymus ap. Stob. 2.70.8 W.: τούς τε φίλους καὶ τοὺς γνωρίμους καὶ τὰ παραπλήσια. D.L. 7.95: τό τε σπουδαίαν ἔχειν πατρίδα καὶ σπουδαῖον φίλον καὶ τὴν τούτων εὐδαιμονίαν.

49. Sextus Empiricus quotes the Stoic view in the context of a discussion of the Academic and Peripatetic classification of "goods," yet that this is legitimately Stoic is confirmed by the fact that he admits there are no goods (in the strict sense, as I read the passage) of the body, and by the parallel passages from Arius Didymus and Diogenes Laertius.

50. See also *Ep.* 74.22–26, 93.4, 94.

will be no larger community unless we start with the smaller one close to home.[51]

Epictetus (*Diss.* 1.11) gives an invaluable glimpse of the value of parenthood when he scolds a Roman official for having abandoned his little daughter on her sickbed because he could not stand the thought of her dying. Family affection, we are told (17–18), is "in accordance with nature, and *good*" (τὸ μὲν φιλόστοργον κατὰ φύσιν τ' ἐστί καὶ κάλον; see also *Diss.* 3.3.8; D.L. 7.120), and is not incompatible with reason (τὸ εὐλόγιστον). Rather than automatically assuming that "good" is diluted here and used in a broader, nonphilosophical sense, we should leave the possibility open that family affection is being upgraded to a status similar to that accorded to friendship. The pair "in accordance with nature" and "good" indicates that here we are dealing with the higher-level *oikeiōsis;* the "reasonable" is coextensive with nature in this sense, whereas affection, as we have seen, can fall under both levels of *oikeiōsis.*[52]

The upgrading of traditional modes of sociability is most striking in the case of the marital relationship. Antipater, Musonius Rufus, and Hierocles in particular apply to marriage language and terminology that in other contexts is reserved for the bond between the sages. As with friendship, the bond between spouses can become an expression of the life of philosophy that constitutes the life of virtue. Antipater (*SVF* 63, 256.31–32 von Arnim) transfers the language of "treating another as oneself" (εἴ τις προσλάβοι οἷον ἑαυτὸν ἕτερον) from the rapport between the wise (see D.L. 7.23, 124) to that between spouses. For Hierocles (Stob. 4.502.9–503.10 Hense = 52.23–53.12 von Arnim), marriage is correlated to the rationality (*logos*) that distinguishes humans from animals and lower-level living beings. Thus marriage cannot be reduced to the sole purpose of producing offspring. Arius Didymus explicitly states that the wise man will marry and have children and that "these things follow from the nature of a *rational* animal designed for community and mutual affection" (Stob. 2.109.16–18 W.). Musonius Rufus, as will be examined in greater detail in the fifth chapter of this study, most fully adopts the perspective of an equal and reciprocal bond between spouses.

51. Contra Mingay 1972, 271. He fundamentally misinterprets the Stoic position. It is not a matter of parallel processes, of us being "related in *biological* status to all other humans, even to all living things, in a graduated way," without this relationship "generating much emotional momentum," on the one hand, and a "grand psychological improbability of their [the Stoics'] *direct leap from the individual to all mankind, in keeping with the transcendental nature of their whole ethic*" (emphasis mine), on the other.

52. Contra Dobbin 1998, 131–36.

The idea that sociability is intrinsic to reason, then, is not unique to the case of friendship, and neither is the idea of the role of memory in coping with absence and loss.[53] This last point, however, is contradicted by some of our evidence. For instance, when discussing the category of the "relatively disposed" (πρός τί πως ἔχον), Simplicius claims that the Stoics would hold that "a father whose son has died ceases to be a father" (*SVF* 2.403). Leaving aside the question whether Simplicius got it right, it is clear that the Roman Stoics at least present a very different picture. In the long run and in the larger scheme of things, the memory of individual people may indeed seem of minor relevance (Marcus Aurelius 8.37). But as Seneca's consolations show (see also *Ep.* 63), memory allows us to hold on to the value of *all* our relationships.

The entire first book of Marcus Aurelius's *Meditations* attests to the importance of memory because it is devoted to the social fabric in which he locates himself. This first book is an unusual "genealogy" for an emperor in that it does not trace a glorious lineage or justify imperial power—at least not directly. The account, which in all likelihood Marcus Aurelius wrote for his own use, is a curious reversal of the motif of a testament: rather than talking about what he would leave other people after his death, he goes through a list of people who bequeathed to him crucial insights and moral examples and who helped him to form the philosophical ideal toward which he is striving, in keeping with the dynamic of ethical development that is expressed in the Stoic notion of "appropriation." In this soliloquy, Marcus Aurelius remembers the relatives, teachers, and friends who charted his course not to power but to the good life, which entails political responsibility. Their influence on and importance for him cannot be affected by death.[54]

The testament motif is even more explicit in Tacitus's rendering of Seneca's final moments. We are given a short excerpt of a speech to his friends on the philosopher's attitude toward impending evils (*Ann.* 15.62). Tacitus's Seneca is modeling his behavior after Socrates in Plato's *Phaedo.* Unlike Plato's Socrates, however, Seneca consoles his friends by telling them that they could hold on to their memory of him and to the image of his life. The centurion sent to Seneca refuses to have the tablets of his will brought out, so Seneca (in Tacitus's rendering) claims that "as he was prevented to show his gratitude for their merits, he left them his only but most beautiful possession, the image of his life. If they guarded this in their memories,

53. See, e.g., Sen. *Ep.* 35.3, 55.8–11, 63.4ff., 64.1, 93.5, 98.11, 99 passim.

54. See Martinazzoli 1951, esp. 29–42, 131–50.

they would be carrying with them the renown of virtuous accomplishments as the reward for loyal friendship." In the closing pages of the *Phaedo*, Plato gives the impression that Socrates' true self is already elsewhere and that he is present merely in body. By emphasizing the memory of his life which he leaves others, Seneca, on the other hand, could not be more present. Here a testament has turned into a channel, not for distributing traditional goods, but for bequeathing moral and philosophical benefits.

We are now in a better position to understand Seneca when he says, "No school [other than the Stoic] is kinder and more gentle, none more full of affection for human beings nor more attentive to the common good" (*Clem.* 2.5.3). Self-control in the case of the loss of loved ones indeed implies holding back emotions and coming to terms with bereavement. Yet such control is not a matter of cold detachment but a response that in reality allows us to serve others better.[55] A wise man who helps in times of sorrow will be more efficient in his help if he can hold back his own tears (*Clem.* 2.6.1). In contrast to the self-restrained person, someone who is under the sway of passions is neither a good defender of his country nor a successful advocate for his friends (*Vit. Beat.* 15.4). And a recurrent theme in Seneca's consolations is that one who indulges in mourning overlooks her responsibility to loved ones who are still alive.

Epictetus tells us (*Diss.* 2.22; see also 1.23) that unless we make the right kind of value judgments, we will not be able to love other people truly. If we invest our "selves" in our bodies and in the ordinary externals, self-interest will always drive a wedge between us and other people, and we could quite literally betray a spouse for a necklace. If, on the other hand, we locate our selves in our *prohairesis* (our moral character as governed by reason), which is something only the sage can truly accomplish, only then can our country, parents, and friends safely rely on us. But again, this form of self-control does not entail that we *reduce other people* to the status of (preferred) indifferents.[56] One could also argue, taking this line of thinking beyond Epictetus, that insofar as a woman is not treated as a piece of property, she cannot become the "pretty little wench" who wrecks the relationship

55. On the point that the sage is a more reliable friend, see also Lesses 1993, 68–69, with reference to D.L. 7.117–18. See also Cic. *Fin.* 3.71; Arius Didymus ap. Stob. 2.101.21–102.3 W.; Plut. *Comm. Not.* 1076A.

56. Contra Sorabji 2000a, 183–84. He also underestimates the importance and role of the *eupatheiai* (47–51).

between father and son or causes a war between host and guest. And if we are going to attach value to people in exactly the same way as we do to ordinary external objects, then they had better be indifferents, or else the quarrel over a woman could lead to war. But this still leaves open the option not to treat people as run-of-the-mill objects at all.

Loss and exile are not supposed to affect a Stoic's happiness. Our affective rapport with other people is, in the final analysis, not a matter of need but an injunction from reason, or what Seneca calls "natural promptings" (*naturalis inritatio, Ep.* 9.17).[57] Yet, there is an important sense in which the Stoic's spouse, children, kin, friends, and indeed all her fellow human beings will always be with her, wherever she goes. Of the Stoic sages it is said:

> If a single sage anywhere at all extends his finger prudently, all the sages throughout the inhabited world are benefited. This is their amity's work [τῆς φιλίας ἔργον]; this is the end in which for their common benefits the virtues of the sage issue . . . the amazing benefit which sages receive <from> the virtuous motions of one another even if they are not together and happen not even to be acquainted. (Plut. *Comm. Not.* 1068F–1069A, trans. Cherniss)[58]

Hierocles does not limit this idea to the community of sages. In an echo of Homer,[59] which is both transmitted via Plato's Socrates in the *Apology* (34D) and at the same time radically transposed, he claims that brothers help each other even when they are far apart, and due to nature's forethought, "nobody is alone; we do not come from a tree or a rock, but out of parents and with brothers, relatives, and other close relationships. And of great assistance is reason (ὁ λόγος), which appropriates even strangers, people with whom we do not have blood ties, and provides an abundance of allies" (Stob. 4.663.17–19, 664.6–11 Hense = 60.26–30 von Arnim). Here the manner in which Hierocles has anchored intimate relationships in the broader community of reason recaptures the main theme of this chapter. The Roman Stoics significantly upgraded the relational mode of human existence, both within the context of the preferred indifferents that correspond to our lower-level

57. This would allow a comparison between Kant and the Stoics, a trend in current research, but one from which I am deliberately refraining in this context.

58. See also Arius Didymus ap. Stob. 2.101.21–102.3 W.

59. Homer *Il.* 22.126, *Od.* 19.163; see also Plut. *Cons. Uxor.* 608C.

oikeiōsis and, even more importantly, as an intrinsic feature of reason itself, and hence of the moral good, in the strict Stoic sense. The relational aspect of reason, in turn, is no longer limited to the friendship among the wise but opens up to embrace more traditional relationships such as marriage and parenthood, as long as they are transformed in order to meet the conditions of the shared life of reason.

CHAPTER THREE

Politics, the Philosophical Life, and Leisure

How this passion which Cosimo always showed for communal life fitted in with his perpetual flight from society, I have never properly understood. . . . One would say that the more determined he was to hide away in his den of branches, the more he felt the need to create new links with the human race . . . . What he had in mind was an idea of a universal society.

Italo Calvino, *The Baron in the Trees*

He who rests should act and he who acts should rest.

Seneca, *Epistulae* 3.6

Except for its function as mediator, all aspects of the self, as stipulated in the working definition of the first chapter, have been brought into relief by now. We have seen how the Roman Stoic notion of self entails that it is both held by all human beings in common and endowed with features that are specific to any given individual. The Roman Stoic self is also fundamentally embedded both in the structure of nature as a whole and in a web of relationships. The notion of the self as a mediator, however, is really the capstone of this project. We need it in order to do full justice to the importance of individuality and social embeddedness in Roman Stoicism.

The mediating self captures an all-important feature of the Stoic stance by bringing the philosophical life to fruition wherever and however one finds oneself situated in the spatial and temporal conditions of everyday life. This act of mediation requires that we try to transform traditional modes of engaging with others from within, and that we continuously strike a balance between engagement and detachment, the latter ranging, in different degrees, from voluntary inner reserve and *otium* to extreme, imposed conditions, such as bereavement and exile. Whereas the subsequent chapters examine how this mediating self handles parenthood and marriage, this one focuses on the question of political responsibility:

how does the act of mediation play itself out in the field of political forces?

Cicero and the Roman Stoics were very much preoccupied with the circumstances and manner in which the philosopher should become involved in the state. They framed these questions against the theoretical background of Plato's *Republic* (520B ff.), a work that attempts to present the best possible form of political government. In practice, however, both Cicero and the Roman Stoics had to face political responsibility in conditions that were not only far from ideal but also quite unstable and threatening. And whenever the sociopolitical situation did not pose a direct threat, at the very least this situation created a kind of void for Rome's leading class, which had no real power under the emperor's rule, yet was still required to go through the motions of decision making, particularly in the Senate. Under these circumstances, the Roman Stoics came up with a specific combination of commitment to philosophy and political duties, in a symmetrically calibrated and dialectical relationship between detachment and activity.

"Don't hope for Plato's *Republic*"

In ordinary states, Plato's Socrates tells us, philosophers are allowed to stay aloof from the political scene because they have acquired their knowledge in spite of, and in opposition to, a corrupting environment. This reasoning does not apply to the "beautiful city" (*kallipolis*) Socrates develops as an alternative, because its entire structure of education is aimed at the acquisition of appropriate knowledge. Only under these nurturing circumstances do the philosophers "owe" the state the proper management of its affairs. Only in the transformed state, which has come as close as possible to the desired perfection, will the philosopher, if reluctantly, accept the burden of rule and be king. This dispensation also stipulates that through his rule he will maintain the state in as good a condition as possible. Yet just as perfection is ultimately absent from our world, so Plato's true sage would much prefer to be detached and aloof from his bodily existence and surroundings, and he considers political involvement a necessity (520E). In this sense the philosopher-king possesses a "tragic" trait.

The Platonic view has left its mark on the Stoa's defense of political responsibility: "the wise man takes part in politics, especially in such political systems as display some progress [προκοπήν] toward being complete [or "perfect," τελείας] political systems" (Stob. 2.94 W., trans. Pomeroy).[1] And

1. For this chapter, I have benefited from discussions with Eric Brown, who graciously shared the

"The man with good sense [τὸν νοῦν ⟨ἔχοντα⟩] will sometimes [ποτε] be king and associate with a king who shows natural ability [εὐφυίαν] and the love of learning [φιλομάθειαν]. For we said it is possible to take part in government in accord with preferential reasoning [κατὰ τὸν προηγούμενον]" (Stob. 2.111 W., trans. Pomeroy; see also Sen. *De Ot.* 3.3). So, if politics allows for progress toward the ideal, and if a ruler is open to change and learning, the wise man may enter into public life. Under such circumstances, the energy he would invest in society would be worth the effort. Unlike in the Platonic context, it is not perfection but progress that is required, and for progress it is sufficient that a ruler merely have a "love of learning"; a king does not need to have already reached the stage of wisdom.

If, on the other hand, political conditions fall below a critical threshold, then abstention becomes a legitimate option for the sage: "but [it is possible] also not to take part if something <prevented him> and especially if he was not going to benefit his country, but assumed that great and difficult dangers would follow directly from political life" (Stob. 2.111, continued, W., trans. Pomeroy; see also Sen. *De Ot.* 3.3–4). This last attitude mirrors Socrates' stance in the *Apology* (31D–32A): given his uncompromising take on virtue and the good life, his actual participation in politics would have led much sooner to his downfall and so would have prevented him from benefiting the city as much as he ended up doing from a safer distance.

But from a pragmatic perspective, this double-edged advice would not have been of much use to Seneca. If one takes on the task of tutoring a future emperor like Nero, the main problem is that one cannot always predict whether political affairs will take a turn for the better or for the worse. Or to put it differently, often only the benefit of hindsight allows one to assess whether one's political involvement was worthwhile. In his old age, Seneca has to admit, in a radically un-Stoic manner, that he wasted most of his life because he failed in his attempts to steer Nero and imperial politics in the right direction (*QN* 3, *Pref.* 2; see also *Ep.* 102.2; *De Ot.*). And in a strongly pessimistic streak, he draws the conclusion in his reflections on leisure that no real city is ever in good enough condition to warrant active participation in politics (*De Ot.* 8.3–4). Whatever time he has left, he wants to devote not to politics but to a study of the universe.[2]

The Roman Stoic who is not quite ready to go Seneca's route would find herself facing not Plato's *kallipolis* (nor Zeno's utopian counterpart to the

---

work on Seneca and Marcus Aurelius from his forthcoming manuscript *Stoic Cosmopolitanism*. See Gill 2000, with good bibliography.

2. Lana 1996.

Platonic proposal, for that matter) but the messiness of real-world politics. If she wants to adhere to the Stoic ideal, she faces the challenge of accepting the burden of involvement in everyday circumstances. One is more likely to run into a king with philosophical aspirations than into a philosopher with any real chances of rising to power. Plato himself emphasizes the role of the philosopher who would be king, but he leaves the door open for rulers to become philosophers (*Rep.* 473D; Musonius Rufus 8 Lutz), and the latter is the approach the Stoics seem to have developed, to which the passage quoted above and Musonius Rufus (8 Lutz, 38.8–11 Hense) attest. Because a king ought to be a "living law" (νόμος ἔμψυχος), as Musonius claims, he should embody the four cardinal virtues of justice, self-control, courage, and wisdom, and he should practice philosophy to attain this goal. A statement of this kind acquires a sharper focus only if we take into account that Rome's leading class was not always convinced of the practical value of philosophical learning. Suetonius (*Nero* 52), for instance, claims that Nero's mother discouraged him from studying philosophy, on the grounds that it would be useless for, and even conflict with, his aspirations to be a ruler. This did not prevent Seneca from addressing his *On Clemency* directly to Nero, with a clear set of instructions on how a good ruler ought to behave.

But what happens if the ruler is not just being nagged by people intent on giving him good advice but is actually himself motivated to adhere to philosophical principles, as was the case with Marcus Aurelius? According to the *Historia Augusta* (*Marcus* 27.7), Marcus Aurelius was fond of quoting Plato's stance on the king-philosopher. His own *Meditations*, however, reveal a markedly critical attitude toward Plato. "Don't hope for Plato's *Republic*," he tells himself (9.29). So what can and should a ruler hope for? Marcus Aurelius has nothing but contempt for the traditional motivations to enter public life. He questions thirst for glory as a serious motivation and denies the greatness of Alexander of Macedon and rulers like him. What nature demands of us at any given point in time is an alternative and much more modest standard for behavior. His second critique entails modesty too, but in another sense, namely, that any ruler should have realistic expectations about the changes he can effect. By describing—in the opening line of this entry—the world-cause as a "rushing torrent," Marcus underscores the fact that most external matters are not under humans' control, to the point of undermining the Stoic notion of a well-ordered divine plan.

Marcus Aurelius was not the first author to have used the phrase "Plato's *Republic*" as shorthand for unrealistic and utopian expectations. In the tradition it became associated with Cato the Younger because he refused to make any concessions to realpolitik.[3] In his *De Oratore* (1.227ff.),[4] Cicero also uses the phrase to portray defendants who refuse to lower themselves and play on the emotions of their judges (or who forbid their counsel to behave in this manner on their behalf) so as to obtain a favorable verdict. They refrain from such behavior, Cicero quibbles, "for fear, no doubt, of being reported to the Stoics." And he connects this attitude to Socrates' similar behavior at his trial. But Cicero, it has to be said, was not entirely consistent on this point: in a letter to his brother Quintus, Cicero compliments him on having achieved Plato's ideal in his propraetorship of Asia (1.1.29). Leaving aside the question of Cicero's self-consistency, we may turn to the Stoic Epictetus, who actually questions the behavior of a friend who tried to imitate Socrates at his own trial over a relatively minor issue and thus lost his case. One always has to keep timing, circumstances, and what is proper to oneself (τὰ ἴδια) in mind, Epictetus warns, and not engage in provocation for the sake of provocation (*Diss.* 2.2.17–20).[5] Here Epictetus's thinking appears to be in line with Marcus Aurelius's sense of restraint. Musonius Rufus, at any rate, allegedly claimed that, unlike Socrates, he fully intended to defend himself at his trial (Philostr. *VA* 4.46).

So the first problem with people who "hope for Plato's *Republic*" is a certain intransigence, which in Cicero's account is attested for both the Stoics and Socrates. They refuse to make any concessions. But such an attitude would have been impossible for an emperor. Marcus Aurelius would have had to aim at an equilibrium between holding on to his philosophical principles and striving toward effective leadership. His reluctance to compromise is evident in claims that we have discussed in the second chapter, such as the one that people who are obstacles to doing the right thing should be relegated to the category of absolute indifferents (5.20). Yet this injunction does not imply that he simply walks away from people and situations that do not suit him: according to Marcus Aurelius, a wise person will be able to convert even obstacles into opportunities to promote the good.

Unwillingness to make any concessions or compromises can lead to further problems. Pierre Hadot suggests that the phrase "Plato's *Republic*" indicates that one wants to surround oneself exclusively with philosophers, or

3. Cic. *Att.* 2.1 = 21 Shackleton Bailey, 8; Plut. *Phocion* 3.1.

4. See also Plut. *Cato Minor* 4. The Roman Stoic P. Rutilius Rufus also became a stock example of this kind of behavior, as in Cic. *Brut.* 110, 113–16; Quintilian *Inst.* 11.1.13. On this topic, see Lévy 2000.

5. I owe this connection to Julia Annas.

at least with those who have inclinations toward philosophy.[6] If one keeps company only with like-minded people, the potential for conflict disappears. But Marcus Aurelius knows that responsibility for community will involve working on behalf of many people who come nowhere close to the ideal and who do not even care. And so one of his regular exercises is to fortify himself to face and have patience with difficult people.

Intransigence can also lead to the kind of grandstanding that, far from being effective, actually has serious negative political consequences. From Cicero's perspective, Cato's attempt to bring corrupt jurors to trial merely succeeded in unleashing political unrest. Marcus Aurelius rejects the trappings of traditional power exemplified in Alexander, Philip, and Demetrius but also refuses to buy into a utopian alternative. Hinting at and rejecting Plato's notion of social conditioning, he claims that if we cannot change people's convictions, obedience turns into slavery. As we have seen before, a Stoic refuses to impose his own views on other people; he can set an example and try to work for the common good, but he cannot preempt others' decisions. An earlier Stoic like Posidonius (135–51 BC) apparently could still believe along Plato's lines that people would voluntarily submit to rulers gifted with reason because they recognized that this submission would be in their interest. Posidonius both projected this scenario onto a previous Golden Age (Sen. *Ep.* 90.5) and thought he had discovered an actual historical example in the Black Sea tribe of the Mariandynians.[7] Marcus Aurelius, in contrast, altogether discarded such hopes.

The position Marcus defends here is the most difficult imaginable: to work for the best and do what one can, but without ostentation and expecting only modest results. "Even the smallest advance" would be "nothing contemptible." And to achieve such modest goals, one should not wait or hope for optimal conditions to do "what nature demands of one at this very moment." No trappings of power, no rewards of glory, and no spectacular results: is this a Roman emperor or someone trying to stem a tide with his bare hands? The answer is neither. Marcus Aurelius was an emperor who had at his disposal a court, an impressive administrative apparatus, and a formidable military force, yet who also refused to have his sense of self be taken over by this role and status:[8]

6. P. Hadot 1998, 303–6.

7. F60 Edelstein and Kidd; see also Plato *Lg.* 776D.

8. See also the debate about how much of Marcus Aurelius's Stoicism actually influenced his actions as a ruler: Hendrickx 1974; Noyen 1955; Stanton 1969.

Take care that you are not turned into a Caesar, that you are not stained with the purple; for such things do come about. Keep yourself simple, then, and good, sincere, dignified, free from affectation, a friend to justice, reverent towards the gods, affectionate, and firm in the performance of your duties. Struggle to remain such a man as philosophy wished to make you. Honour the gods, protect your fellows. Life is short; and our earthly existence yields but a single harvest, a holy disposition and acts that serve the common good. (6.30, trans. Hard)

Alcibiades Again

Picking up the thread again of Plato's influence, one could argue, of course, that there is more to Plato's political views than what such texts as the *Republic*, the *Laws*, and the *Statesman* reveal, and that he also had a genuine interest in improving politics in the all-too-real city of Athens.[9] Socrates does not operate under the most ideal of conditions, and Alcibiades, as portrayed in the *Alcibiades I*, is not interested in becoming a philosopher-king. Alcibiades wants to be successful, both in the politics of Athens and in his love life. In giving advice to Alcibiades and presenting himself as the best lover Alcibiades could wish for, Socrates faces the challenge of a more pragmatic incorporation of his values into the political game as it is actually being played; his task is to turn Alcibiades into a better man, so that he may become both a better politician (in the moral sense) and a better lover. In this practical context, as Foucault remarks,[10] we find an important occurrence of the expression τὸ ἑαυτοῦ ἐπιμελεῖσθαι, "taking care of oneself" (123D; see also *Ap.* 36C—as opposed to other expressions, such as περὶ ψυχῆς θεραπείαν).[11] "Taking care of oneself," more so than the Delphic injunction "Know thyself," firmly connects the project of philosophy to action and political ambition: those who want to rule others had better be able to rule themselves first.

As is the case with so many of Plato's characters, at the beginning of the dialogue Alcibiades is not yet fully receptive to Socrates' teachings. In order to get him to reach that point of receptivity, Socrates has first to corner him and confront him with the limitations of his expertise. Socrates' first line of attack, therefore, uses a trick to which the young and ambitious Alcibiades is highly susceptible: an imaginary judgment of him by someone who has

9. For a broader background to this issue, see Schofield 2000. He, however, does not draw on the *Alcibiades I*, which, as I pointed out in the first chapter, was considered authentic in antiquity.

10. Foucault 1988b, 23–26.

11. As in *La.* 185E, *Grg.* 464C.

a very high social status, the Persian queen mother (123C). By her standards, as Plato represents her reaction, all of Alcibiades' accomplishments and so-called assets of birth and education turn out to be quite trivial and insignificant. Once Socrates has trapped Alcibiades in his own contradictions and made him, much to his dismay, realize how ill-equipped he in fact is to realize his ambitions (127D), then the philosopher finds the would-be politician open to his advice and knowledge.

Socrates, of course, has a response to Alcibiades' predicament: "But don't despair. If you had noticed this problem only when you'd turned fifty, then it would have been difficult for you to take care of yourself. But now you have exactly the right age at which one should perceive it" (127E). It is not too late for Alcibiades to turn himself around and embark on a better course of action. This passage makes one wonder what the best time in life is to "take care of oneself" through philosophy. What Socrates says to Alcibiades here resembles a view the character Callicles elsewhere is made to defend (*Gorgias* 484C ff.): that taking care of oneself is merely an educational phase in youth, when one acquires necessary knowledge once and for all. But in the *Republic* (498A–C), Socrates explicitly lashes out against those who want to study philosophy at a young age merely as a prelude to "running a household and making money." Young people, he claims, should take very good care of their bodies, and only as they grow older and their souls begin to reach maturity, should they devote progressively more attention to philosophy.

So, which course should we follow? Study philosophy first before embarking on the major undertakings of life, as the *Alcibiades I* suggests—in agreement with much of what Xenophon has to say about Socrates in his *Memorabilia*—or wait until we have reached a more mature stage in life? The Stoics argue that the preoccupation with oneself is a lifelong and ongoing activity. As soon as one acquires the faculty of reasoning, one starts this project, but because life experience matters, an older person is, in fact, better at it. The question which comes first, theory or practice, is not relevant to the Stoics, because philosophy is always inextricably linked to one's being in the world and in society.[12]

To be sure, experience will remedy some of Alcibiades' shortcomings. After all, Socrates makes the queen mother chastise the young Greek upstart because of his lack of experience and of the kind of dignity that ad-

12. See also Epicurus, opening of the *Ep. ad Men.* 122: "Let no one either delay philosophizing when young, or weary of philosophizing when old. For no one is underage or overage for health of the soul" (LS25A).

vanced age bestows. Experience and dignity traditionally do carry a lot of weight in public life. But for Socrates, the crucial knowledge Alcibiades needs— knowledge of matters pertaining to the soul—has little to do with actual experience in the ordinary sense, and that knowledge always has absolute priority (even if ultimately it is virtually impossible to attain). The turn toward the true self—the soul as opposed to the body—will have a salutary effect both on Alcibiades' love life and on his political ambition. He should favor the lover who is in love with his soul, because this is the kind of lover who will remain with him even when the bloom of his beauty has withered (131C–132A). And the knowledge of his "self" will teach him what he needs for the political sphere of action (132B).

What is striking about Socrates' conclusions is a certain naive optimism, which suggests that everything will be all right once one knows what one needs to know. The same optimism of *Alcibiades I* is at work in book 10 of the *Republic*, in the description of the external rewards for the just man, and also in the *Apology* (30A ff.), in which Socrates claims that Athens would do very well if only the city followed his advice. But would a politician such as Socrates envisions not run into all kinds of trouble, encounter a great deal of resistance, and become, in fact, quite vulnerable? Given the challenges of Athenian politics, being just and wise could cost one dearly. At the end of the *Alcibiades I*, Socrates does hint at the difficulties that might arise for one who attempts to be morally upright. His ultimate answer to such challenges (as in *Ap.* 30C8–D5, 41C8–D2) moves far beyond any kind of naive outlook: nothing can harm the wise man. Taking their cue from this answer, the Stoics recommend becoming fully involved in public life while openly acknowledging the risks. A true Stoic's art does not consist in avoiding trouble but in rising above it by knowing how to deal with it so that it does not affect him.

It is not so much in the idealized approach of accounts such as the *Republic* that we can find similarities between later Stoic attitudes and what Plato's Socrates advocates. An *Alcibiades I* would yield more points of comparison because it seems more pragmatic and advocates incorporating philosophical values into the given sociopolitical framework. But crucial differences still remain: for Stoics, the turn toward the self is a lifelong balancing act between two parallel sets of norms, philosophical and sociopolitical, that can create serious and far-reaching tensions. As I stated in the first chapter, the Stoic unified and individualized self is eminently suited for this continuous act of mediation. And the notion of a self mediating between ideal and practical constraints best captures Marcus Aurelius's realistic sense of his political responsibility.

Precisely because the Roman Stoics' highly developed notion of a "core" is so intimately connected to the mediating function it has to fulfill, it becomes easier to understand why the notion did not arise in philosophies such as Cynicism and Epicureanism, which thrived on the margins of ordinary life and on the outskirts of society.[13] Nor is it surprising, from the Stoic vantage point, that Aristotle did not devise the concept,[14] because in his utopian vision of the polis, essentially no conflict exists between philosophy and society (even though in his writings there might be an unresolved tension between the politically active life and philosophical contemplation, to which the enormous amount of secondary literature on the topic testifies!).

To be sure, Socrates himself impressively walks a tightrope between heaven and earth: he operates on the margins of the polis, but he does not keep his views to himself, and he tries to convince his fellow citizens to become better people. For someone who never fully took part in politics and who left Athens only under exceptional circumstances, he knew the city inside out, together with its inhabitants. Ultimately, nothing can harm the good man, he claimed, and at the end of his life, he himself emptied the cup of poison calmly. He could participate in military expeditions and remain his unperturbed self, drink without getting drunk, sleep next to the attractive young Alcibiades without getting sexually aroused, have a wife and children and yet be by himself (with that relentless fellow, his inner voice) when he went home. This is the Socrates the later Stoics primarily claim as a model.[15] "Ask yourself: 'What would Zeno or Socrates have *done* under these circumstances?'" is the key injunction in Epictetus's *Encheiridion* (33.12; see also Sen. *Ep.* 6.5–6). It was not Plato's elaborate theoretical constructs but Socrates' attitude, heroic behavior, and method of questioning to which these Stoics felt most drawn. They tailored their Socrates to fit their own vision.

13. Griffin 1989. As Cicero testifies (*Off.* 1.70ff.), for Stoics noninvolvement would be the exception (*Fin.* 3.68). Epicurus (ap. Plut. *Tranq.* 465F–466A) makes the opposite claim. See also Sen. *De Ot.* 3.2–3, D.L. 7.121, discussed in ch. 2.

14. Though we find an adumbration of the notion in *EN* 1178a2–4, with the claims that reason or the best thing in us "would seem to be each man himself" and that its life is the "the life of oneself." This is not unlike Plato's appeal to a turn inward. See also O'Connor 1999.

15. See Döring 1974. See also the earlier study by Jagu (1946). Dio Cassius (61.15.4) puts the famous dictum "Anytus and Meletus can kill me, but they cannot hurt me" (based on *Ap.* 30C–D) into the mouth of the Roman senator Thrasea Paetus, substituting Nero for Socrates' accusers. In *Diss.* 3.1.42, Epictetus makes the connection with the *Alcibiades I* 131D.

Cicero's Predicament

We now have an important aspect of the Stoic commitment to political involvement: that self-reflection and the lifelong care of the soul are prerequisites for realizing practical goals. But that realization in itself is not yet sufficient to understand the self's mediating role. For this notion, the pull between the ideal and compromise with which Cicero struggled at the end of his life offers a useful perspective. In trying to come to terms with challenges, Cicero is primarily interested in a reading of the Stoics and their ideal of wisdom that brings the sage closer to real communities and prevailing structures of sociability. For one thing, in Cicero's *De Finibus* (3.69), it appears that sages do not merely benefit one another—benefits that would fall under the strict category of the "good" (the *emolumenta* as opposed to the *commoda* that belong with the preferred indifferents)—but that they are benefactors of all of humanity.[16] With this extended responsibility, the philosopher's social role asserts itself even more strongly.

Scholars such as Pierre Grimal and M. Isnardi Parente, as well as others in their wake, have emphasized that the views of Antipater of Tarsus were central in this move toward a more pragmatic view of Stoic virtue, while others have highlighted Diogenes of Babylon's contributions.[17] This process, in other words, did not start in Rome, but in Hellenistic Greece and the East, though Roman culture accelerated it. In the previous chapter we have already come across the possibility that Antipater may have contributed significantly to the upgrading of more traditional modes of sociability.[18]

In his analysis of Cicero's *De Officiis*, Christopher Gill focuses on the four-*personae* theory that Cicero inherited from another Stoic, Panaetius, and that we already discussed in the first chapter. The four *personae*, which Gill defines as "normative reference-points in rational moral choice,"[19] appear in the first book, in the context of the discussion of the notion of *decorum* (1.93ff.), that which is proper. The first pair of normative reference

16. Fuhrer and Howald 2000.

17. Grimal 1989, 1971–72; Isnardi Parente 1989. For the importance of Diogenes of Babylon in this development, see Obbink and Vander Waerdt 1991; Vander Waerdt 1991. See also the still valuable work by Valente (1956) and the general overview by Inwood and Donini (1999), as well as Schofield 1999.

18. Cato Minor for his part had close ties with Antipater of Tyre: Plut. *Cato Minor* 4.2–3; Morford 2002, 47.

19. Gill 1988, 176.

points (1.107) are, on the one hand, our common human nature, endowed with reason, and, on the other, our individual dispositions. Another pair combines with the first (1.115): the circumstances in which one happens to live (*casus aliqui aut tempus*) and the kind of career one chooses, which is to a certain extent both determined by the other three *personae* and a *persona* in its own right. Gill sees the essence of the Panaetian innovation of Stoic ethics in an "increased interest in actual, differentiated human beings" (the second *persona*) "and a reduced interest in the normative 'sage.'" But, it has to be added, this new interest in individuality is itself embedded in "a highly social perspective," because "the individual is viewed in a social setting and judged by social norms."[20]

It is clear from Cicero's rendering of the four *personae* that for him the social framework takes precedence over other normative reference points. For instance, the examples Cicero gives us of different individual dispositions (1.108–9) can only be understood in a social context: the people he quotes are "distinguished" in the sense of "accomplished and notable in society."[21] The emphasis on social success even contradicts certain higher moral values, as illustrated by the cases of Sulla and Crassus. The curious result of all this is that Cicero's adoption of the Panaetian scheme yields a value system in which the philosophical norm of a rational human nature has become fused with the *mos maiorum*, which is a construct of social values with a distinct Roman coloring.

Now, Cicero makes it very clear that he is not interested in the potential conflict between social and philosophical values. What he cares about is the decline from past to present *within* the sociopolitical framework. From his perspective, the former ideal of the *mos maiorum* and of the good of the community, the *res publica* (which really is omnipresent in the *De Officiis*), has, as the result of the civil war and Caesar's bid for power, given way to fragmentation and to individualization. The philosophical values that Cicero embraces help him to justify the old order, for which no justification was needed as long as it could maintain itself, and to condemn what he wants to condemn.

When Cicero discusses the notion of *societas*, for instance, he does mention the common bond of our universal nature, which is *ratio* and *oratio* (1.50) (reason/concepts and language), but he also strongly emphasizes the *res publica* and the fatherland (1.57), with a particularly Roman twist to the

20. Gill 1988, 170, 171; in 175 n. 27, Gill refers to the work of Brunt and De Lacy on this issue. He also adds the caveat (n. 29) that most of our evidence is post-Panaetian.

21. Thus Gill 1988, 181.

Stoic notion of the universe–city (cosmopolitan) community.[22] Cicero's political concerns, the frustration and horror he feels vis-à-vis the sociopolitical changes of his times, could not have been expressed more explicitly. Precisely because he embodies the old value system, Regulus is the moral foundation of the entire *De Officiis:* as he had promised, this Roman returned to Carthage and to certain death because the hostages would be of more use to the common good than he (1.32ff., 3.92–115). Cicero firmly rejects any claims for extenuating circumstances that could have justified Regulus's breaking his oath; he is not willing to subscribe to any philosophically motivated casuistry. When Cicero claims that one is allowed to follow one's own nature as long as it does not go against the encompassing common human nature (1.110), we, the readers, must keep his political interpretation of the common good in mind.

The following passage illustrates how he harnesses philosophical values to convey his political views:

> But those who have natural skills for running public affairs should let go of all hesitation, take on public office, and run the state. There is no other way for the body of citizens to be governed, nor for magnanimity to show itself. For those who take charge of the state it is no less necessary—and perhaps even more so—to have greatness and a perspective from above on human affairs, which I often mention, as well as tranquility of mind and steadfastness, at least if they are to be free from anxiety and to live with dignity and self-composure. . . . Therefore it is not without reason that those who govern the state are beset by greater emotions as well as ambitions than inactive people. So there is all the more reason for the former to hold on to greatness of spirit and freedom of cares. (1.72–73; see also the entire context of this passage)

The aloofness from the blows and difficulties of fortune, and the inner calm that Cicero advocates have a double function. First, these attitudes give the politician the courage to continue performing his duties in a political context that has become very dangerous and unpredictable (see also 1.71). Tacitus attests to this point for the Stoic senator Helvidius Priscus: "he devoted himself to philosophy . . . to take up public life, protected against the blows of fortune" (*Hist.* 4.5, trans. Griffin). It is not hard to see that, at different times and under different circumstances, senators and emperors alike could have had use for this kind of courage.

22. Gill 1988, 196–97. Gill remarks that the *De Officiis* has a strong tendency to equate conventional values with the common human nature, but he does not elaborate on the consequences this has for its incorporation of the Panaetian theory.

Second, and even more fundamentally according to Cicero, detachment would have prevented the degeneration of the *res publica* in the first place, because only the politician who is indifferent to personal advantages, or to the advantages of a single group of people, can truly serve the common good (see, e.g., 1.85). Cicero condemns the parties of the civil war (Caesar, especially) precisely because their personal ambitions prevailed (1.26, 1.43, 1.57, 1.62ff., etc.). Elsewhere, he even mentions a *persona* that would apply specifically to a statesman bound by duty: "It is, thus, the proper responsibility of a magistrate to understand that he takes on the *persona* of the body politic [*persona civitatis*], and that he has to maintain its dignity and honor, to preserve the laws, to order their application, and to remember that these matters have been entrusted to his care" (*Off.* 1.124). Another striking point in the passage from *De Officiis* about the greatness of spirit required in statesmen is the definition of what I term "the balancing act" between conflicting values; a politician needs even more composure than a philosopher because he is constantly under fire—or, we might say, constantly tempted to give in to the wrong values. The Ciceronian politician should be engaged, yet detached at the same time, because only then can he make the best of his job.

Cicero's treatment of Plato and Socrates continues along the same lines: on the one hand, he seems to agree with Plato's viewpoint, especially where the latter defines justice as responsibility for the common good (1.85); on the other hand, he criticizes Plato and others for their inconsistency and lack of involvement.[23] For those with the right "natural" disposition, Cicero himself advocates political courage even under difficult circumstances. He is willing to make an exception for men of extraordinary philosophical genius and for those who have weak health or a serious motive for withdrawal (1.71). This viewpoint is in keeping with the type of exception clause we examined in the previous chapter and at the onset of this one: unless there are valid contraindications, a Stoic should participate in public life.

Whatever role was attributed to social values in Panaetius's theory, we can no longer divorce this theory from the Ciceronian context in which it appears. But we can witness how crucial and predominant the sociopolitical values are for Cicero, and in what sense; they become so crucial, in fact, that the philosophical values are completely drawn into a nonphilosophical framework. In the *De Officiis,* Cicero turns to philosophy from a very Roman viewpoint and from a markedly contextualized per-

23. *Off.* 1.19, 1.28, 1.69, 1.70, 1.72–73, 1.92, etc.

spective.[24] The combination of involvement and detachment that will become so essential in later Stoicism manifests itself here already in the specific concerns of politicians like Cicero. Because the conflict between individualism and the common good has peaked in a formidable public crisis, "the right thing to do" no longer appears to be self-evident but must instead be continually evaluated and justified.

Not only does Cicero criticize noninvolvement, but he is also deeply suspicious of philosophical values that oppose the social norms to which he adheres.[25] This is why his discussion remains within the parameters of public life, and he does not make it his primary concern to analyze the tension between public involvement and philosophical detachment. A strong notion of the "self," as examined in the first chapter of this study, would run counter to the ideal of the *mos maiorum* and the common good to which this Roman, as he presents himself, adheres. In fact, if anything, this notion of selfhood approaches the attitudes of the politicians whom Cicero severely condemns.[26] From this perspective, it is very revealing that unlike Hierocles, Cicero (1.53ff.; see also 3.69) puts not the individual but the marital relationship and the family unit at the center of his image of social relationships as concentric circles. Cicero, we have to remind ourselves, is not a Stoic.

Unlike Cicero, Seneca and Epictetus reemphasize the importance of a philosophically defined human nature over and above all other roles, including those that are socially defined. But the legacy we find in Cicero cannot be ignored in later developments of Stoic ethics, and we need to keep it in mind in order to understand a Seneca or a Marcus Aurelius and, especially, their involvement in public life, even on the highest level of power and prestige. Cicero's interpretation of the *personae* theory firmly assimilated Roman social values.[27]

If we imagined a day in the life of an ideal Roman Stoic, who, as Seneca presents him to us, is not the perfect sage, we would notice that every day he has a loaded agenda of activities. Although the concentration of power

24. The *De Officiis* was written after Caesar's death. See Long 1995; Heilmann 1982. For the Early Stoics, see *SVF* 3.611–24, 686, 694–700, 702; D.L. 7.117–31; LS 1.434–37; Gill 1994, n. 39. Yet the context in which Cicero addresses the issue of involvement in politics is strikingly Roman.

25. See Gill 1988, 193–94.

26. Miriam Griffin (1989, 9–11) explains the attraction the Peripatetic and Academic sects exerted for Romans of the Late Republic as the result of the training these schools could provide in oratorical skills, which were at that time still essential to political activity.

27. See, e.g., Epict. *Diss.* 2.10.1–12 (LS59Q), 4.12.15–19 (LS66F). See also Brunt 1975.

in the person of the emperor would be an accomplished fact, a political forum would still remain, with the obligations it entailed. And there would always remain the care of one's own household (in the largest sense) with all its possessions.[28] Unless extreme circumstances create obstacles, even rendering suicide the only valid option, the Stoic would not withdraw to the margins of society but would assume his role in the community. Nor would he devote his time to considering how to *change* the fundamentals of the sociopolitical structure in which he lives; even if some of his beliefs could be considered quite radical, he moves within the given parameters of public life.[29] But this attitude does not imply a priori that a Stoic will waffle and be caught between fundamentally incompatible demands, having to settle for an uneasy juxtaposition. Rather, he internalizes neither the values of public life nor its judgments of his successes or failures. And how he goes about his daily business is a reflection of his philosophical views. Thus, at the end of the day, when he evaluates what he has done, in a moment of self-contemplation, in a letter to a friend or in an entry in his diary, he will ideally set aside the praise he has earned or the profit he has made. In determining whether or not he has done well, he will consider only his degree of rationality and self-composure in assessing the value of indifferents. This distance of the inner realm is highly determined by a framework of philosophical values that find their justification in our nature as rational beings—a framework that possesses its own authoritative tradition of teachings, precepts, and examples.

The metaphor of an inner fortress sometimes used to describe the Stoics' attitude could be misleading. The closure of the self toward the end of life may be more pronounced than at the end of a day in an active political career, especially in a case such as Seneca's. Yet the closure of a Stoic is always open to the world, to social obligations as well as philosophical norms. History properly construed and the examples of great men and women, most of whom were themselves once public figures, maintain the connections between these two normative realms (Sen. *Ep.* 104.21ff.). Or as Pierre Hadot has aptly put it, the inner fortress is not an ivory tower.[30]

28. On the background for this, see Natali 1995. Pliny the Younger's correspondence gives one a good picture of how Romans continued to construe these responsibilities.

29. For an excellent analysis of this, see Brunt 1975, 13ff., 23, 26 (slavery not challenged), 32. This study is very much inspired by Brunt's claim (1975, 23) that an antithesis of Roman and Stoic would be false. See also Sen. Ep. 14.14.

30. P. Hadot 1998.

Because it detaches happiness from the outcome of involvement, Stoicism would help any Roman to stay involved in public life under uncertain and dangerous circumstances, while at the same time protecting him. Seneca's Stoicism then effects for him what the turn to philosophy did for Cicero as well; as I have already indicated, calling this psychological evasiveness misses the point that Stoicism is the least evasive of the ancient models because it motivates political courage and systematic engagement. Things might be much more pleasant and less dangerous on the outskirts of public life, especially under the rule of some of the emperors, but, then again, it is precisely this kind of safety that a Roman from a certain mold would have been unwilling to countenance.[31]

Yet no matter how attractive a solution the Stoic balance may have appeared, it remained very hard to realize in practice—an ideal equilibrium that in reality turned out to be very vulnerable. But if equilibrium mattered, and if holding on to the sage's values implied a tension with other norms, it is not that hard to understand why a Stoic like Seneca could break down in exile. Hierocles (7.5–10 Bastianini and Long) points out that children are afraid of the dark because the lack of external, sensory stimuli generates the impression that their extinction is at hand. They need outside stimuli to keep their sense of self. Sages would be above fear, of course, but they too interact with others and the world in order to keep their "selves" in good standing.

Otium

We could examine more closely the Roman Stoics' views on society and politics from several vantage points: the debated senatorial opposition to the emperors' rule, Seneca's notorious oscillation between participation in politics and retirement, or the philosophical discussions about the political and the contemplative lives. Here, however, I would like to focus on the Roman Stoic perspective on *otium* and on withdrawal, whether voluntary or through exile. But there are some general questions regarding political responsibility that we need to address first.

First, the community of reason, and even the well-known tag of "a city and state shared by men and gods," are not in themselves sufficient grounds for Cato's conclusion in Cicero's *De Finibus* that the "wise man should want to play a part in governing the state" (3.68). In theory, at least, we, like Plato

31. André 1989, 1776–78. He gets the nuance exactly right in connection with Seneca when he speaks of a "paradoxical reversal of the *mos maiorum*" and claims that Seneca's *De Otio* "demonstrates the intellectual scruples of a Roman social conscience that refuses to die." See also André 1966.

and Aristotle, should be able to think of other ways to create communities that would do justice to humans as rational and social beings. Why would we want to participate in "business as usual" politics rather than creating a radical alternative? Yet, the Stoics did not want a revolution: to give but one notorious example, although Seneca indicates that Zeno did not have any slaves (*Cons. Helv.* 12.4),[32] and the Stoics may have expressed respect for slaves as human beings, they nevertheless did not advocate abolishing slavery. We have already noted Marcus Aurelius's rejection of idealized alternatives.

Second, the previous chapter posited that if there is a normative conflict between those political attachments and the common good, personal relationships fall under the heading of the indifferents. Similar normative conflicts can occur because of what Seneca calls one's allegiance to a "double" community:[33] the fatherland in which we happen to find ourselves and the universal community of gods and men. The good of the universal community does not always align itself with national interest. The idea that what would be good for Rome could be at odds with the well-being of other peoples or with universal humanity was not unfamiliar to the Romans. During his embassy to Rome (156–155 BC), the Academic Skeptic Carneades provoked consternation with his speeches for and against justice on consecutive days. In his case against justice, he drew the attention of his audience to the conflict between national interest, that is, the self-interest of one state, and the good of others as conceived in geopolitical terms: "For what are the 'advantages of the fatherland' except the disadvantages of another state or tribe, that is, to spread territories violently seized from others, to increase empire, to get greater tax-paying dominions?" (Lactantius *Inst. Div.* 6.6.19, trans. M. F. McDonald).[34] According to this scenario, Romans and non-Romans are locked into a zero-sum game.

As it so happens, our main source for Carneades' speeches is Cicero. In spite of the fragmentary state of the third book of Cicero's *De Republica,* this much is clear: the character Laelius reflects on the conditions under which Rome's rule could be made compatible with the common good. Some of the rationalizations in the extant text run as follows: (1) a war undertaken for the purposes of restitution or in defense is justified; (2) a

32. Compare this to the claim preserved in Aulus Gellius 2.18 that Zeno had Persaeus as his slave and that Persaeus became a Stoic philosopher in his own right; D.L. 7.36.

33. Sen. *De Ot.* 4.1; Sen. *Ep.* 68; see also Epict. *Diss.* 1.9.

34. See also 5.16.4, 6.9.3–4; Hahm 1999; Zetzel 1996.

war has to be declared officially and after reparation has first been demanded; and (3) Rome had expanded its power base and waged war at the request of its allies, who were seeking protection, the weaker from the stronger (*Rep.* 3.35). The question of justice in dealing with other peoples would become even more pressing once Rome had fully acquired the status of a world power ruled by an emperor.

Epictetus does not reject the *pax Romana* as such (*Diss.* 3.13.9). That universal humanity is served not in opposition to Rome but *through* Rome, just as it is served through personal relationships, he appears not to question. There is no critique of the pitfalls of "imperialism" (in our sense of the word) analogous to the critique of the risks of personal relationships. Rome can indeed be ruled by the wrong emperors in the wrong manner, and philosophers can be the first in line to receive hostile treatment, but its right to rule, if the rule is just, is taken for granted. One could argue, however, that the claim that Rome is justified to rule if its emperors are philosophers does match the conditions that personal relationships have to meet in order to be compatible with virtue. Such an argument would leave the door open for criticism of prevailing practices. And there are indications of a rejection of war, such as when Epictetus claims that wars occur because of misguided value judgments (*Diss.* 2.22.22; see also Sen. *Ep.* 95.30–32). Even more interesting, when viewed in the light of his own military campaign of the 170s, which earned him the title Sarmaticus, is Marcus Aurelius's comparison of the man "who catches some Sarmatians" to a "mere robber" (10.10). But this critique would not solve the problem of Rome's claim to power, because one could still argue that there is a fundamental difference in the way in which universal humanity is served through personal relationships, on the one hand, and through Rome, on the other. Rome "serves" universal humanity by its rule and dominance over other peoples, which involves overruling similar claims that other peoples may make, whereas ideally one person's intimate circle does not have to weigh more than another's in serving the common good.

Yet, in practice, and given the social stratification the Roman Stoics do not question, the latter ideal scenario vanishes altogether: the intimate circle of the emperor, let us say, or of a senator does have a much greater impact on the larger community than that of an ordinary citizen. In other words, the connection between specific Roman social circles and the community is as much shaped by the power dynamic between ruler and ruled, or master and slave, as is the relation between Rome and its empire. If beyond book 1 of his writings, Marcus Aurelius cares primarily for universal humanity rather than for individual people, he does so because as the emperor he in fact bears responsibility for a large part of humanity.[35] The difference in the impact of hierarchically structured social circles is a serious problem if one is bent on contextualizing universal norms in local settings, as I have argued the Roman Stoics were. If an unquestioned and rigid social stratification affects how one's intimate circle opens up to the community at large, then being "allowed to serve" turns into a privilege. In that case, looking at the issue of contextualization from the perspective of the relation between one's fatherland, if that fatherland happens to be Rome, and universal humanity merely aggravates a problem that is already deeply entrenched within Roman society itself.

If we turn to the topic of *otium* now, we will find that this notion which plays a central role for the Roman Stoics is already embedded in Cicero's writings. It is a concept of "leisure" that, as we will examine in greater detail, is fundamentally symmetrical: political activity both requires and is an expression of philosophy, and a more exclusive focus on philosophical studies is still relevant and beneficial for society at large; theory and practice mutually reinforce each other, and the relation between them works in both directions. Hence we find Cicero claiming about himself:

> I did not start to study philosophy as a whim, and from my youth I devoted considerable effort and care to this study. When I seemed least to be doing so, I was actually most involved in philosophy. . . . And if all philosophical precepts are relevant for life, then, I think, in both my public and my private affairs I have fulfilled the prescriptions of reason and philosophical teaching. (*ND* 1.6–7)

His philosophical erudition, he claims, was exemplified throughout his life, in his political activity, in his speeches, as well as in the company he chose to keep. At the times of his life during which he was forced to withdraw from the forum and the court, his philosophical studies and *otium* still served his political purposes (*Brutus* 304–16).

The French rendering of the term *otium* (as in the title of one of Seneca's treatises, *De Otio*) as *disponibilité,* "being available," gets to the heart of the matter: for the Roman Stoics withdrawal and *otium* are not ends in their own right but modes of retreat that remain fundamentally oriented toward community. Here too the distinction between the contemplative and the active life becomes blurred (Sen. *De Ot.* 5.8, 5.7), as with the analysis of reason's intrinsic sociability, in the second chapter of this book. Epictetus, for one, claims that the philosopher's "activity" is analogous to, and can hold its own against, the activities of everyday life (*Diss.* 1.10.7ff.).

35. Brunt 1974.

Otium in a political sense is a form of caution because under threatening circumstances it allows one to withdraw from an overtly active life. Seneca freely admits (*Ep.* 22.7ff.) that the Stoics stand out less for their courage than for their caution; caution (*cautio,* εὐλάβεια) is one of the Stoics' good emotions. And if *otium,* even of the voluntary kind, is an option when political circumstances become too hazardous, then it becomes the equivalent of a self-imposed exile, albeit under more comfortable conditions (Sen. *De Ot.* 8.1). This connection allows us to compare attitudes in times of *otium* with how the Roman philosophers recommended one should behave when in exile.

Let us turn our attention first, then, to those conditions under which a Stoic may choose or be forced to withdraw from active life so as to concentrate on his own thoughts and studies. Musonius Rufus, for one, seems to have remained faithful to the Stoic ideal; he behaved more honorably in exile than did Seneca, who did not shun any of the political expedients necessary to promote his return. Musonius Rufus earned a glorious reputation for the manner in which he comported himself. Not only did he bravely put up with his plight, but supposedly he also managed to make himself useful even in as desolate a place as the island Gyara, which became proverbial for being the harshest possible place of exile. If Musonius made light of a serious condition such as exile, Favorinus tells us, it was certainly not out of hatred for his fatherland or his fellow citizens (Περὶ φυγῆς, 76.17–20 Barigazzi). Rather he embraced events as they came his way, on the grounds that they were part of the human lot. He never found himself to be utterly alone and drew students to wherever he happened to be (Philostr. *VA* 7.16). In the passage "That Exile Is Not an Evil" (9 Lutz), he is apparently giving instruction as one man in exile to another. Even in exile, he benefited the community to which he belonged: he is said to have discovered a well on the arid island (Philostr. *VA* 7.16) and "to have concerned himself with the welfare" of the place (Julian *Ep.* 16 Wright).

When he was not in exile, and throughout his life, Musonius Rufus never seems to have directly involved himself in politics, though apparently he did not altogether stay out of society or the fray of political crises. Whether he found himself in Rome or on Gyara, his basic conduct remained the same. The tradition has it that he tried to talk an army of soldiers into peace, though the only responses he got were expressions of boredom, ridicule, and even aggression.[36] In addition, he indirectly affected public life by mentoring a string of the influential people of his day:

36. See Tac. *Hist.* 3.81.

Rubellius Plautus, Thrasea Paetus, Borea Soranus, the younger Seneca, Euphrates of Tyre, Epictetus, Dio Chrysostom, and his own son-in-law Artemidorus.[37] The image our sources give of Musonius Rufus is the hagiography of a Stoic active in exile and reserved at home. And by the time of Musonius, this hagiography already had an impressive Roman lineage in figures such as P. Rutilius Rufus, who, after his condemnation in 92 BC, gave up his Roman citizenship in exile and adopted the local citizenship of the community in which he lived, Smyrna.[38]

What are the implications for political activity of the attitude modeled by Rutilius and Musonius? On the one hand, the value of political office is not an absolute good and the correctness of one's choice to engage depends on circumstances. On the other, political responsibility nevertheless belongs to the social duties that require a special reason for dispensing with them. Hence we should refrain from being overly ambitious and yet, as Seneca advised Athenodorus (*Tranq.* 4.1ff.), not throw in the towel too easily. It is also possible for leisure to become the kind of "external" that causes anxiety if we hanker after it too much, as Epictetus warns (*Diss.* 4. 4). The upshot of this point of view is that we should literally serve where we find ourselves through circumstances. If we retreat, the retreat ought to be gradual. Because "the service of a good citizen is never useless," even a silent person can have a political impact by setting a good example (*Tranq.* 4.6). And if one does not get enough opportunities for displaying civic virtue, one can still "frame laws for the human race without running afoul of those in power" (Sen. *Ep.* 14.14).

This recommendation of social responsibility in the face of challenges could be projected onto Socrates. A very telling anecdote portrays him as a Roman Stoic *avant la lettre* during the regime of the Thirty Tyrants:

> Socrates was in the thick of things [*in medio erat*]; he consoled [*consolabatur*] mourning city fathers, he encouraged [*exhortabatur*] those who despaired of the state, he scolded [*exprobrabat*] the wealthy who were dreading their possessions because their regret for their dangerous greed had come too late, and for those who wanted to imitate him, he carried with him a great example, by walking freely among thirty masters. (*Tranq.* 5.2)

This Socrates is not engaged in a Platonic dialogue but relies on the modes of discourse Seneca himself uses (*Ep.* 94 and 95), as do the other Roman Stoics: consolation, exhortation, reprobation. Here, Socrates is a model for

37. Claassen 1999, 66.

38. See Cic. *Balb.* 28; Tac. *Ann.* 4.43.

Seneca himself, again according to a philosophical mode that emphasizes the importance of precepts and examples.

Continuing the argument along the lines of progressive withdrawal, one can serve the community of which one becomes a part as a result of exile, and if that is not possible, one serves universal humanity and the community of gods and men, from which one can never be banned. By studying, reflecting, and teaching when possible, philosophers are always on call: *numquam privatum esse sapientem* (Cic. *Tusc.* 4.51; Sen. *Tranq.* 4). This responsibility has several implications. First, the studies of the Stoic at leisure differ from the traditional *otium litteratum* because they do not serve mere erudition (Sen. *Brev. Vit.* 13.1ff.) but have the good life as their goal. Second, in contrast to the lifestyle of Servilius Vatia, who withdrew into the luxury of his villa by the sea (Sen. *Ep.* 55), to "live for oneself" is not a matter of mere self-gratification for the Stoics. Nor is it a matter of painstakingly trying to preserve and project an illustrious image of oneself by constantly wearing a mask that comes at the cost of great anxiety (*Tranq.* 17.1–2). By concentrating on the pursuits of philosophy, as Seneca has resolved to do in his old age (*Ep.* 8.1, 8.6), Stoics can follow Zeno's and Chrysippus's example, who were more useful, so Seneca claims (*De Ot.* 6.4–5), to the people around them, to future generations, as well as to all nations, than if they had actually participated in politics or commanded armies. According to a testimony preserved by Philodemus (*De Stoicis* col. 12.1–6 Dorandi), Zeno, at the opening of his *Republic,* claimed the work "to be of benefit" to his own time and place.[39]

When in the most extreme situation one finds oneself cut off from fellow human beings, one still converses with oneself (Epict. *Diss.* 4.4.26), remains connected to the social fabric, and enjoys the company of the gods, who are present in nature, particularly in the heavenly bodies, as Seneca also agrees: "when we have assigned to the sage that community [*rem publicam*] that is worthy of him, namely, the universe [*mundum*], he will not stand outside the community [*rem publicam*] even if he withdraws. . . . never is a sage more active [*numquam plus agere*] than when divine and human matters have come under his gaze" (Sen. *Ep.* 68.2).[40] In this passage Seneca, like Cicero, plays on a pun in the term *res publica:* the term can stand for both a sociopolitical entity (what we would call a "state") and the universe, the

39. παρορῶντες ὅτι κατ' ἀρχὰς τοῦ γρά[μ]ματος ἐμφαίνει τὸ πρόσφορον αὐτὴν [*Republic*] ἐκτιθέναι καὶ τοῖς τόποις, ἐν οἷς ὑπῆρχε, καὶ τοῖς χρόνοις, καθ' οὓς ἔζη; Obblink 1999, 183.

40. See also *Ep.* 74.27–29, 85.36–40. On this, see Annas 2001–2.

community of gods and men, which is ruled by the divine principle, also called Zeus.

The analogy between state and universe allows one to compare Zeus's "governance" with human forms of involvement in community. Epictetus, for instance, draws on this analogy to highlight a striking parallel between Zeus's situation as the active divine principle at the point of universal conflagration (*Diss.* 3.13.2–7; see also 1.12.21) and the human condition of vulnerability to loss, a parallel we also find rendered in Seneca (*Ep.* 9.16–17; *Vit. Beat.* 8.4–6). At the stage of universal conflagration, the order of the universe has become undone, and Zeus has reabsorbed everything, including the other gods, into himself. Yet, although he is by himself, he is not forlorn, we are told, and does not pity himself for being alone. Epictetus criticizes those who would claim otherwise and who would thus undermine divine self-sufficiency: "For they do not grasp the condition of one who is alone, starting from a certain natural principle, that by nature we are social beings, dear to each other, and taking pleasure in human company." Though Epictetus himself would not challenge the claim of natural sociability, his Zeus does just fine by himself. He does not fret but instead: "dwells in his own company, is at peace with himself, contemplates what his governance is like, and remains with thoughts that are fitting to himself." According to Epictetus, then, there is no radical opposition between Zeus's self-sufficiency and his relational identity, because when he is alone, the highest god thinks about his relation to, and governance of, the world. When humans, for their part, find themselves alone, they should imitate the divine principle and engage in an analogous mode of contemplation:

> likewise we should be able to converse with ourselves, not to be in need of others, not to be at a loss for an occupation; we ought to pay attention to divine governance, as well as to our disposition to other things; to examine how we used to react to whatever happened to us, and how we react now; what the things are that still weigh on us; how these too can be remedied, how they can be removed; if any of these things still require perfection, to perfect them in accordance with the reasoning that pertains to them. (*Diss.* 3.13.2–7)

Humans should contemplate god's ordering of the universe, think about how they fit into the larger scheme of things, and reflect on how further to improve their attitude to life. They have to master the "need" for others, but even at their most isolated moments, as in exile, they remain part of a larger whole and are supposed to guide their reason accordingly.

Now this is all very well and good as far as it goes, but unfortunately for the Roman Stoics, the political relevance of withdrawal did not just result from a magnanimous choice on their part. Under imperial rule, opting for *otium,* or settling too easily into exile, had, whether intentional or not, a political impact in a different sense: such choices could be perceived as an act of criticism and opposition. Given their claim that substandard forms of government could justify withdrawal, Stoics certainly left themselves vulnerable to suspicion.[41] In addition, Roman collective memory could still recall the case of a certain M. Marcellus, which for us has been preserved in Cicero's correspondence: he chose voluntary exile over submitting himself to Caesar's power and made it very clear that this act should be perceived as criticism. To Cicero's considerable embarrassment, the man even refused to return after Caesar had pardoned him, a gesture for which Cicero had, in his *Pro Marcello,* heaped praise on the ruler. It required all the diplomatic skills Cicero could muster to persuade Marcellus to agree to return to Rome.[42]

The implications of a story such as Marcellus's are clearly on Seneca's mind in letter 73 (1–12). In order to get out of the bind of having his voluntary withdrawal register as criticism of the emperor, Seneca compares Nero's role as the father of the empire to Zeus's role as the ruler of the universe, who has all human matters under his care (*tutela*). The emperor as guarantor of peace (*pax*) and liberty (*libertas*) actually allows for the ideal conditions under which his subjects can devote themselves to philosophy. Subjects benefiting from these conditions for *otium,* in turn, are in a better position to be grateful to and sing the praises of the emperor than are subjects who are politically active. The latter are never satisfied in their ambition, Seneca avers, and have ulterior motives for fawning on the emperor. The picture he draws is clear: *otium* is a situation from which both the emperor and his subjects benefit. The tone of this letter is more than a little ominous and, in its flattery of the emperor, reads like a supplication to let go of Seneca. Seneca is clearly all too aware of the fine line he is walking here; he tells us himself, through his advice to Lucilius, that "an important part of one's safety lies in not seeking safety openly; for what one avoids, one condemns" (Sen. *Ep.* 14.8).[43]

So far we have looked at the relation between detachment and engagement from the perspective of withdrawal, whether in exile or through *otium.* If we pursue this relation now in the other direction, we discover

41. Lana 1996; Veyne 2003, 25–29, 160–63.

42. See Cic. *Fam.* 4.7–12; Claassen 1999, 82–83. Before he could return, Marcellus was assassinated.

43. See also Suetonius *Nero* 35.5; Tac. *Ann.* 14.53–56.

that in action, as I have already indicated, Stoics are supposed to keep a certain measure of distance, even if merely to insert a pause between impressions and impulses, and to hold off on assenting in order to examine and question the impressions so as to make correct use of them. The mediation between philosophical ideals and traditional social values never stops. This attitude points to the remarkable symmetry in the Roman Stoic constructions of both the active life and *otium:* the most withdrawn life still embraces political responsibility, and the most active life still requires a measure of detachment.[44] Seneca claims (*Ep.* 62) that he merely "loans himself to his affairs": even when he is politically active, he never fully invests himself and is ready to withdraw if need be.

That the Roman Stoics are trying to keep a sense of perspective in whatever they undertake is also borne out by the topic of "inner reserve," (*reservatio, hupexairesis*), to which we need to return one last time. The argument here would be that the Stoic notion of inner reserve is structurally analogous to their perspective on *otium.* Another way of looking at this structural analogy would be to posit that inner reserve is meant to allow us to hold on to some of the philosophical advantages of leisure when leisure is impossible. In the first chapter of this study, we have already examined what reservation entails for social responsibility and why our evidence for the notion comes primarily from the Roman Stoics. Here the question becomes how exactly reservation is related to social responsibility.

The Arius Didymus doxography applies "reservation" to a range of psychological notions, including "desire" (ὄρεξις), "impulse" (ὁρμή), and "inclination" (ἐπιβολή; Stob. 2.115 W.). Epictetus, by contrast, limits the application of reservation to our impulses, because he leaves aside desire and inclination and recommends that desire be suspended until the discipline of impulse is firmly established (*Ench.* 2; F27 = 177 Schweighäuser). Marcus Aurelius appears to have followed Epictetus in limiting the domain of reservation to impulse. But to which type of impulses is reservation connected? Seneca applies reservation to just about any social action following from impulse, including going to a dinner and a wedding or providing bail for somebody (*Ben.* 4.39). Most of the evidence, however, including the Epictetus fragment, comes from Marcus Aurelius, and for Epictetus and Marcus Aurelius, impulse has a privileged sphere of application in the domain of matters pertaining to justice—in other words, to a more specific

44. Armisen-Marchetti 1996.

range of social actions. So, with the latter two Stoic thinkers, we are zooming in on a privileged connection between reservation and the specific goal of *promoting justice* in the sphere of human interaction.

This is the Epictetus fragment preserved in the writings of Marcus Aurelius:

In the exercise-theme which deals with the impulses, we must never relax our attention,

1. so that these impulses may be accompanied by reservation (μεθ' ὑπεξ-αιρέσεως)
2. that they may have as their goal the service of the community (κοινωνικαί),
3. and that they may be proportionate to value (κατ' ἀξίαν). . . . (F27 = 177 Schweighäuser = Marcus Aurelius 11.37, trans. Chase, slightly modified)[45]

The second requirement focuses on the goal of service to the community and encompasses the social duties. The third requirement, proportionality according to "value," can cover both the good in the strict sense and the indifferents that are according to nature, because both are "valuables" (Arius Didymus ap. Stob. 2.83 W.).

Marcus Aurelius himself considers the discipline of impulse the discipline of action, and action, in turn, serves the community. Let us take a more detailed look at the relevant passages. One reference to reservation occurs in the passage we have discussed at greater length in the previous chapter, about the sense in which other human beings can become indifferents: "Now these [the indifferents] may hinder one or other of my actions [ἐνέργεια], but they are not hindrances to my impulses or my disposition [διαθέσεως], because I have the power to act under reservation [διὰ τὴν ὑπεξαίρεσιν] and to turn circumstances to my own advantage [καὶ τὴν περιτροπήν]" (5.20, trans. Hard). What Marcus Aurelius means by *peritropē,* "turning things around," is clarified by another passage about reservation, in which he explains that when the ruling power in us is in agreement with nature, "it converts into material for itself any obstacle that meets it, just as fire does" (4.1).[46] That which would have been an obstacle to the original intention becomes in itself an opportunity for the exercise of virtue insofar as it amounts to accepting the divine plan and order of fate.

45. See also P. Hadot 1993a.

46. This specific idea is attested for Chrysippus as well, in a passage preserved by Epictetus (*Diss.* 2.6.9–10).

The last passage that is relevant for Marcus Aurelius's view on reservation again highlights the theme of social action in the service of promoting justice:

> Try to persuade them, but act even if they themselves are unwilling, when the principles of justice demand it. Should anyone, however, use force to block your way, have recourse instead to equanimity and refusal to yield to distress, and so use the setback to display another virtue. Remember, moreover, that your original impulse was not unconditional, and you were not aiming at the impossible. At what, then? Simply to exercise an impulse subject to certain conditions. And this you have achieved; just what we have proposed to ourselves to come to pass. (6.50, trans. Hard)

If we connect this passage to his doubts about the possibility of changing the conviction of others (9.29), we realize again how modest he had to be in his expectations. The outcome of this analysis, then, is that the Roman Stoic who is the most committed to political action because he has the most power to affect outcomes also emphasizes reservation the most strongly. This correlation hits home the point that inner distance, to an even greater extent than *otium*, is the very condition of the soul itself that makes sustained and responsible political involvement possible.

As with previous questions, the answer to how the Stoics provided a philosophical anchoring for inner reserve in all one's actions is not to be found in passages pertaining to doctrine only. Two motifs help to underscore the point: the first, that of the rustic life at the countryside, and the second, that of an individual surrounded by a crowd. Musonius Rufus uses the traditional Roman theme of the moral value of the simple agricultural life (11 Lutz) almost as an allegory for detachment. Being a farmer is really the best occupation for a philosopher, he contends, because it is a hardy and self-sufficient lifestyle in close contact and agreement with nature. Seneca too praises this lifestyle as a mode of "working with one's own hands."[47] One of the biggest advantages of life in the country, according to Musonius, is that it takes one away from the humdrum and corrupting influence of city life. Hence the countryside is the best context for a philosopher to pass his teachings on to his pupils, provided there are enough periods of rest. The setting is ideal, however, not only for teaching, strictly speaking, but also for the pupil to observe his teacher putting theory into practice. The constant association between teachers and pupils is to the advantage of both. And because it remains firmly rooted in activities of everyday life, this association is of a fundamentally different type from what one would expect

47. On the theme of *autourgia*, see ch. 5; see also *Ep.* 86.5; on Scipio, 86.10.

to find in a philosophical school or lecture room. In the Stoic appropriation of this theme, "country life" comes to stand for that point halfway between full and thoughtless immersion in Rome's hustle and bustle and irresponsible withdrawal among dusty books and useless theoretical quibbles.

The topos of life in the country is well represented in the younger Marcus Aurelius's letters to Fronto, as when he writes that he helped out with the harvest of the grapes:

> Greetings, my sweetest master. We are in good health. I went to sleep rather early last night, on account of my little cold, which seems to have died down. So, from the eleventh hour of the night until the third of the day, I spent some of the time reading parts of Cato's essay *On Agriculture,* and some of it writing—less dreadfully, thank goodness, than yesterday. . . . I went to see my father and joined him at the sacrifice; after that on to luncheon. What do you think I had to eat? A tiny portion of bread, as I saw the others hogging beans, onions, and fish well-advanced in pregnancy. After that we spent some time on the grape harvest, sweating and shouting away together, and as our author has it, "left but a few survivors of the harvest, hanging in the trees." We made for home at the sixth hour of the day. (From letter 8, trans. R. B. Rutherford = 1.180–83 Haines = 62–63 van den Hout)

With this letter, Marcus Aurelius is trying to prove to Fronto that he is paying attention to his masters' teachings. The countryside is clearly a better training ground for discipline and simplicity than Rome with all its temptations. The structure of Marcus's entire day is governed by ground rules of the correct way of life: part of the day is devoted to studies, the other to working with one's own hands. But in spite of the pretense at seriousness, the tone in the younger Marcus Aurelius's letters is often playful. "Wishing for a plank bed covered only with a skin and for everything else that formed part of Greek discipline" as a young man (1.6) was, after all, quite a bit easier than holding on to simplicity and due measure as an emperor at court. And the asceticism of the earlier, rural life would have been more enjoyable than hardships resulting from protracted military campaigns.

The second literary device that serves to underscore the goal of detachment in action is the motif of the "crowd" (*turba,* ὄχλος).[48] As we have seen, the notion of universal humanity implies an affective bond among all human beings because they have reason in common. Do not call being by yourself "solitude," Epictetus warns us, and do not call being in a crowd "turmoil" (*Diss.* 4.4.26–27). "If you fall in with a crowd, call it a game, a

48. Business of the Forum: Sen. *Ep.* 7, 8.1, 18.3, 25.6–7, 28.6; see also Sen. *Ep.* 32.2, 36.2ff., 43.5; *Vit. Beat.* 1.3–2.4.

festival, a feast; try to celebrate together with the people. For what is a more pleasant sight to one who loves mankind than to see a gathering of many people?" The other side of the coin, however, is that most human beings not only fall short of the ideal of the Stoic sage but are also nowhere close to it. Seneca, in particular, often displays pessimism about the human condition[49] and slips into Hieronymus Bosch–style depictions of human behavior, as in the passage in which he goes on at great length about the perverse use Hostius Quadra made of mirrors in his sexual debauchery (*QN* 1.16).

Faced with these two sides of reality, the Stoic will not remove herself from the group but will bolster herself against the waves of possibly disturbing influences:

> And there is a great need to withdraw into ourselves; for mingling with disparate company disrupts proper composure, renews passions, and aggravates whatever in the mind is still weak and not fully healed. Yet these things must be combined and alternated, solitude and company. The one will make us hanker after humans, the other after ourselves, and the one will be the remedy for the other: solitude will heal loathing of the crowd; the crowd will heal the boredom of solitude. (*Tranq.* 17.3)

The way he describes it here, Seneca falls short of Stoic orthodoxy, in an oscillation between two kinds of aversion that somehow have to cancel each other out. We already know what Epictetus would have said in response. Yet Seneca too is capable of displaying the authentic self in mediation:

> It is a sign of greater courage to remain dry and sober when people around you are drunk and vomiting; on the other hand, it is a sign of greater temperance not to remove yourself, draw attention, or blend in with the crowd, and to do the same things, but not in the same manner: you may celebrate a feast day without excess. (*Ep.* 18.4)

In this chapter, we have unfolded the implications of the Roman Stoics' call to public involvement. Stoic doctrine in action and displayed in the self-assessment of the Roman Stoics' writings has yielded a self that finds its meaning in, and that is constituted by, being poised between diverging demands. Poised as that self is, it is not frozen or paralyzed. It may have difficulty avoiding contamination by values it ultimately must reject, but its philosophical reserve does keep it involved in the life that we face every day, in our ordinary concerns, and in the affectionate care for human beings

49. As in *De Ira* 2.9.2, 3.26.4, 10.6; *Tranq.* 15.1; *Brev. Vit.* 3.2ff.; *Ben.* 1.10.1, 2.14.4, 4.37.2, 5.15.1, 6.38.2–3, 7.26.4–5.

around us. In the recently reopened Alte Nationalgalerie in Berlin, a double herm is on display that on the one side shows the head of Seneca and, on the other, Socrates.[50] It is an apt image: the Roman Stoics saw themselves as continuing Socrates' legacy; nonetheless, they were looking in a different direction. As Seneca puts it, a Stoic continues to "do the same things, but not in the same manner" (*Ep.* 18.4, 5.2–3).

50. Staatliche Museen, Berlin, cat. no. 371; see Richter 1965, 114.20; Zanker 1995, 198–210.

CHAPTER FOUR

Parenthood

> I am glad your little daughter gives you pleasure and that you agree that affection for children is a part of nature.[1] Indeed, if this is not the case, there can be no natural tie between one human being and another, and once you abolish that, you abolish all society. "And good luck!" says Carneades—an abominable thing to say, but not so naive as the position of our friends Lucius and Patro [Epicureans]; when they make self-interest their only yardstick while refusing to believe in any altruistic act and maintain that we should do good only to avoid getting into trouble and not because goodness is naturally right, they fail to see that they are talking about an artful dodger, not a good man.
>
> Cicero to Atticus, *Att.* 7.2.4 = 125.4 Shackleton Bailey (Cambridge edition)

The image of Marcus Aurelius's spouse Faustina appears on coins as a symbol of fecundity (*fecunditas Augustae*). If Klaus Fittschen's reconstruction is on the mark, Faustina gave birth to six children between 147 and 152 and then, after an interval of seven years, to seven additional children between 159 and 166 (?).[2] The twin boys she bore in 149 raised the hopes of an imperial lineage, but both infants died the same year. In 161 she gave birth to another set of twin boys, one of whom, Commodus, survived into adulthood and succeeded Marcus Aurelius. As I have already noted, the imperial couple lost many of their children: of the attested thirteen, probably only six survived to adulthood. Faustina herself died not very long after her childbearing years, at the age of forty-five. But it is in itself, of course, a small miracle that she survived so many births in the first place (not to mention miscarriages that may never have been included in the count). Clearly, for Roman thinkers parenthood would be a focal point for any discussion of life's challenges and the moral value of human relationships.

1. Cicero uses a Greek phrase here: φυσικὴν . . . τὴν <στοργὴν τὴν> πρὸς τὰ τέκνα.

2. Fittschen 1982.

After the challenges of politics and public life treated in the previous chapter, this chapter and the next will consider the second major component of involvement, namely, close relationships, with an emphasis on parenthood and marriage. The emphasis on these relationships, rather than on the more commonly discussed case of friendship, is justified by the Roman Stoics' tendency to upgrade traditional relationships, a tendency I discussed at length in chapter 2. When Seneca mentions in one and the same context both the loss of a friend and the loss of a child (*Ep.* 74.22–26), this is a sign that both friendship and parenthood belong to the same type of discourse. So here we will take a closer look at how the Stoics evaluate the bond between parents and children. My assessment of family affection does not rely on a problematic "evolutionary" view that presupposes that somehow the Roman Stoics were more affectionate than their cultural predecessors.[3] Rather, I will examine how Stoic philosophical discourse specifically responds to and, to some extent, challenges accepted cultural standards of affection.

Socrates' Sons and Marcella's Children

In one of the pseudo-*Letters* of Socrates, the author draws on the motif of a "kinship of soul" (τὸ ἐν τῇ ψυχῇ συγγενές) between Socrates and his pupils and among the pupils themselves (6.11.83 Giannantoni 1.307 = 6, p. 239 Malherbe). This "kinship" motif is meant to justify the idea that after Socrates' death, his biological children could count as much on his friends and pupils for guidance as they could have on their father. With this argument, spiritual kinship subtly but undeniably takes precedence over biological ties. If this letter is dated correctly to the first century AD, then we have here a valuable case of contrast that will allow us to discern more clearly what is distinctive in the Stoic approach to parenthood.

Where did the motif of "kinship of the soul" come from? In Plato's *Phaedo,* the friends witnessing Socrates' last moments not only seem to take up the role of beloved, as when Socrates caresses Phaedo's hair and hints at the traditional mourning gesture of having it cut (89A9–B6), but also displace his children. Right before Socrates gives his final instructions to his household and sends his biological children away, Plato has Phaedo comment that he and Socrates' other companions "all felt as if they had lost a father and would be orphaned for the rest of their lives" (116A–B). This is Plato's view of the situation, and we do not hear whether Socrates himself acknowledged his pupils as his spiritual offspring. The other key text

3. For a poignant critique of this view, see Saller 1994, esp. ch. 5. See also Golden 1988.

to mention in this context is, of course, the *Symposium,* which emphatically distinguishes between "labor of the body" and "labor of the soul" (206B ff.).

In the second book of Xenophon's *Memorabilia,* one can find additional information about how Socrates' attitudes to relationships could be perceived by his followers. As in Hierocles' writings, this book contains Socrates' recommendations for different types of relationships: how to treat one's parents, which attitude to have toward a brother or one's friends, how to manage one's household well and preserve harmony. But the marital relationship is conspicuously absent from the stories. Olof Gigon suggests that marriage was left out because of the awkwardness of Socrates' marital relationship with Xanthippe.[4] Most interesting for our purposes is the exchange between Socrates and his son Lamprocles, who complains about Xanthippe's prickly behavior. Socrates makes Lamprocles acknowledge the care he received from his mother, the pains she took on his behalf when he was little, and the good intentions she had and still has toward him. In short, Lamprocles owes Xanthippe respect simply because she is his mother. But Socrates' advice has a peculiar detached quality to it: he could be advising any young person to respect his or her mother. The fact that this is *his* son complaining about *his,* Socrates', *wife*—whose name he does not mention—is irrelevant to the advice given. Although Socrates has taken on the parental and marital relationships, here—as in the *Phaedo*—he appears to be standing outside and above such relationships. It is in part this aloofness that led to an emphasis on spiritual kinship in later texts such as the letter attributed to Socrates. The Roman Stoics, in contrast, want to argue for a much stronger form of commitment: it will not do to be present merely in body to one's immediate family and household while being absent in one's mind.

Platonist philosophers in particular seem to have had a predilection for the motif of spiritual kinship. The Neoplatonist Porphyry (third century AD) married Marcella when he was old and she was already the mother of five daughters and two sons.[5] In a letter addressed to Marcella, he tells us about his attitude toward those children: "[I chose to wed you] not in order to produce bodily offspring, for I had decided to have as children those who are lovers of the true wisdom, along with your children, should they someday embrace the correct philosophy as they are brought up under our guidance"

4. Gigon 1947. See also Xenophon's testimony at *Symp.* 2.10.

5. Another interesting case for comparison would be the story of the fourth-century AD woman Neoplatonist Sosipatra of Pergamum, who did marry and had three sons. On this, see Dzielska 2001.

(*Ad Marcellam* 1.5–8, trans. K. O'Brien Wicker). To be sure, Marcella and her children are not a priori barred from the shared life of philosophy. Yet the message is all too clear: that Porphyry will recognize as his children only "those who are lovers of wisdom," and that Marcella's biological offspring will have to rise to the challenge if they want that kind of recognition from him.

From this first passage one can already deduce that Porphyry did not have a high opinion of bodily procreation. In the same letter, he restates this view in even more explicitly negative terms: "The most blessed offspring come from virginal soul and unmated Intelligence. For the incorrupt come from the incorruptible, while what the body begets is considered contaminated by all the gods" (33.515–17, trans. K. O'Brien Wicker). This claim hinges on a very stark dichotomy between a pure, spiritual offspring and a contaminated bodily counterpart. In this Platonist view affection between parents and children is, at best, misguided and is, at worst, a threat to the life of contemplation.

A similar kind of standoff between spiritual and biological parenthood comes through more subtly in anecdotes as well, as when a boy raised in Plato's household discovers that his biological father is prone to anger and compares negatively to the philosopher (Sen. *De Ira* 2.21.10–11). It is no coincidence that the anecdote mentions a boy raised in Plato's household, as opposed to that of a philosopher of any of the other ancient schools of thought: by this time, the Platonists have come to stand for a view that intensely questions the value of human parenthood. It is only a relatively small step from this view to the story of Plato's miraculous birth from a virgin mother and the god Apollo.[6] Ancient thinkers, Jerome informs us, could not imagine the fountainhead of wisdom as being conceived in any other way.

Not surprisingly, while the Roman tradition uses Socrates as a role model, it also tries to correct Plato's and Xenophon's portraits of him and relates anecdotes that have a different ring to them. Epictetus is the one to tell us that Socrates did love his children, but as was fitting for a free philosopher (*Diss.* 3.24.60), and Seneca shows us Socrates playing with small children (*Tranq.* 17.4).[7] By now we have accumulated plenty of evi-

6. Jerome *Adv. Iov.* 1.42; D.L. 3.2. For a good discussion of this and overview of the secondary literature, see Tarán 1981, 228–37.

7. See also the anecdote that Socrates was not in the least embarrassed when one day Alcibiades came upon him as he was playing with his children and laughed at him (Valerius Maximus 8.8, ext. 1; see also Aelianus *VH* 12.15).

dence that an author's own views are revealed by which Socrates he happens to pick from the possibilities transmitted in the tradition and how he adapts those possibilities to his own concerns. Plato's and Xenophon's accounts of Socrates and texts such as Porphyry's letter to Marcella bring into focus how parenthood relates to the project of the philosophical way of life.

Cicero's Daughter and Epictetus's Advice

Cicero and the Roman Stoics write against the background of a society that highly values the reciprocal, dutiful, and affectionate bond of *pietas* between parents and children. The rhetorical treatise *Ad Herennium* (erroneously attributed to Cicero) states: "There is a law by nature, observed because of kinship and loyalty [*cognationis aut pietatis causa*], by which parents are esteemed by children, and children by parents" (2.19). For an author such as Valerius Maximus too "the first law of nature is to love parents" (5.4.7). And in Aulus Gellius's ranking of the duties (5.13), which he claims to have received from a long and hallowed tradition, duty to parents stands at the top of the list, followed by the guardianship of orphans (*tutela*).

The expectation of mutual affection between parents and children also underlies the passage of Cicero's letter to Atticus quoted at the opening of this chapter. Cicero rejects both the Academic-Carneadean and the Epicurean stances on affection for children because the former, he claims, undermines the very existence of such a "natural" bond, and the latter tries to make self-interest its prime motivation. In contrast to both of these positions, Stoics view affection for children as "natural," and they hold that care for offspring cannot be reduced to self-interest but instead embodies a crucial transition from self to other. For the Stoics parenthood on both the human and the cosmic level has exemplary moral value.

Cicero's correspondence and *Tusculanae Disputationes* provide a good point of entry for a discussion of human relationships in a Roman context. If Cicero had started to write the *Tusculanae Disputationes* in the summer of 45 BC, then he did so after several months had passed since the death of his daughter Tullia around mid-February of the same year.[8] The *Consolatio* he wrote after Tullia's death is no longer extant. But the epistolary consolation that Sulpicius Rufus wrote to Cicero (*Fam.* 4.5) and Cicero's response explicitly acknowledge his sorrow: "the grief I incur in the public life, my home can no longer offer a consolation for; nor can the public forum make

8. For a different interpretation of the same material, see Erskine 1997.

up for the domestic kind" (Cicero in *Fam.* 4.6.2, trans. Shackleton Bailey). However, the expositions on death, pain, and suffering in the *Tusculanae Disputationes* appear to have no room at all for either Tullia or his sorrow.[9]

After having given birth to a boy around mid-January, Tullia appears to have died as a result of complications. In his assessment of this type of suffering, Cicero again shows inconsistencies. In a letter (*Fam.* 6.18.5), he expresses concern about Tullia's delivery and acknowledges the risks of her weak condition; but in the second book of the *Disputationes,* which focuses on physical pain, men are those who suffer pain and toil in war, athletics, or the public arena. Women are "womanish in weeping," the term "virtue" is derived from the Latin word for "man" (*vir,* 2.43), and the only examples of tough women are old ones, who are able to do without food (2.40), and Spartan women, who are subjected to the same kind of drills as are the men (2.36).[10] In the fourth book (11–14), Cicero follows the tough Stoic stance that there is no good use of distress.[11] He strengthens the hard line on grief further by rejecting even vocal expressions of pain (4.55). The same section of the text also includes a reference to legal restrictions on women's mourning practices. And when Cicero mentions the example of mourning the loss of a child, or even a daughter, and refers to his own loss, it is only to reject such mourning.[12] Amid all of these stipulations, Tullia has vanished: not only does Cicero repress his grief, but he cannot even acknowledge the physical and emotional ordeal his daughter must have gone through. His affection and concerns for his daughter can be expressed in letters, but philosophical discourse (apart from the genre of consolation) in his opinion apparently leaves no room for such topics.

Such severity is, of course, not unique to the Stoics. To return to the *Republic,* a text I have used as a backdrop before, when Plato discusses the poets' negative influences on how people should deal with pain or enjoyment (603C ff.; see also 395C–E), we hear that if a decent man is to mourn at all—and the implication is that men well versed in philosophy will not—he will do so only in private, so as to avoid effeminate behavior.

9. See also Plut. *Cic.* 41.7; Cic. *Att.* 12.18a.2, 12.28.3, 12.30.1; Cic. *Fam.* 6.18.5.

10. As Susan Treggiari pointed out to me, an exception to the generally negative evaluation of women is Cicero's inclusion of women among the heroes who supposedly have gone to heaven (1.27–28). If we take into account that Cicero considered erecting a shrine for Tullia, he may have been thinking of her in this passage.

11. S. White 1995.

12. As in *Tusc.* 3.63 (loss of a daughter), 4.40 (loss of a child), 5.36 (loss of a child), end of treatise (reference to his own loss and sorrow).

Along similar lines, Aristotle thinks that only women and womanly men indulge in mourning and want other people to share in their sorrow (*EN* 1171b6–12).

But if one can express reservations about the feasibility of a godlike aloofness in one's management of public affairs, or even question whether aloofness is the most desirable course of action under all circumstances, surely one must be even more critical of that same attitude in more intimate rapports, and one can question whether it is a good thing or an appropriate response. Maybe we *ought* to feel and express grief at the loss of a child. This was a matter of debate for the ancients as well. In a letter to Atticus of March 8, 45 BC, Cicero himself is still wavering on the issue of whether to mourn Tullia's death or not, and he is still willing to consider that suppressing his grief would not be the right thing to do: "And I try all I know to bring my face if not my heart back to composure, if I can. While I do this sometimes I feel I am committing a sin, at others that I should be sinning if I failed to do it" (12.14.3, trans. Shackleton Bailey; see also 12.15). In contrast, in the *Disputationes* Cicero categorically denies that one ought to grieve (3.61ff.); and although in his letters he discusses the possibility of erecting a shrine for Tullia,[13] in his *Disputationes* once again a woman, Artemisia, stands for the weakness of excessive grief, because she had a lavish burial monument built for her husband, Mausolus (3.75).[14]

Given that Cicero is reporting Stoic doctrine when in his *Tusculanae Disputationes* he rejects grief, one cannot help being surprised to read what the Roman Stoics actually have to say about how one deals with the vulnerability of close relationships. For instance, just as Epictetus invokes the case of a father who accompanies his son on a dangerous sea voyage (*Diss.* 3.7.3), he also talks a Roman official into staying by the bedside of his daughter when she is dangerously ill (*Diss.* 1.11).[15] As we have seen before, Epictetus attempts to teach the man that family affection is natural and good (1.11.16ff.) and that the only evils are in "our opinions and the decisions of our will" and not in events. The corollary of this sermon that is most relevant here is that the official too, and not only the girl's mother or servants, should have stayed with the child to attend to her.

Epictetus's injunction that a father attend to a sick child *himself* goes far beyond the customary expectation that the head of the household look after

13. See D. Shackleton Bailey, *Cicero's Letters to Atticus*, vol. 5, Cambridge Classical Texts and Commentaries, vol. 7 (Cambridge: Cambridge University Press, 1966), 404–13.

14. Loraux 1998, 29–34.

15. On this, see also Long 2002, 77–79.

the needs of his household, including their medical needs. Making sure that such needs were taken care of did not prevent the head of the household from keeping a comfortable distance and delegating actual tasks to someone else. It was an accepted cultural practice for parents of the Roman upper class to delegate day-to-day care of children to servants, particularly in the case of newborns and infants. Keith Bradley suggests that the high infant mortality rate can help account for this phenomenon in Roman society.[16] The point here is not that the Romans did not love their children, or that they loved them less than our culture does; they loved them all too dearly and when they could afford to do so had recourse to techniques of emotional cushioning to protect themselves from the pain of bereavement and the pangs of a sharpened sense of vulnerability. In this context, Peter Garnsey speaks of a "stern realism" and also points out that ritual practices indicate that in the first days of its life, up to the *dies lustricus,* a newborn was considered to be in a state of limbo between death and the realm of the living and fully human.[17] Roman culture acknowledged this technique of emotional cushioning explicitly enough for Seneca to be able to draw on it in a consolation as an argument against excessive grief: a man, he said, should not go overboard in mourning for a son "who was as yet better known to his nurse than to his father" (*Ep.* 99.14).

Like Seneca in his consolations, Plato and other authors use the more traditional topos of the father-son relationship to raise the issue of one's attachment to children. In his *De Officiis,* Cicero tells us (1.32) that a Roman is allowed to walk away from his public duty in order to stay close to a son who has become ill. And in a passage about child mortality attributed to Seneca (*De Remediis* 13 Haase), the loss of a son weighs heavily—most heavily in the case of an only son.[18] Against this background, Epictetus's testimony stands out because it focuses on a father's responsibility toward a small child who is also a daughter.[19] This unusual twist to a familiar theme must have made Epictetus's audience sit up and notice that more was going

16. See Bradley 1986, esp. 213–20; 1991; 1994. I am grateful to Keith Bradley for having commented on an earlier version of this chapter. For recent updates on some of these issues and bibliography, see Rawson 2003; see esp. the chapter on relationships, 210–68.

17. Garnsey 1991.

18. See also Marcus Aurelius to Fronto and reply, late AD 164/early 165, *De Nepote Amisso* 2.220–33 Haines = 235–40 van den Hout; Quintilian *Inst.* 6, preface; Plut. *Cons. Apoll.* But for cases of concern about daughters, see, e.g., Marcus Aurelius to Fronto, with reply, 1.202 Haines = 3.11–12, 3.65–67 van den Hout; Plut. *Cons. Uxor.*; the Demosthenes episode in Plutarch's *Cons. Apoll.* 119B–C (also mentioned in Cic. *Tusc.* 3.63); Pliny the Younger *Ep.* 5.16.

19. For a story about the affection between mother and daughter, see Valerius Maximus 5.7.4.

on in this context than a merely conventional reference to affectionate duty. It would have drawn attention to and underscored Epictetus's strong claims about the value of family ties.

Epictetus builds a much stronger case for parental responsibility than does Seneca. Even if one is not convinced by the hypothesis that mechanisms of emotional protection may have been at work in Roman treatment of infants, this much is clear: the Roman official in the Epictetus passage is running away because he cannot face his daughter's illness, and it is precisely in such a situation that the Stoic attitude toward death does not dissolve but radically strengthens commitment to loved ones. Because philosophy provides an entirely different strategy for coping with potential loss, the Roman official can no longer invoke his sense of vulnerability in order to justify blocking the presence of his child. Hence the Roman Stoics hold a powerful card to challenge prevailing practices in the treatment of children.

Comparing the death of one's wife or child to a broken jug and accepting losses "beginning with the very least things," as Epictetus recommends (*Ench.* 3), are, to be sure, no easy matters. We cannot let our affection blind us to the reality of vulnerability. We must instead exert "a counter-pull" (ἀντίσπασον) and "control" (κώλυσον); we must maintain a reserve by "calling to mind the opposite impressions" (*Diss.* 3.24.84–87). But this injunction is only half of the equation: while urging restraint, Epictetus does acknowledge human love for offspring and the expression of that love as commitment. And so in this balancing between affection and detachment too we see the mediating self at play. Inner reserve and familial affection are not, as in Cicero's own case, segregated in different modes of writing, such as letters and philosophical expositions, each with their own literary conventions and normative and cultural constraints. For Epictetus, both are integrated into *one and the same* philosophical discourse.

A Divine Father and Human Parents

Which features of Roman Stoic philosophical discourse allowed for such an integrated approach to parenthood? Contrary to its Platonic counterpart, Stoicism does not pit spiritual parenthood against the biological kind. In the earliest Stoic accounts, the human process of procreation is already inextricably intertwined with the process of generation in the universe as a whole. The divine principle that structures all of reality is in itself a corporeal and physical entity, namely, creative fire or "breath" (*pneuma*). At the most fundamental level of reality, the Stoics posit two principles: (1) the generative principle just mentioned, which the Stoics also called *logos* and Zeus, and (2) an entirely passive principle matter, which is meant to be entirely malleable by the divine active principle. A human soul is a "piece broken off" (*apospasma*) from the divine principle: it is made of the same corporeal stuff (*pneuma*) as is god and in its rational aspect is structurally and functionally analogous to divine reason. When human beings procreate, they in turn pass on a piece (*apospasma*) of their soul *pneuma* to their offspring.[20] Hence a continuous chain is established from divine *pneuma* through the substance of parents' souls down to their offspring.

A key difference between the mode of interaction of the divine active principle and passive principle matter and the human procreation process, however, is that in the case of humans, *both parents* contribute *pneuma* to the formation of the offspring. A woman is not analogous to the passive principle matter, and so a mother plays an active role in the process of procreation. Only when the formative powers of both parents (δυνάμεις καὶ ποιότητες) are a good match for each other (ὁμόφυλοι) can successful conception occur (*SVF* 2.752). It has to be said, though, that not all of the extant Stoic evidence is unambiguous on this topic. One passage attributed to Zeno claims that women merely ejaculate a watery substance akin to sweat.[21] In addition, Sphaerus (a pupil of Zeno and Cleanthes, third century BC) and his followers are said to have claimed that female sperm is infertile because it lacks tension, is scant, and has a watery consistency.[22] This could be an explanation, as Föllinger suggests,[23] for the fact that women cannot conceive by themselves, without necessarily excluding that they can pass on hereditary material. Or it could merely be an indication of dissent in the Stoic ranks. Another Stoic account, that of Hierocles, is ambiguous: he distinguishes between seed and matter (ὕλη), and although the activated seed draws matter from the pregnant body,[24] the womb plays a role in activating the male seed.[25]

20. *SVF* 1.123–33, 2.738–60.

21. *SVF* 1.129.

22. D.L. 7.159; see also Censorinus *De Die Natali* 5.4.

23. Föllinger 1996, 256–65, with many references to Lesky 1951, 163–72. For a general background, see also Dean-Jones 1994, esp. the third chapter: "The Female's Role in Reproduction."

24. *Elements of Ethics* 1.5–30 Bastianini and Long = LS53B.

25. [τὸ σπέρμα] ὑπ᾽ ἐρρωμένου τοῦ ἀγγείου συλληφθὲν (compare this to the Zeno fragment at *SVF* 1.128: [τὸ σπέρμα] ὅταν ἀφεθῇ εἰς τὴν μήτραν, συλληφθὲν ὑπ´ ἄλλου πνεύματος, μέρους ψυχῆς τῆς τοῦ θῆλεος) οὐκέτι ἠρεμεῖ, καθάπερ τέως, ἀλλ´ ἀνακινηθὲν ἄρχεται τῶν ἰδίων ἔργων (1.6–8; "if . . . [the seed] is gripped by the receptacle in good health, it no longer stays still but is energized and begins its own activities"; trans. LS53B).

Some of our evidence of the Stoic view mentions a two-seed model in which both males and females carry a type of sperm.[26] Human "seed" is either itself soul *pneuma* and fire or a vehicle. The male formative power resides in semen in the strict sense, whereas our sources leave open which substance actually carries the female formative power, whether blood or some other bodily fluid. It is also worth noting in this context that inside and outside are not that easy to distinguish in the Stoic formation process of a human being: a human being receives its finishing touches and has its plantlike "nature" (φύσις) fashioned into a soul only right after birth, when the impact of cold air solidifies it (*SVF* 2.804–8).

On the cosmic level, divine *logos* makes and structures reality through "seminal" *logoi.* Hence Chrysippus notoriously allegorized a painting of Hera fellating Zeus as the passive principle matter receiving seminal *logoi* "for the purpose of arranging all things in a beautiful ordered way" (*SVF* 2.1074 = Origines *Contra Celsum* 4.48; see also *SVF* 2.622 = Dio Chrysostom *Oratio* 36.56–57). This markedly physicalist interpretation of divine action apparently provoked quite a bit of scandal and consternation, so much so that Diogenes Laertius bluntly refuses to "soil his lips" by repeating "language more appropriate to streetwalkers than to deities" (7.187–88). Be that as it may, one Stoic fragment states explicitly that the *logoi* in human sperm are the same as those at work in the universe (*SVF* 1.128). And a fragment attributed to Cleanthes compares the universe's process of generation to the process in which the *logoi* contained in human sperm separate into the different parts of the human being (*SVF* 1.497).

If the biological model can be writ onto the cosmos at large, where and how do the chains of divine fatherhood and human procreation intersect? Censorinus says that, according to Zeno, the first human beings (in each cycle of the universe's existence presumably) are born of earth "with the aid of divine fire, that is, of god's Providence."[27] We can infer that, from that point onward, human beings keep passing on this initial spark of divine fire to their offspring. Censorinus's rendering evokes the mythical image of humans and other living things being born from seed of the gods implanted in the earth. Marcus Aurelius expresses the idea that humans eventually return to earth as follows: "I proceed along a path laid down by nature until the day arrives for me to fall and take my rest, yielding my last breath to the air from which I daily draw it, and falling to that earth from which my father drew his seed, my mother her blood, and my nurse her milk" (5.4, trans. Hard).

26. *SVF* 1.128 (including D.L. 7.158), 2.741–43, 2.747, 2.749.

27. *SVF* 1.124, *adminiculo divini ignis id est dei providentia.*

This is how Epictetus renders the connection between divine and human fertility:

> Anyone, though, who has come to understand the administration of the universe, has learned that the supreme and greatest and most inclusive government is the one composed of men and god. He knows that from god have descended the seeds of being [τὰ σπέρματα], not only to his father or grandfather, but to all things born and engendered on the earth, but chiefly to rational beings, since they alone are equipped by nature to share in god's society, being entwined with him through reason. (*Diss.* 1.9.4, trans. Dobbin)

Epictetus addresses an audience that would have been made up exclusively of male pupils. Thus he tends to take the male line of descent, through grandfathers and fathers, as his starting point. But this perspective does not prevent him from occasionally also drawing attention to a relationship such as the one between father and daughter, discussed above (*Diss.* 1.11). All of nature owes its existence to the "seeds of being" that come from god, but humans have a privileged connection with the divine principle and, because of reason, share in a special kind of community.

One important and paradoxical consequence of the connection between human and divine seed is that although parents do contribute parts of themselves to their offspring, there is a very important sense for the Stoics in which children are not mere "parts" of their parents, which they are according to Aristotle (*EN* 1161b18–20).[28] Children cannot be reduced to existing merely as parts of their parents because each human being has its own connection with the divine principle.

The formative influence parents have on their offspring does not stop with birth, of course. Breast-feeding in particular is a topic of concern to authors of this period, because it appears to combine biological formation with a normative influence. Whereas Marcus Aurelius, in the passage quoted above (5.4), still relies on the widespread practice of using wet nurses, Musonius Rufus enjoins women to breast-feed their babies themselves (3 Lutz), a claim echoed by other moralists. Such a claim falls under the general heading of moral injunctions for both men and women to perform tasks themselves (αὐτουργία) rather than to rely on others, mostly slaves. A gulf of anachronisms separates us from what Musonius Rufus

28. In the statement that Plutarch attributes to Chrysippus (*Stoic. Rep.* 1038B), "that we have an appropriate disposition relative to ourselves *as soon as we are born* and to our [body] parts and to our *own offspring*" (οἰκειούμεθα πρὸς αὑτοὺς εὐθὺς γενόμενοι καὶ τὰ μέρη καὶ τὰ ἔκγονα τὰ ἑαυτῶν), the word "parts" (μέρη) is used in the sense of "members," that is, body parts. See also Cic. *Off.* 1.11–12; Cic. *ND* 2.128–29; Inwood 1996; Whitlock Blundell 1990.

intended with his recommendation about breast-feeding. We cannot interpret his injunction from the perspective of a New Age "return to nature," the latest trend in pediatrics, Tolstoy's nineteenth-century-Russian take (epilogue to *War and Peace*), or Simone de Beauvoir's notion that women are enslaved to the species (*The Second Sex*). The most fruitful perspective, I would argue, is to read this as a response both to Plato's *Republic* and to social concerns in Musonius Rufus's own cultural context.

But before we turn to Plato, let us first take a look at other statements about breast-feeding that appear to fall in line with the Stoic view. Aulus Gellius (12.1) has preserved a scene in which the philosopher Favorinus is lecturing to the mother-in-law of a pupil who has just become a father. After having asked about the length and difficulty of the labor, Favorinus enjoins the mother-in-law to ensure that her daughter breast-feeds her baby herself. In a text erroneously attributed to Plutarch, we find a similar plea (*Lib. Educ.* 3C–D).[29] Both passages emphasize the value of the natural affection between mother and newborn, using animal behavior as a point of comparison and stating that the relationship between mother and child will inevitably deteriorate if the mother does not nourish the child herself. These authors themselves explicitly draw attention to the connection between an affectionate disposition and the explicit expression of that affection; this concern is not an anachronism. Roman authors were aware of the problem that loving one's children in the Socratic, hands-off manner may not do them much good.[30]

These authors also give valuable glimpses of some of the motivations behind the use of wet nurses: the mother-in-law of Favorinus's pupil would like to "spare her daughter . . . , in order that to the pains which she had suffered in childbirth there might not be added the wearisome and difficult task of nursing" (trans. Rolfe). The pseudo-Plutarch passage points out that some women are "in a hurry to bear more children."[31] (Breast-feeding temporarily interrupts the fertility cycle.) And we have to keep in mind that many women actually died in childbirth. Such deaths would create an emergency situation in which the availability of a wet nurse would determine the chances of the infant's survival.

29. See also Tac. *Dial.* 28–29; Tac. *Germ.* 20.1; Plut. *Cons. Uxor.* 5; Plut. *Am. Prol.* 3–4; Plut. *Cato Maior* 20.3; ps.-Quintilian *Decl. Mai.* 18.3; Soranus *Gyn.* 2.19.24–25. See Bradley 1986, 1994; Fildes 1986, esp. 17–36.

30. See Dixon 1988, esp. 104–40.

31. *Lib. Educ.* 3D.

In a manner that is analogous to Stoic embryology,[32] Favorinus's psychophysiological account of breast-feeding entails that, just as she did with the fetus, through her milk the mother continues to shape both soul and body of her child, in her likeness as well as the father's. After birth the same blood that *fashioned* the fetus in the womb (*sanguis opifex*) "rises into the upper parts, ready to cherish the first beginnings of life and light, and supplies the newborn children with the familiar and accustomed food" (12.1.13–14, trans. Rolfe). "For the milk, although imbued from the beginning with the material of the father's seed, *forms* the infant offspring from *the mind and body of the mother* as well" (12.1.20, trans. Rolfe, emphasis mine).[33] It follows that bad nurses do not corrupt children merely through neglect and setting a bad example, as Chrysippus too noted,[34] but quite literally through the milk they are providing.

All of this is a far cry from Plato's stipulations in the *Republic*. In that context, women-guardians and would-be philosophers are not exempt from the duty of childbearing for eugenic reasons, precisely because they constitute the best stock available.[35] Plato describes this civic obligation in the most impersonal of terms. The mating occurs by assignment, there is no affective bond between parents, and all ties between offspring and parents are deliberately cut off. One could interpret the fact that the women get help with the child rearing as a positive feature. As Socrates' interlocutor puts it: "This is childbearing made very easy, as you tell it" (460D6–7). But that is far too optimistic a reading. Just as in his argument against biological procreation Porphyry is not primarily concerned with Marcella's physical well-being, here Plato does not have "child care" arrangements in mind. For the social reality in both Plato's and Musonius Rufus's milieu was that women of the upper class would have had access to slave labor and hence

32. The case has been made that this passage betrays a Peripatetic influence (Holford-Strevens 1988, 72–92; 1997). But it also carries traces of a Stoic influence, emphasizing the role both parents play in the formation of offspring; see T38 Barigazzi, p. 114. The context in Aulus Gellius could reinforce this claim: Aulus Gellius himself has sympathies for the Stoics and has Favorinus cite Epictetus with admiration (17.19). The treatise *On Exile* (περὶ φυγῆς), if it is by Favorinus, also shows Stoic influences. A good example of a very one-sided, negative interpretation of this passage is Gourevitch 1984.

33. Compare this passage with Plut. *Am. Prol.* 495D–496A, which grants the blood-turned-into-milk the function of nourishment only and no formative power, unlike the Favorinus passage: see Aulus Gellius 12.1.11, 12.1.13 (*sanguis opifex*), 12.1.14 (analogy between formative powers of semen and mother's milk), 12.1.20.

34. Quintilian *Inst.* 1.1.4, 1.1.16, 1.10.32.

35. On this see also Gardner 2000.

would have had help with child rearing. They could have delegated breast-feeding to a wet nurse, who would have been the one to get up in the middle of the night to take care of the baby.

Though the arrangement in the *Republic* helps women save their energy for other tasks, such as participating in war and ruling (philosophy is reserved for menopause), it aims primarily at severing all ties between parents and children, because such ties would undermine the common good. For women, this means that they would have to give up their babies immediately after birth. Illegitimate and deformed offspring would be disposed of. To prevent deeper attachments (460B–D), women are required to breast-feed randomly assigned infants on a schedule. A community in which all children of one generation are considered siblings, and all adults of an older generation their parents, is in effect a community in which guardians are systematically cut off from emotional bonds with their heterosexual lovers and children.

Against this background, Musonius Rufus's plea that women breast-feed their own babies can be seen in a new light. This is at first glance a rather banal stipulation, one that is easy to ridicule. The scene that Aulus Gellius depicts (12.1) admittedly smacks of unacceptable patronizing: while the young woman who has just given birth is sleeping and recovering from the delivery, Favorinus pontificates to her mother about the moral imperative for women to breast-feed their children. Yet though Musonius's claim and Favorinus's plea are seemingly banal, the philosophical implications are not minor if Musonius's reply to Plato's *Republic* is interpreted in the context of Stoic ethics. According to Musonius, the bond between parents and children is indispensable to the moral fiber of a human being. As I have indicated in the account of *oikeiōsis,* this bond embodies the primordial transition from self-centeredness to social behavior. To be sure, all relationships carry with them the danger of corrupting influences (*perversio,* διαστροφή), but parenthood is not a priori and intrinsically problematic, in terms of being beyond redemption for the philosophical life, and women are not intrinsically corrupting merely because they are women. Hence, for Musonius an intimate bond between mother and child is in the first instance not an obstacle or a danger, as it is for Plato.[36] In the case of thinkers such as Musonius, what the Stoic view amounts to is that the parental bond can be integrated into the philosophical life.

36. Walcot 1987. See also *Lg.* 694D. One could argue that the Stoics preferred to develop more fully another strand of thinking present in Plato's *Laws,* about giving expecting mothers advice on the diet and exercises that would be conducive to the fetus's prosperous development (788A ff., 792E; cf. Posidonius F31 Edelstein and Kidd).

The moralizing about parenthood is not limited to the case of breast-feeding; the Stoics systematically emphasize the moral implications of parenthood itself. Once a child is born, Epictetus points out, we have no choice but to love it and care for it; the option is literally not up to us (1.23). Hence we do have to think twice before taking up parenthood, and we have to think through the consequences. We cannot hold back our affection when we see our child fall and cry. And provisions do need to be made for the material needs of mother and infant, from warm baths to ointments and clothes (3.22.71–72, 74). In contrast, one of the so-called Cynic letters of Crates to Hipparchia praises her for having given birth without much effort or fuss—in fact, Crates is made to say that he did not even know that she was pregnant (*Letter* 33 Malherbe). Her hardy lifestyle as a Cynic philosopher has prepared her well for the physical exertions of pregnancy and childbirth. As a result of her optimal physical condition, her son is strong and healthy, and it will not be long before he will be a child version of the Cynic, a puppy born of "Dog" parents, complete with staff, cloak, and wallet.

This Cynic version of "childbirth and child rearing made easy" has more than a touch of the unreal about it and could merely be a different version of the Socratic and Platonic lack of concern for biological offspring. I would like to argue that Epictetus has got it right here, that women and infants are more likely to need special care, which lovers and fathers cannot choose to withhold and simply walk away from. But if that is true, Epictetus's claim does sound striking in the context of the Greek and Roman practice of child exposure. It is probably a "that is the way things are" claim which is in fact a moral injunction, an "ought," to love one's children.

Musonius Rufus categorically rejects the practices of infanticide, child exposure, and abortion, as well as other deliberate attempts at limiting the number of children in a marriage (15 Lutz). Rejecting the duty of procreation, he argues, goes against the stipulations of society's original law-givers, "godlike men" who are "dear to the gods." And such behavior also constitutes a transgression against Zeus, "guardian of the race." Having children not only is the honorable thing to do, in the community of gods and men, but is also profitable, because children can take care of their parents in old age, and siblings can support each other. In an echo of the utopian Cynic stance, Musonius claims that even poor people do not need to refrain from having many children: if even the birds can take care of their offspring, humans, who have so much more endurance and ingenuity, should not shrink from this responsibility. And if there is no good reason for the poor to refrain from procreation, there is even less reason for the wealthy to do so, even though the latter are intent on maintaining the family fortune.

Just as Cicero teases his friend Atticus that his Epicurean stance is not consistent with the affection he feels for his little daughter, so Epictetus turns the tables on Epicurus by claiming that even Epicurus's own parents would not have exposed him despite knowing that he would grow up to claim that parental affection is not natural. Hierocles, in turn, would have given Epictetus something to think about, by pointing out that people who do not want to marry and have children are criticizing their own parents (ap. Stob. 4.604.9–13 Hense). Simplicius (*In Ench.* 44.77-80 I. Hadot), however, testifies that to save a child from being exposed, Epictetus in his old age did adopt the child of a friend who was too poor to raise it. Epictetus also took on a woman to take care of the child (though Lucian claims that he never married, so we are probably dealing with a nurse).[37] Yet we have to be cautious with this evidence: Simplicius's testimony reads like a projection of Platonist practices onto a Stoic.[38]

So far we have examined the moral dimensions of parenthood. Yet in spite of the value the Stoics do attribute, contra the Platonists, to this type of human interaction and for all its potential contributions to the good life, they too will admit that the parental relationship has its limitations for four reasons: it ranks second to divine parenthood, it cannot be fully subject to rational selection, the obligations it involves are not absolute, and it cannot be a fully symmetrical relation among equals. Let us take each of these limitations in turn, starting with the higher rank of divine fatherhood. The Stoic notion of a scale of nature implies that although the bond between humans and their offspring is stronger than in the case of animals, this bond pales in comparison with Zeus's care, as father and divine Providence, for the universe. There is no fundamental difference in kind, as the Platonists would have it, between divine and human parenthood, but Epictetus in particular does emphasize a difference of degree (*Diss.* 1.3). Human parents, as we have already seen, are mere transmitters of a spark of reason that originates from Zeus.

A second limitation the Stoics acknowledge is that although adults have some measure of freedom in deciding whether or not to take on the responsibilities of parenthood, parents and children do not choose each other. This situation is further complicated in the Roman social context because

37. *Demonax* 55.

38. See Simplicius *In Ench.* 37.211–19 I. Hadot; Sen. *De Ira* 2.21.10–11; Porphyry *Vita Plotini* 9. For the broader context of this discussion, see Reydams-Schils, forthcoming-c.

biological parents are far from the only mechanism of child rearing: in addition to the use of wet nurses and slaves, the social dynamic of divorce and remarriage, adoption, and tutelage (*tutela*) of orphans brings many more possibilities of adult care into children's lives. The blood relationship of parenthood itself comes without a guarantee clause: a son who has been studying philosophy may notice that his biological father is not a paragon of virtue, and even if parents have the philosophically correct hopes for their children, those hopes may not come to fruition. Nature gave us parents, siblings, and children, but no assurance that they be good.

Hence, in Roman Stoicism, the mutual duty of care and affection between parents and children is not an absolute. It is true that adult children are still expected to accept the authority and even physical abuse of their parents; as Epictetus's claim proves, nature expects us to put up with fathers even if they are bad. Yet, the question whether parents' duty toward their children and children's obedience to their parents had limits or were to be preserved under all circumstances was genuinely open for the Roman Stoics.[39] Epictetus lets Heracles off the hook (*Diss.* 3.24.16): he could abandon his wives (plural) and children and delegate his parental obligations to Zeus, the father of all mankind, whenever some new and urgent business required him to move on. As in Socrates' case, presumably, a special divine mission can overrule other duties. But in Heracles' case, given that he is a direct descendant of Zeus, the matter would presumably still have been a family affair.

The father and head of a household, the so-called *pater familias,* had the theoretical right to preside in judgment over the life and death of his child. Richard Saller has pointed out that many concrete Roman examples of the *pater familias* exercising his right to dispose of the life of his children in fact deal with conflicts between the parental bond and the father's duty to the "common good" politically construed.[40] But the Stoics would not necessarily have accepted this type of reasoning. Chrysippus, for instance, may have rejected Agamemnon's decision to sacrifice his daughter for the sake of the military expedition to Troy,[41] considering such a decision an error of judgment. In the other direction of the parental bond, from children to parents, we have already encountered the case in which, in Cicero's words,

39. Aulus Gellius 2.7 has preserved a doxographical schema of the debate. See also Arist. *EN* 1164b23–25.

40. Saller 1994, 114–17. See also the critical assessment of this notion by Shaw (2001, 56–77), with further bibliographical references.

41. Galen *Plac. Hipp. et Plat.* 4.2.26–27, 242–44 De Lacy.

a son ends up "preferring the well-being of his fatherland over that of his father" (*Off.* 3.90). And there is Dio Cassius's insinuation that Seneca actually instigated Nero's murder of his mother, Agrippina (61.12.1). If that is the case, Agrippina's misgivings about having a philosopher as her son's tutor were well founded.

Musonius Rufus too grapples with whether a son ought to obey his father under all circumstances (16 Lutz). The question is particularly poignant when a father forbids his son to study philosophy, in which case the son would presumably already be disobeying his father merely by asking Musonius what he ought to do. It is not just the mother of a future emperor who could be suspicious of philosophy. Seneca tells us his own father "detested philosophy" (*Ep.* 108.22). The study of rhetoric was often considered a much more fitting occupation for an ambitious Roman of high rank. So what is the son of a Roman parent to do? True obedience, Musonius tells the young man who asks him for advice, consists of always doing what is right and honorable and refraining from what is wrong and disgraceful. One should not necessarily obey the letter of a father's commands but heed the father's intention to have his child's best interest at heart. Any father could be wrong about what that best interest consists of, Musonius claims, and in fact, as Stoic authors such as Seneca and Epictetus do not neglect to point out, most parents are on the wrong track in wishing worldly success for their children.

The young man in Musonius Rufus's scenario has a couple of options for dealing with his father. Actually, as in the case Cicero discusses, he is being given a script for conflict mediation. First, he can reason with his father. Then he can try to convince his father by putting what he has learned into practice, which would make him the best son any parent could wish for. But if the father refuses to be impressed and the conflict persists, the son should disregard his biological father's commands and heed instead the commands of the "common father of all men and gods, Zeus," who demands that humans lead a life of virtue. Even if a father then went to the extreme of locking up his son, such a radical intervention could not keep the son from studying philosophy. The son's mind could work anywhere, as we have seen already, whether in prison or in exile or under any other constraints. Musonius's advice clearly builds on the assumption that human parenthood ought to be in alignment with Zeus's fatherhood. When it is not, the latter prevails.

Finally, the relation between parents and children is not one between equals. Children in the prerational stage of their lives cannot partake of virtue. Seneca brings the point home in a sweet-and-sour vignette:

"Children hit their parents in the face, and the infant messes up and tears his mother's hair, and sprays her with spit, or uncovers for the household to see body parts that should remain hidden, and does not shrink from using bad words" (Sen. *Const.* 11.2). And people who do not make the right value judgments according to the Stoic norm of wisdom are like children in comparison both to humans such as Socrates, who have true insight, and to the divine principle.

Scholars working on sociocultural history will be quick to point out that the theme of parenthood has an additional complication in the period we are examining in that an emperor saw himself as "father of the fatherland" (*pater patriae*) and sometimes even took over the role of *pater familias,* as in the anecdote related by Seneca (*Clem.* 1.14.2, 1.15) in which Augustus attends a household council. Increasingly the emperor's own household became part of the official iconography.[42] And Seneca clearly uses the analogy between the emperor's care for his subjects and divine fatherhood not only to cover his back but also to prod the emperor toward virtuous behavior.

Mourning Mothers?

The final aspect of parenthood I would like to examine is the Stoics' assessment of a mother's emotional attachment to her children. In Seneca's view, mothers tend to be more tenderhearted toward their children than are fathers, pampering and overindulging them (which is not the same as saying that they will automatically exert a bad influence). Two of Seneca's consolations allow us to assess how this theme of a mother's attachment might play out. Both are addressed to mothers, one to his own, to console her over his exile, and one to Marcia, who has lost a son. Any reader of these texts would notice that Seneca appears to make allowances for moderate grief, a position for which Cicero's report on the Stoics in his *Tusculanae Disputationes* left no room. Has the Stoic stance shifted in Seneca's works?

According to Cicero's assessment of the Stoic position (*Tusc.* 3.52ff.), in any situation there are two types of judgment that could trigger an excessive and inappropriate emotional response: (1) that something *y* or *z* is good or evil and (2) that a certain response *w* or *x* is appropriate. In the case of the loss of a loved one, the first judgment would state that such a death is an evil; the second, that one ought to grieve in response to this evil.[43] As Cicero indicates (3.76ff.), Cleanthes and Chrysippus propose different

42. Severy 2000.

43. Graver 2002; Sorabji 2000a; S. White 1995.

strategies to cure this erroneous state of mind: whereas Cleanthes proposes to focus on the first judgment, the erroneous assessment of the presence of a good or an evil, Chrysippus prefers to tackle the second one, that a certain response is called for.

Cicero sides with Chrysippus and has two main reasons for doing so. First, there is only one case of a real evil, namely, the lack of wisdom or moral progress, in which the first judgment would be right. This first judgment in itself, however, is not sufficient for a reaction of distress, which would be triggered by the second judgment. So, because Chrysippus's approach can also take the case of lack of wisdom into account, it covers more ground. Second, therapy is a matter of timing and also of adjusting one's strategy to individual dispositions. Even though in the long run a combination of as many techniques as possible may be most effective, to argue that death is not an evil (Cleanthes' line) could be counterproductive with individuals of a less philosophical disposition or when a death has occurred recently and an emotional wound is still fresh. On the other hand, Chrysippus's strategy—that one ought to bear the loss bravely and not sacrifice one's dignity to distress—can be used immediately and in most cases.

It appears then that Cicero primarily targets the emotional response as being inappropriate and requiring suppression. Seneca, in contrast, allows for moderation in mourning as the appropriate response. So whereas Cicero appears to apply a strategic leniency to the first type of judgment involved, and is strict in the case of the second, Seneca is less strict concerning the second type of judgment. Yet the difference is more subtle. To follow the Stoic line, Cicero's grieving person eventually has to arrive at the proper value judgment concerning death, that it is an indifferent; only initially and merely for therapeutic reasons does the judgment that death is an evil stand unchallenged. In contrast, Seneca's defense of moderate mourning as an appropriate response may not fall under this restriction; that is, we are not supposed to realize at a later stage in the healing process that we should not have mourned at all. But if this reading of Seneca is accurate, the key question becomes whether any Stoic could consistently argue in favor of moderate grief.

A first oddity to notice is that Seneca allows for moderation only in the case of grief; he does not make a similar allowance for anger, which falls under the heading of another passion, namely, desire (for revenge, D.L. 7.113): he categorically denies that anger is in accordance with human nature and argues for its total eradication (*De Ira* 1.5–8; 3.42).[44] Second, he is running the risk of crossing over into the terrain of Peripatetic doctrine,

44. On the complexities of Seneca's views on anger, see Nussbaum 1994, 402–38, with further bibliography there.

which generally adheres to the doctrine of moderate emotions, a position that Seneca himself rejects in his letters (85.3ff. and 116).[45] At first glance the Stoic theory of *apatheia* and *eupatheiai* does not seem to be able to accommodate Seneca's stance. As I have noted, in Cicero's account of the *Tusculanae Disputationes,* distress is the only passion that does not have an acceptable counterpart, an *eupatheia,* that would be concomitant with the correct use of reason. The other three main passions do: the passion exuberance has the good emotion joy as its counterpart, desire is balanced by wish, and fear by caution. Yet this implies that the symmetrical schema of this Stoic doctrine appears to have one box left empty, and Seneca's position could be an attempt to fill it.

Before we turn to his letters, let us first take a look at his exact wording in a number of key passages from his three consolations. In his consolation addressed to Marcia, who has lost a son, Seneca says:

> Nor shall I direct you toward precepts of a sterner sort, so as to order you to bear human matters in an inhuman manner, so as to dry a mother's eyes on the funeral day itself. I shall appear with you before an arbiter with this question to settle between us, whether grief ought to be great and enduring. (4.1)

The matter under consideration here, and this is crucial, is not whether one ought to grieve; the issue is whether to curb *excessive* grief. A grief that is "great and enduring" surpasses certain limits in quantity and time. Not grief itself but an excessive expression of this emotion turns out to be the problem.

In his consolation to Polybius, Seneca also refuses to extirpate grief altogether:

> for some measure [of grieving] nature demands of us; more [is contracted] through vanity. But never will I demand of you that you not mourn at all. I know there are certain men who adhere to a harsh wisdom rather than a brave one, who would deny that a sage will ever grieve. (18.4–5)

I take it that Seneca here is not reacting against Stoic doctrine in general but against a strict strand of it, as reflected by the position defended by Cicero in the *Tusculanae Disputationes* that there are no good uses for distress. The Platonists, and Crantor in particular, held that not allowing people to mourn would amount to barbaric inhumanity (Cicero *Tusc.* 3.12–13). The Stoics would have left themselves vulnerable to this charge, and in both passages quoted so far, Seneca is mounting a defense against an accusation

45. See Manning 1974, 1981. See also Grollios 1956; Abel 1967, esp. 15–46. On the consolation tradition in general, see also Kassel 1958; Horst-Theodor 1968.

of *inhumanitas*.[46] The claim that it is nature that prescribes a moderate measure of sorrow, which we find in the passage of the consolation to Polybius, is also present in the consolation to Marcia: "'But to experience a sense of loss for loved ones is natural.' Who denies this, as long as it is within bounds [*modicum est*]? . . . But what opinion adds is more than what nature ordered" (7.1).[47] And so the consolations appear to be consistent: Seneca answers the inhumanity charge by stating that nature prescribes grief in moderation, while also rejecting excessive grief as misguided.

But Seneca does not always couch his position in such unambiguous terms. In one of the letters in which he rejects the Peripatetic line on grief (116.3), Seneca's claim about the role of nature is much more moderate and hesitant, as the qualifications (in italics) reveal: "Who denies that all the emotions flow, *as it were*, from *a certain* natural starting point?" In a Stoic context, "nature" for human beings does not encompass only the reasoning ability but can also refer to the lower-level, nonrational nature that humans share with animals and that is part of the overall order and scheme of things. All Seneca could be saying in the letter is that a certain physiological response is unavoidable, just as when we cut an onion, we cannot help but get tears in our eyes. Which "nature" does Seneca have in mind in the consolations?

The Stoics allow for "involuntary reactions" that even the sage would not have under control, such as a sudden pallor of the face, yawning, or even crying (Sen. *De Ira* 2.2ff.).[48] In his reflections on anger, Seneca postulates (2.4.1) that "there is a first stirring that is not voluntary but, as it were, the lead-up to a passion, and a kind of threat." These involuntary reactions are not passions in the Stoic sense. Passions require a voluntary assent of the mind, a judgment that a good or an evil is at hand and that it is appropriate to respond in a certain manner. Earlier on, in the first book of the same work, Seneca had claimed that the wise man's mind will "experience a light and slight stirring; for, as Zeno says, in a sage's mind too, even when a wound has healed, there remains a scar. Thus he will feel certain suggestions and shadows of passions, but he will be free of the passions themselves" (1.16.7).[49] Involuntary reactions of body and soul are mere "bites" (*morsus*, the equivalent of the Greek δηγμοί); they are "slight and superficial," mere "suggestions and shadows" rather than passions as such. Could such reactions

46. See also Plut. *Cons. Apoll.* 3.102C–E.

47. See also *Cons. Helv.* 16.1; *Tranq.* 15.6; but in the latter passage *natura* has been added as an emendation.

48. Stowell (1999, esp. 46–103) makes a strong case for this thesis.

49. See also Sen. *Const.* 10.4; Sen. *Ep.* 72, 74.31ff.; Cic. *Tusc.* 3.83; Plut. *Virt. Mor.* 449A; SVF 3.574.

be what Seneca has in mind when he allows for some response to the death or absence of loved ones?

There is a problem, however, with ranking the emotions evoked in the passages of the consolations among involuntary reactions. Animals and children do not reflect on whether their arational emotional reactions are appropriate or not. In contrast, what Seneca has in mind appears to presuppose the ability of humans to reason, at least in a second-order process of reflection: the consolations' strong claim of a prescription by nature does appear to imply assent and a correct judgment of the mind that the emotion is the appropriate response. But if Seneca were to leave reason aside, then the question arises how effective his use of the preliminary reactions and "bites" could be as an argument against the charge of inhumanity. At best his sage can argue for the lukewarm position that such responses are unavoidable. Because they involve no judgment whatsoever on his part, he cannot claim that they are appropriate. Only the category of *eupatheiai* leaves room for proper emotional responses that are compatible with reason.

Philo of Alexandria provides help for this dilemma by making a revealing "mistake" (*QG* 2.57): in his list of the four main types of passion and their positive counterparts, the good emotions, he does list a counterpart for distress but calls this counterpart "bites and contractions" (Archner: *punctio et compunctio*).[50] "Bites," however, is a term applied elsewhere to involuntary reactions, which strictly speaking are not full-fledged emotions at all. Neither good emotions nor involuntary reactions are passions, but for different reasons: the one because they are the good counterparts to passions, the other because they fall below the threshold of emotions altogether. But it is possible after all that Philo's mistake is an indication that there were attempts in contemporary Stoic doctrine to fill the empty box in the system of passions and good emotions by coming up with an acceptable counterpart to distress.[51]

Other Roman Stoics besides Seneca show signs of an interest in tweaking the category of distress. Whereas Cicero's account, using Alcibiades as role model, rejects even the type of distress we can feel at our own lack of progress and ineptitude, Epictetus seems to think the distress of the novice justified,[52] along with reactions of shame (*aidōs*),[53] rejoicing,[54] and

50. See Dillon and Terian 1976–77; Graver 1999.

51. Cf. Philo's passage with Plut. *Virt. Mor.* 449A; Cic. *Tusc.* 3.82–83, 4.12–15; Graver 1999, 316–18.

52. As in *Diss.* 3.19.1–2, 4.9.10ff., 4.10.3.

53. Kamtekar 1998. For "shame" as ranked under the good emotion "caution," see *SVF* 3.432; D.L. 7.116.

54. As in *Diss.* 2.5.23, 2.11.22, 2.18.12–14, 3.7.5, 4.4.45–48; *Ench.* 6; F52.

caution.[55] In the case of the wise person, rejoicing, caution, and *aidōs* (in the sense of reverence) are *eupatheiai.* Given the company it is keeping, the novice's distress may be crossing over to the good side. The affective range of the good life is in general widening in the Roman Stoic authors, and the relevant material is not limited to technical lists of passions and good emotions.

But here another objection bars the way to setting up a positive counterpart for distress. The reactions described by Epictetus are, after all, attributed not to the sage but to the novice. The novice is not yet supposed to be in full control of his reasoning ability, and the "good emotions" are concomitant with the correct use of reason, so that, strictly speaking, only the sage can experience good emotions. With the passages of Seneca's consolations we may be coming up against the limits of Stoic theory and the restraints of context and literary genres. Consolations constitute the therapeutic genre par excellence, which comes with rhetorical requirements of its own and adapts itself to the emotional and psychological strength of its addressee.[56] The passages are mostly addressed to women, who in Seneca's view, and in keeping with a well-established tradition, are the weaker sex and more prone to emotional excess. He may judge it "appropriate" for women and mothers to mourn in moderation; given their natural dispositions that is the best they can do. And he may choose not to be too demanding on a slave imperial official such as Polybius, of whom he is expecting something in return. Yet this would be an odd strategy in a consolation addressed to Marcia that opens with the compliment that she has never been prone to any of the usual womanly weaknesses, including excessive mourning. And Seneca gives his mother, Helvia, the same compliment (16.2).

The claim that Seneca allows weeping in moderation only in the specific contexts of addressing "weak" women (and other humans of a lesser capacity) does not work for a different reason as well. Women are not the only ones prone to mourning, as Cicero's case demonstrates and Seneca's letters reveal. Seneca himself gives us a justification for keeping the consolations together with the consolatory parts of the letters. In two famous letters, Seneca defends the position that neither general doctrine by itself, without concrete precepts, nor precepts without doctrine will be effective (*Ep.* 94 and 95). In these letters he casts his net even wider to include, in addition to precepts, the hortatory techniques the Stoics would regularly use to

55. As in *Diss.* 2.12.13, 3.16.3.

56. The strongest case for this view is to be found in Shelton 1995. See also Sorabji 2000a, 178–80.

convey their views to different audiences, such as persuasion, reprobation, and consolation. Once we have noticed this unity of approach behind the different philosophical writings, we can worry less about where Seneca is being a philosopher and where he is not, and rely more on continuity throughout his philosophical works.

So, turning to those consolations that are scattered in and among the letters, what can we discover that throws more light on the issue of moderate grief? In letter 63, a consolation for Lucilius, who had lost a friend, Seneca tells us how he himself was once *overcome* by sorrow (*dolor vicit,* 14) and that he now condemns his *excessive* grief (*inmodice flevi*). Seneca does not exempt himself from the weakness of distress. What he condemns in his past behavior is not the fact that he mourned at all but that his grief got the better of him. The letter Seneca addresses to Marullus in order to console him for the loss of his son (*Ep.* 99) is strikingly analogous to the consolation for Marcia; like Marcia, who is in her fourth year of mourning when Seneca addresses her (1.7), Marullus should not be humored but scolded for indulging in his grief and being too soft (*molliter ferre*).[57] His trouble is a mere "bite"—*morsus,* the term used for the involuntary reactions. It is he himself "who turns it into pain" (*dolor*). Yet in spite of using the term that is reserved for the pre-emotions, it is precisely this letter that comes closest to admitting there is a type of grief that could be considered an *eupatheia.*

It is possible to have one's memory of dead loved ones be governed by the good emotion joy (not pleasure, contra the Epicureans) rather than pain (99.23ff.). But more importantly,

> tears can flow from the eyes of those who are calm and composed. They often flow without impairing the sage's authority, in such moderation that neither humanity nor dignity is lacking. It is possible, I say, to follow nature while preserving one's serious demeanor. I have seen men who deserve respect at the funeral of dear ones on whose face love [*amor*] stood out— with all the show of mourners removed— and nothing was present except for what was granted to honest emotions [*veris adfectibus*]. There is proper behavior even in grieving; this the sage has to preserve, and as there is a due measure in other matters, so there is also in tears; it is with the foolish that sorrows, like joys, overflow. (99.20–21)

Granted, here Seneca is walking a fine line between using the well-established categories of his Stoic predecessors and breaking new ground. Tears as involuntary reactions could suffice to obey the call of nature, if by nature we mean everything that corresponds to a human being's constitution,

57. For a detailed literary analysis of *Ep.* 99, see Wilson 1997.

including the aspects it has in common with animal nature. And joy and love are *eupatheiai* that are counterpoints, not to distress, but to exuberance and desire. In other words, here we already have two different strategies to allow for some type of emotion in response to a death. The first strategy enhances the role of the "preliminary reaction" of grief. This strategy, however, Seneca refuses to use for the first reactions related to the passion anger: there is nothing natural or useful about even the seeds of anger. The second strategy finds room for an emotional response among the *eupatheiai* that are deemed acceptable by Seneca's Stoic predecessors, such as joy in remembrance and love. The last lines of the passage, however, cross over into a third strategy by positing an acceptable counterpart to the passion distress that is analogous to joy, the proper counterpart for exuberance. Seneca is struggling to find a way compatible with Stoic doctrine to tell Cicero (and indirectly Plato) that even in public and at a burial not only a mother but also any philosophically inclined human being has neither to be stone-faced nor stone-hearted in order to preserve dignity and virtue.

* * *

The high opinion the Roman Stoics have of the relationship between parents and children is philosophically anchored in their views of procreation and embryology, which intertwine the physical generative aspect of the divine principle with human biology. Human parenthood mirrors the divine care for the universe, and mothers play a valuable role in this process; they are neither mere passive matter nor a predominantly weak and corrupting influence. Seneca's consolation to Marcia bridges the gap between Platonists and Stoics by drawing on material from Plato's *Phaedo*,[58] which contains Socrates' famous arguments against the claim that death is an evil. The remarkable outcome of this chapter, then, is that the Roman Stoics consider the loss of a child a serious enough occasion to use arguments and strategies that Plato applied to the loss of a friend-teacher. And far from giving up on women's potential for a philosophical attitude, Seneca takes a mourning mother seriously enough to have expectations of her similar to the high expectations that Plato's Socrates had of his pupils and philosophical companions.

58. Stowell 1999, 140–45. Further bibliographical references are included there.

CHAPTER FIVE

Marriage and Community

> *Yoke:* An implement, Madam, to whose Latin name, *iugum*, we owe one of the most illuminating words in our language—a word that defines the matrimonial situation with precision, point and poignancy. A thousand apologies for withholding it.
>
> Ambrose Bierce, *The Devil's Dictionary*

Unlike parenthood, marriage does allow for the possibility of a relationship between two human beings who are equal in their capacity for wisdom. This is the primary reason that some of the later Stoics prefer to portray the marital bond as the paradigmatic traditional relationship, rather than parenthood. Musonius Rufus, for example, explicitly considers the bond between the spouses to be much stronger than the bond between parents and children: "no reasonable mother or father would expect to entertain a deeper love for his own child than for the one joined to him in marriage," and "the love of a wife for her husband surpasses the love of parents for their children" (14, trans. Lutz). By ranking marriage above parenthood, a Roman Stoic can undo the alignment of women and children that is nearly ubiquitous in ancient thought, as in the variations on the stock phrase of a man handling "his wife and children," among his other possessions.

The potential that marriage offers for achieving the philosophical way of life is the subject of the final chapter of this study. In this context, let us return one more time to Socrates and the first generations of his admirers, such as Xenophon, who wrote about marriage. Maybe it would be too much to expect that Xenophon, who, after all, exalted the blessings of a well-managed household (*Oikonomikos*), would mention his own marital troubles. But apparently he could use some advice, and in a dialogue by the

Socratic Aeschines, Socrates recounts how Aspasia once used his method of questioning to effect a reconciliation between Xenophon and his spouse.[1] If a contemporary reader wonders why Socrates did not apply the same remedy to his own household, given his turbulent relationship with Xanthippe, the ancients did as well. Another Socratic, Antisthenes, is on record for having asked Socrates why he did not practice at home what he preached, that husbands could educate their own wives (Xenophon *Symp.* 2.10). Socrates' response was that Xanthippe's difficult behavior was his training ground: if he could handle her, he would have no difficulties in dealing with the rest of mankind.[2]

If the story is true that Socrates actually had two wives, the pandemonium in his household could have been even worse.[3] At any rate, there is an anecdote that Socrates made fun of his two wives for quarreling over as ugly a man as he was, and that they then turned their anger against him, chasing him out of the house.[4] The Stoic Panaetius, however, was not amused and categorically rejected the rumors of Socrates' polygamy as false.[5] Did he do this because such an image of Socrates' marital life would have been an obstacle to using him as a moral example? The Stoic views on marriage discussed in this chapter could lead one to believe this to be the case.

A question that the ancients writers—whether the sources in general or the philosophers—do not allow us to raise is the extent to which Socrates himself was responsible for Xanthippe's sour moods. It is curious that we can discover a more positive picture of Xanthippe in a passage of the first century AD (probably) that describes her behavior in the aftermath of Socrates' death and portrays her as a dignified widow who apparently did learn from his example.[6] It is almost as if, after Socrates' death, she comes into her own, accepting with philosophical equanimity a very simple lifestyle for herself and her children. But if the dating of this passage is accurate, it would, of course, be contemporary with Roman accounts, including Stoic ones, in which the virtuous and dignified widow comes to the fore.

1. Giannantoni 1990, F70, 2.615–17. See Cic. *Inv.* 1.51–53; Quintilian *Inst.* 5.11.27–29; Victorinus *In Rhet.* 1.31, pp. 240.20–241.15 Halm.

2. See also Aulus Gellius 1.17.

3. See Giannantoni 1990, sections IA36, 1:19; IB7, 44, 45, 48, 49, 54, 57; ID1 (26), 2; IG56, 90; IVA, 226.

4. Sen. *De Matrimonio* 62 Haase.

5. See F132–34 van Straaten.

6. Gigon 1947, 121–23. See ps.-*Letter* of Aeschines, "Socratics" *Letter* 21, Malherbe 1977, 270–71.

So if we cannot cross-examine Socrates on his attitude toward his wife, which questions do the Roman Stoics allow us to raise, and which answers did they provide?

To Marry or Not to Marry

The Early Stoics' contributions to the lively debate pro and contra marriage[7] are not consistent. In one passage (7.121), Diogenes Laertius reports that Zeno believed that the wise man ought to marry and have children; in another (7.131), Zeno is said to have endorsed the position from Plato's *Republic* that women and children are to be held in common. Diogenes Laertius attributes the second position, in strikingly similar wording to Zeno's, also to Diogenes the Cynic (6.72). This attribution is plausible because one could expect a rejection of conventional modes of sociability from a Cynic. Max Pohlenz tries to argue away the conflicting Stoic evidence by claiming that marriage and parenthood would be appropriate in ordinary circumstances, whereas the sharing of women and children would be appropriate in the ideal setting of a community of sages.[8] Cicero too seems to indicate that, as in the case of a career in politics, circumstances could enter into the decision whether to marry. He alludes to Stoics who take the Cynic's stance into consideration: "As to the way and life of the Cynics, some say they are applicable to the sage *under certain circumstances;* some say not at all" (*Fin.* 3.68, emphasis mine). His wording implies that "some" Stoics would have endorsed the Cynic lifestyle if conditions had warranted it.

Elizabeth Asmis proposes a different solution for the inconsistency in the Stoic sources. She suggests that our sources misunderstood and misrepresented Zeno's claim about the common possession of wife and children, and that he must have meant that women participated in the community of virtue of the wise.[9] So "common" would not primarily refer to sexual promiscuity, even though the Early Stoics did not shrink from holding shocking views. It may be impossible to ascribe this view with certainty to the Early Stoics, but the Roman Stoics and others thinkers at a later stage do appear to have followed such a line of thought. Given that Plato's injunctions constitute the background of the discussions of marriage, it is not surprising that authors of the imperial period engaged in amusing attempts to rewrite Plato's phrase of friends "holding everything in com-

7. See the collection of source material in Gaiser 1974. For Epicurus, see Brennan 1996.

8. Pohlenz 1948, 138–39. See also Baldry 1959, 9–10; Schofield 1991, 119–27.

9. Asmis 1996.

mon." Epictetus, for instance, claims that in his *Republic,* Plato intended to replace the traditional bond between a man and a woman by another type of marriage (F15 = 53 Schweighäuser). Seneca uses the phrase to underscore that a child belongs to both of his parents (*Ben.* 7.12.1), an interpretation that strengthens rather than annihilates the parental bond. And Plutarch proposes an interpretation in terms of the union of *souls* between spouses (*Am.* 767E).

Whatever the merit of Pohlenz's explanation for the conflicting evidence of Zeno, it is quite clear that Epictetus endorses exactly the reverse in his rendering of the Cynics' view (*Diss.* 3.22). In society as ordinarily given, there would be a conflict between the life of reason and the demands resulting from relationships; under these conditions, it would be best to take up the Cynic's mode of life and to "make all humans one's children, having the men as sons, the women as daughters. In this manner he approaches them all; in this manner he cares for them all" (3.22.81–82). In more ideal circumstances, however, the wise man could marry and be a parent, "for his wife will be another person of this kind [i.e., like himself], and so will his father-in-law, and his children will be brought up in the same manner" (3.22.68–69). In other words, if they fulfill the right conditions, traditional relationships can be transposed into the community of the wise, as I have noted previously. In that case, the wise man will not have to "descend" to marriage (Stob. 2.94.8–20 W.); marriage will be lifted up in order to become compatible with the pursuits of reason. The Cynics Crates and Hipparchia, of course, were so exceptional that Crates found in Hipparchia another self. Both of them could manage their relationship even in society as given (76), and according to another source they were even able to raise a child in the Cynic vein, as we have seen in the previous chapter.[10]

Although Epictetus does allow for marriage in his version of the ideal community, we may be running into another problem. Like other ancients in their accounts of *eros* and friendship, Epictetus would have difficulty doing full justice to unique traits in a beloved. How could one account for the personal preferences of more intimate relationships in the community of shared reason? If, according to the ideal, we are all the same, then why choose as one's spouse this person rather than someone else? One answer the Roman Stoics could provide would be that affection is colored according to the range of social duties. There would be different types or *modalities* of affection (σχέσεις) according to the type of kinship, including the one among the sages, but there are no different *degrees* in affection. It would

10. See the ps.–*Letter of Crates to Hipparchia*, 33 Malherbe 1977, p. 83.

indeed be absurd for the Stoics to claim that one loves one's spouse in exactly the same way as one does one's mother. What one should strive for is a level of parity in the different types of affection. If, however, we also take into account Panaetius's theory of the four *personae* that define each individual, the Roman Stoics would be able to make room for different types of personalities as well, in addition to different types of relationships. From this vantage point, it would not be hard to see that some personality types would be more compatible than others, even if they were all equal in being virtuous. Finally, for the relationship between lover and beloved, even the deus ex machina kind of *eros* can be retrieved by the doctrine of good emotions (*eupatheiai*).[11] Why do spouses like each other? Because they do, meaning because Eros is at work in the relationship.

Looking at this same question from a different perspective, we should also keep in mind that the Roman Stoics aim not primarily at the sages but at those struggling to make progress; they do not address an ideal society but try to mediate with society as given. Their audience works with the concept of arranged marriages; the selection of a partner is very much a function of where and how one happens to be situated in society. In this context, arguing for alternative criteria of selection constitutes a meaningful challenge to prevailing norms, bringing the point home that marriage too can be a legitimate vehicle for the philosophical ideal.

Musonius Rufus, Antipater, and Hierocles

The evidence for the Stoic defense of marriage comes primarily from Antipater of Tarsus, Hierocles, and Musonius Rufus. I will assess Antipater and Hierocles from the vantage point of what we know about Musonius Rufus's views, who provides the key to this chapter.

Given our current knowledge of Stoic sources, Musonius Rufus, Epictetus's teacher, takes the importance of personal involvement, and of marriage specifically, the furthest. Perhaps it is a bold move to use the lesser-known Musonius as the focal point of an analysis of Stoic views on relationships, but his contemporaries, at any rate, had a very high opinion of him. We know that Fronto, Marcus Aurelius's teacher of rhetoric, presents Musonius as a philosopher who instructed an entire generation of famous philosophers and orators.[12] Admittedly the originality in the limited number of Musonius Rufus's extant expositions is not easy to detect

11. By distinguishing between *eros* and ἀφροδίσια, "sex," Roman Stoics can lift *eros* out of the category of passions, contra Stephens 1996, 196.

12. *Epistulae ad M. Antoninum Scriptae de Eloquentia* 1.4, 135.3–5 van den Hout = 2.50 Haines.

because they are governed by rhetorical topoi (i.e., stock arguments and phrases).[13] This mode of discourse, however, does allow a speaker to present crucial points through subtle changes in the repertoire.[14] Where Musonius breaks through the traditional conventions, he must have caught the listener's attention, as he now holds the reader's gaze (in the texts others recorded). Musonius's accounts will also yield fresh insights if interpreted in the context of Stoic doctrine.

What value, then, did Musonius Rufus, Antipater, and Hierocles assign to marriage? Unlike Cicero, who is said to have refused to remarry because "he could not possibly devote himself to a wife and to philosophy,"[15] Musonius answers the question "whether marriage and living with a wife is a handicap to the pursuit of philosophy" (14 Lutz) with an emphatic plea in favor of marriage. In addition to the pronouncements quoted in the first paragraph of this chapter, Musonius asserts that "marriage is manifestly in accord with nature." "Whoever destroys human marriage destroys the home, the city, and the whole human race." "One could find no other association more necessary or more pleasant than that of men and women." "To whom is everything judged to be common, body, *soul,* and possessions, except man and wife? For these reasons all men consider the love of man and wife to be the highest form of love [φιλίαν]." "Where indeed does Eros more properly belong than in the lawful union of man and wife?" To underscore the importance of the marital union and procreation, Musonius echoes Chrysippus's invocation of Zeus by invoking the gods Hera, Aphrodite, and Eros (14 Lutz) as guarantors of the sanctity of these duties.[16]

In line with Musonius Rufus, Antipater (*SVF* 3.62–63)[17] highlights the importance of the household for the larger community. He calls the union of the spouses one that entails "the truest and most genuine goodwill" (τῆς ἀληθινωτάτης καὶ γνησίου εὐνοίας) and compares it to a complete, "whole through whole" mixture (ταῖς δἰ ὅλων κράσεσιν) of wine in water. The

13. For a thorough analysis of parallel passages, see Geytenbeek 1963; Praechter 1901. For an excellent assessment of the tradition of philosophical writings on marriage, see Deming 1995; Treggiari 1991 (both with very good bibliographies). See also the very fine and succinct analysis of Benabou (1987).

14. A background is provided by such texts as Xen. *Oik.*, the so-called Pythagorean letters, the so-called Cynic letters, and ps.-Aristotle *Oik.* 3.

15. Sen. *De Matrimonio* 61 Haase; see also 48, attributed to Theophrastus. See also Wilhelm 1915.

16. Jupiter Gamelios and Genethlios in Latin; Sen. *De Matrimonio* 46 Haase.

17. A translation is provided by Deming (1995, 226–29, with notes).

union is described in terms not merely of sustenance and children but of body *and soul*. He explicitly tackles the problem of misogyny (he actually uses the word) and men's rejection of marriage, a theme Musonius leaves implicit. He compares the union to regaining a missing hand or foot or to acquiring an extra pair of eyes or hands; it makes our tasks so much easier if we "take the other as ourselves, regardless whether that other is man or woman." As discussed in chapter 2, the phrase "treating the other as oneself" is reminiscent both of Aristotle's friendship among equals[18] and of the bond among the members of the Stoic community of the wise;[19] hence this phrase indicates how highly Antipater values the spousal union.

Hierocles' "most necessary *logos* on marriage" (ἀναγκαιότατος . . . περὶ τοῦ γάμου λόγος) is also very similar in tone to Musonius Rufus's exposition.[20] Community lies at the heart of what humans are according to their nature as rational beings, and without homes there would be no cities. A marriage's purpose is not limited to procreation but finds its full realization in the shared life between the spouses. "No one holds a closer affinity to a man than his spouse; no one comes closer to his skin than his child." The pairing, or "yoking" (ζεῦγος), of husband and wife intertwines the fate of both; harmony exists between them; they do everything together, in body and, even *more so*, in soul. Like Antipater, Hierocles tackles arguments against marriage. Why do men scorn marriage? Because they have married for the wrong reasons. It does not make any sense to try to turn friends into allies against the hardships of life while ignoring the prime alliance given to us by nature, the laws, and the gods: that with spouse and children. As we have seen in the previous chapter, Musonius too draws on the theme that the family provides natural allies (15 Lutz).

From this general overview of what Musonius Rufus, Antipater, and Hierocles have to say about marriage, let us now turn to some of the details and crucial nuances. Musonius Rufus mentions Socrates' marriage, together with Pythagoras's and Crates' marital relationships, as examples of the compatibility between marriage and philosophy. That he *presents* this claim as self-evident, in a context, no less, in which he puts a heavy emphasis on affection, strongly suggests that he is rewriting the script.[21] On an audience

18. See *EN* 1170b6ff., *EE* 1245a30.

19. See D.L. 7.124 = *SVF* 3.631.

20. Stob. 4.502–7 Hense = 52–55 von Arnim.

21. See also Döring 1979, 43.

accustomed to the entertainment that topoi could provide, this understated innovation would not have been wasted. Socrates? The husband who is said to have paid about as much attention to Xanthippe as one would to the geese around the house, which one keeps for the sake of their eggs even though in themselves they are a nuisance?[22] This move on Musonius's part is a vast departure from Plato's one-paragraph dismissal of Xanthippe in the *Phaedo* (60A), the Xenophon passages discussed in the previous chapter (*Mem.* 2), or even Epictetus's praise for Socrates' patience with his difficult wife.[23] Antipater too (*SVF* 65), unlike Musonius, refers to the difficult relationship between Socrates and Xanthippe, as does Seneca.[24] What is Musonius trying to get across?

First, in Musonius's opinion, marriage does not exclusively serve the function of procreation. Contrary to what some scholars have claimed, he lifts the value of this relationship far above the utilitarian concerns of household management and civic duty. Daniel Babut, for instance, has put too much emphasis on the procreationist aspect of marriage as Musonius presents it.[25] Another distortion surfaces in analyses of the Stoics' impact on the Christian tradition. Scholars such as J. Stelzenberger[26] and, much more recently, W. Deming focus on the role marriage plays in regulating the sex drive, as the infamous "remedy against lust" (*remedium concupiscentiae*). Perhaps damage control is the one aspect of the Stoic view by which the Christians were most struck, but possibly, in the case of Stelzenberger, it is the scholar himself who has not noticed that a long-term rapport between a man and a woman could serve more positive purposes as well. As a matter of fact, Musonius Rufus considers affection and *eros* to be as important as the care for offspring and social duty—so much for the stereotypical image of the Stoics as being cold and detached. Musonius's view can be said to be procreationist only to the extent that he considers child rearing as central to marriage (see also 15) and holds forth against indulging in sex for the sake of "mere pleasure," even within marriage. Let us explore each of these two points in turn.

22. See D.L. 2.37; Teles 2.18–20 Hense.

23. *Diss.* 4.5.3, 4.5.33; see also 3.26.23, 4.1.159ff.

24. Sen. *Ep.* 104.27, *Const.* 18.5, *De Matrimonio* 62 Haase.

25. Babut 1963. For very different accounts, see Eyben 1978 (who was clearly ahead of nearly everybody else on this issue); Foucault 1988a, 146–85; Laurand 2003.

26. Stelzenberger 1933; his twelfth chapter, 403–38, is entitled "Die *Sexual*ethik." See also Broudéhoux 1970; Reydams-Schils forthcoming-a.

Musonius strongly emphasizes that the union between the spouses is the foundation of marriage. Under the heading "What Is the Chief End of Marriage?" (13A) we read:

The husband and wife . . . should come together for the purpose of making a life in common and of procreating children, and furthermore of regarding all things in common between them. . . . The birth of a human being which results from such a union is to be sure something marvelous, but it is not yet enough for the relation of husband and wife, inasmuch as quite apart from marriage it could result from any other sexual union, just as in the case of animals. But in marriage there must be generally [πάντως] perfect companionship and mutual love of husband and wife. (Trans. Lutz)

This passage indicates that procreation is not a sufficient condition for marriage, and we have seen above that the love between the spouses is meant to surpass that between parents and children. Or as Elizabeth Asmis has put it, "the primary purpose of marriage is procreation, the ultimate goal is a harmony of minds."[27] Marriage both embraces and goes beyond procreation. The relationship has a value in and of itself.

In addition to the procreative function of marriage, there is the role of sex to consider. For Musonius Rufus, limiting the sex life between the spouses does not amount to limiting the affective dimension of the relationship. *Eros* is not reducible to sex (ἀφροδίσια); and Plato too limits the latter (limits, not eliminates) in favor of the former. This is a stock version of the Stoic and the Platonist philosophical stance of self-control, that is, reason keeping clear of the passions. Musonius is more original in his strong rejection of double standards for sexual conduct. He holds both men and women to the same expectation of chastity. When he extends this stipulation even to the rapport between master and slave (12), he is all too aware that he is going against the grain of accepted practices in the social circles he frequents.[28] Musonius invites a hypothetical interlocutor who would have no objections against a man sleeping with a slave to consider how he would like it if his wife had an affair with a male slave, giving his audience what to them would be the most shocking counterexample.

Once we have noticed the distinction between *eros* and *aphrodisia*, we are in a better position to assess Musonius's claim that the marital relationship is the highest form of *eros*. Daniel Babut has rightly cautioned, against Flacelière, Pohlenz, and Praechter, that we should not project onto the

27. Asmis 1996, 83.

28. See also Sen. *Ep.* 94.26; ps.-Aristotle *Oik.* 3, pp. 143–44 Rose.

Stoics an evolution from an initial preference for Platonic same-gender relations to the later Stoics' emphasis on marriage as the norm. Persaeus of Citium, a disciple of Zeno, had already written Περὶ γάμου (D.L. 7.36 = *SVF* 1.435), and Cleanthes is said to have written a work entitled Περὶ ὑμεναίου. Furthermore, there is the general Stoic injunction that the wise man should marry and have children.[29] But I disagree with Babut's claim that the Stoic arguments in support of marriage never entail any value judgment against same-gender relations. Musonius's rhetorical question "where indeed does *eros* more properly belong than in the lawful union of man and wife?" (14 Lutz) implicitly critiques homoerotic rapports, and the exposition "On Sexual Indulgence" explicitly rejects homosexual acts (12, 64.4–7 Hense; συμπλοκαί). His defense of marriage as an expression of love cannot avoid being entangled in the dialectic of rejecting other forms of *eros* and in the debate about which sexual acts are acceptable and which are not.

If the marital relationship is to have intrinsic value, as Musonius claims it does, the criteria for selecting a partner become all the more important (13B Lutz). In order to embody virtue as philosophically defined, marriage cannot uncritically fall in line with traditional customs. Hence, far from reflecting standard Roman practice, Musonius's criteria actually constitute a challenge. He tells his audience that social status, wealth, and physical beauty are irrelevant. All that is needed for the body is that it be healthy and fit for hard work. The soul should be naturally disposed to virtue. Again, character, partnership of interest, and sympathy of mind (ὁμόνοια) are as essential as the ability to procreate. Partnership between two base people is impossible, as is a relationship between two partners of unequal ethical worth, a concise but unmistakable reply to Aristotle and the Peripatetic tradition. These criteria, as Musonius lays them out, govern not only a man's selection of a wife, as they do in an analogous passage from Antipater (*SVF* 62), but also a woman's selection of a husband: the "they" refers to husband and wife, as is confirmed by the reciprocal pronouns at the end of the passage. The emphasis on equality, reciprocity, and mutual love runs through all of Musonius's relevant passages.[30]

Marcus Aurelius is said to have used these alternative and philosophically inspired criteria in the selection of husbands for his daughters.[31] But

29. D.L. 7.121 = *SVF* 1.270; Stobaeus = *SVF* 3.611, 3.686; see also *SVF* 1.244, 3.727, 3.729.

30. Compare this to the Pythagorean text Bryson 2, p. 58 Thesleff 1965, which is extant in Arabic and Hebrew versions; see also Plessner 1928, sections 74–103. This text talks about the man's choice of a wife (85ff.) and is markedly more conventional, though it also mentions the topos of both husband and wife being like a straight piece of wood (94–95).

31. Herodian 1.2.2; *HA* 20.6–7.

more important and less ambiguous, perhaps, is Pliny the Younger's testimony (3.11) that Musonius was true to his own principles. Although he could have chosen a suitor from any rank, he preferred the foreigner and philosopher Artemidorus as his son-in-law, a man known for his virtue, endurance, and simplicity of lifestyle. Musonius's reputation was very much based on the fact that he himself practiced what he advised others to do.

Given the importance of selection criteria, how does Musonius Rufus develop further his theme of the quality of the bond between the spouses? "To whom is everything judged to be common, body, soul, and possessions, except man and wife?" (14, 74.7–9 Hense; 13A, 67.9–10). Again, "in marriage there must be generally perfect companionship [συμβίωσις] and mutual love [κηδεμονία] of husband and wife, both in health and in sickness and under all conditions" (13A, 68.5–7 Hense). Musonius uses the strongest terms possible here. First, the union is deemed the most pleasant association. Second, the list of what husband and wife hold in common includes both body and soul. Such lists of what husband and wife share in life (κοινωνία βίου), and of their common interests and possessions, constitute a topos too.[32] In his *Conjugalia Praecepta* (140F, 143A), Plutarch, for instance, considers the union of spouses in terms of body, property, friends, and relations. But Stoics like Musonius Rufus, Antipater, and Hierocles stand out because they pair a union of body with a union of soul, resulting in a harmony of minds. This pairing has far-reaching philosophical consequences, as I will discuss below.

Such a pronounced intimacy between husband and wife comes with a requirement: that women too should study philosophy (3 Lutz) and daughters should receive the same education as sons (4 Lutz).[33] There is no reason why women should not be educated in philosophy, given that men and women share the same nature and have the same virtues. In other words, they have the same ethical and philosophical potential:

> Women as well as men have received from the gods the gift of reason, which we use in our dealings with one another and by which we judge whether a thing is good

32. See also ps.-Aristotle *Oik.* 3 (the Greek title could have been νόμοι ἀνδρὸς καὶ γαμετῆς, included in the Loeb series), pp. 141, 147 Rose, but another passage, p. 146, extols unity of mind, *unanimitas*, between husband and wife. Xenophon talks about the wife being a partner with respect to the household and children (*Oik.* 3.15, 7.11ff., 7.30); he talks about common possessions (7.13, 10.3), a partnership in mutual service (7.17–18), and a union of bodies (10.4). The topos could also be applied to a relationship among friends, as, e.g., in Plut. *Amic. Mult.* 96E, 97A.

33. For a good analysis of the sociocultural background of this issue, see Levick 2002. Levick herself refers quite extensively to Hemelrijk 1999.

or bad, right or wrong. Likewise the woman has the same senses as the male. . . . Also both have the same parts of body, and one has nothing more than the other. Moreover, not men alone, but women too, have a natural desire and inclination [ὄρεξις καὶ οἰκείωσις φύσει] toward virtue. (3, trans. Lutz)

To readers of the post-Freud era, Musonius's claim that one does not have more body parts than the other must seem really startling. It stands in a tradition that sees women's and men's bodies as structurally analogous. Epictetus may have disagreed, though, given his emphasis on the features that nature designed to distinguish men from women, such as the beard.[34]

For Musonius differences assert themselves in the allotment of daily tasks:

since in the human race man's constitution is stronger and woman's weaker, tasks should be assigned which are suited to the nature of each; that is the heavier tasks should be given to the stronger and lighter ones to the weaker. Thus spinning and indoor work would be more fitting for women than for men, while gymnastics and outdoor work would be more suitable for men. (4, trans. Lutz)

With this argument of a distribution of tasks according to capacity, Musonius tries to take the wind out of the sails of those who claim that intellectual exposure would merely make women run wild. That this is not an imaginary concern is brought home by Seneca's testimony that his old-fashioned father checked his mother's studies in order to prevent her from becoming too bold (*Cons. Helv.* 17.4).

Musonius counteracts this concern by claiming (3 and 4 Lutz) that a philosophical education would make a woman a blameless life partner (ἄμεμπτος βίου κοινωνός) and sympathetic helpmate (ὁμονοίας ἀγαθὴ συνεργός). Such an education would also make her more suited to her daily tasks. It would provide her with the skills necessary for being a good housekeeper, a careful accountant, and a skilled director of slaves. The training would make her chaste and self-controlled. She would become an untiring defender of husband and children; she would love her children more than life itself. She would be prepared "to nourish her children at her own breast and serve her husband with her own hands." She would be unwilling to submit to anything shameful and have the courage to stand up even against a tyrant. These points correspond to the four cardinal virtues: wisdom, temperance, courage, and justice.

34. *Diss.* 1.2.29, 1.16.9ff. Compare to Musonius Rufus 21 Lutz.

From a (post)modern perspective, Musonius's claims here sound dangerously reductionist,[35] and they remind us of that period in history when women's education served primarily to increase their chances of finding a suitable husband and of acquiring a veneer of culture that would make them better wives and mothers. But I would claim that these connotations distort Musonius's intentions. These intentions emerge more fully if we take his context into account, which embraces both established contemporary practices as well as the ongoing philosophical debates. Essentially, Musonius's position is a response to Plato's *Republic.*

The first nuance in Musonius's views that goes a long way to correct the reductionist reading is that he does not consider the allotment of daily tasks to be rigidly determined. He actually opens the traditional gender roles to a new dimension. Immediately following the claim that the tasks should be distributed according to physical strength, he makes a rather modest overture: "Occasionally, however, some men might more fittingly handle certain of the lighter tasks and what is generally considered women's work, and again, women might do heavier tasks which seem more appropriate for men whenever conditions of strength, need or circumstances warranted" (4, trans. Lutz). This relatively modest proposal is echoed by Hierocles. Hierocles not only allows for these occasional exchanges of tasks but even recommends the practice as a means of strengthening the bond (κοινωνία) between the spouses (Stob. 5.696–99 Hense, esp. 5.697.4–11 = 62–63, 62.26–32 von Arnim). A man who is secure enough in his manliness, he argues, has no need to shrink from performing so-called womanly tasks. The latter claim reveals the underlying debate with accepted social norms: that certain tasks were beneath men and even threatening to their manliness.

Musonius's subsequent move is a more far-reaching innovation: "For all human tasks, I am inclined to believe [ἴσως], are a common obligation and are common for men and women, and none is necessarily appointed for either one exclusively, but some pursuits are more suited to the nature of one [i.e., in terms of physical strength], some to the other, and for this reason some are called men's work and some women's" (4, trans. Lutz).[36] The more radical claim that all human tasks are a common obligation is embedded in cautious wording and respect for the traditional way, which, however, is presented largely in a pragmatic guise. As a thought experiment, we

35. For assessments of the limits of Musonius's approach, see Engel 2000; Nussbaum 2002, with translations; Wöhrle 2002. See also Favez 1933.

36. Compare this to the more conventional Xenophon (*Oik.* 7.22–32) and the Pythagorean text Phintys 1, 152.6–18 Thesleff 1965.

could ask what would become of Musonius's injunctions in a cultural setting in which physical strength does not matter so much anymore. In such a context his views would allow for a very far-reaching gender equality. The fluidity of the boundaries of gender roles is not mere theory for Musonius either. In his defense of marriage, he mentions the relationship of the Cynics Crates and Hipparchia (14 Lutz), which was notoriously unconventional.[37] He uses the topos of the courage that the Amazons display in war (4 Lutz) to claim that all women can have this kind of courage, though lack of use and practice makes it seem otherwise. As the stories have it, the Amazons were not exactly little blossoms gracing well-established households with their wit and charm.

A second nuance that helps us to understand better Musonius's picture of gender roles comes through in the claim that all of philosophy serves, not merely ethics, but ethics in action. It is not just women who should learn philosophy for the sake of its practical applications. Regardless of who participates in discussion, men or women, the debates should serve a practical purpose (3 Lutz, 11.11ff. Hense), as is the case with the science of medicine. Musonius shares with all the later Stoics a thorough dislike of theory for the sake of theory because it produces mere quibbling and hairsplitting. A section in which practice clearly comes ahead of theory (5 Lutz) for all would-be philosophers, whether men or women, puts the section on the education of women in perspective. And another passage (11 Lutz) posits that agricultural labor and the life of a shepherd are the best means of livelihood for a philosopher. So when Musonius avers that philosophy will exhort "the woman to be content with her lot and to work with her own hands" (end of 3), the broader context in the extant writings reveals that he has these same expectations for men too. Like Musonius, Hierocles extends the benefits of "working with one's own hands" (a phrase that, in chapter 3, we noticed Seneca using as well) to both sexes (Stob. 5.697.12ff. Hense = 62.32ff. von Arnim). As a corollary to this view, the tasks that traditionally go to women are not inferior to or less important than those that are assigned to men.

Antipater provides an excellent contrast here that brings out the key nuances in Musonius's account. As far as we can tell from the limited evidence, in spite of the points of similarity between them, Antipater more closely follows a traditional view on gender roles than does either Hierocles or Musonius. The husband rules over the woman; he is the center of her universe and is in charge of her moral and practical education. Antipater

37. See D.L. 6.96–98.

also strongly emphasizes the political dimension of the man's activities. Having a woman take care of the household duties frees a man for discussions and political activities (*SVF* 63), both of which are traditional aspects of community life that Musonius either transforms or downplays in his ideal life for the philosopher.

The claim that the husband has the authority in the household and the wife is supposed to obey is a good indicator of how traditional or innovative an ancient thinker is. Hierocles alludes to the distinction between ruler and ruled in the household (Stob. 4.503.12–14 Hense = von Arnim 53.15–17) but does not elaborate on it in the extant evidence. Musonius indicates that he is aware of this more traditional view: men fight on behalf of women and children (7 Lutz, 31.6 Hense), and men are stronger than and rule their wives (12 Lutz, 66.15–19 Hense)—or at least they claim (ἀξιοῦνται) to be superior. Yet in the same breath Musonius mentions ruling one's wife and children and ruling one's friends or even ruling oneself (8 Lutz, 39.17–18 Hense). The very juxtaposition of wife and children, on the one hand, and friends and oneself, on the other, throws a different light on the proposition that men are supposed to rule their wives. In the traditional approach, the rapport with wife and children is not to be grouped with friendship. Furthermore, "ruling oneself" in Stoic psychology does not entail a split soul, the rule of reason over lower soul parts, nor the radical opposition between soul and body, as it does in its Platonic counterparts. Platonic psychology allowed later authors to reduce women to the analogue of the body or the lower appetites; Stoic psychology does not.[38] In general Musonius underscores the affection, the symmetry, and the reciprocal character of the spousal relationship. For him chastity is a two-way street as well, as we have seen. In the section on sexual relations (12 Lutz) Musonius uses men's *claim* to superiority to hold them to the same moral standards of chastity as apply to women: if they want to be the stronger sex, they had better be able to rise to the challenge of being virtuous. So here Musonius uses his audience's expectations as a rhetorical ploy to catch male listeners in their own contradictions. And, as we have also seen already, mere superiority in physical prowess does not guarantee men overall superiority.

His views on gender roles reveal Musonius's tendency to transform traditional views and topoi from within, unlocking novel perspectives for his audience. His very mode of discourse, then, reflects the Roman Stoic technique of mediation between conventional social values and the innovative, philosophical kind. Rather than proposing such radical changes as having

38. As in Plut. *Conj. Praec.* 142E.

women discard their traditional roles altogether, as the Cynic Hipparchia did in her life with Crates, Musonius preserves the traditional *decorum* of modest behavior. In that restricted sense, one could argue that he attempts a reconciliation with everyday morality, even though that attempt is only part of the story and should not obscure what is truly groundbreaking in his proposals. The true revolution is a matter, not of transgressive behavior, but rather of an inner transformation of one's attitudes. But the danger with any such concession or mediation is that it can contribute to the reinforcement and justification of conventional values, which thus get in the way of changes that are in fact warranted.

This danger is brought home by the rhetorical analogy between Musonius's defense of women's philosophical education and Seneca's plea for a better treatment of slaves. Just as Musonius wants to preempt the critique that having women study philosophy will make them run wild, so Seneca, after having argued for better treatment of slaves, assures his readers that he does not intend to have the authority of masters undermined, nor to do away with slavery altogether: "Some may maintain that I am now offering the liberty cap to slaves in general and toppling down lords from their high estate because I bid slaves respect their masters instead of fearing them" (*Ep.* 47.18). No, Seneca implies: a good master who rules by the respect he inspires does not have to have recourse to abuse and violence and as a result can afford to treat his slaves more humanely. Humane treatment rather than abolishing slavery altogether is what Seneca advocates. Analogously, rather than discarding the social conventions embedded in marriage and parenthood, Musonius affirms that studying philosophy will not make women shirk their traditional responsibilities but in fact will make women better at performing those tasks. Is Musonius trying merely to lighten the burden of the yoke of marriage for women, just as Seneca is trying to make slavery more bearable?

Seneca's treatment of slavery is obviously problematic. If on the issue of slavery the best one can do is to say that apparently Seneca was not able to look beyond the social framework of his times, this turns out to be a lame excuse at best—and never an appropriate one for a philosopher whose reputation is based on a critical examination of unquestioned assumptions. Is Musonius's treatment of marriage affected by the same problem as Seneca's view of slavery? Both Musonius and Seneca want it to be clearly understood that they have no interest in social upheaval.

Taking these limitations into account, one could argue that the Stoic approach is at its best if and when transformations from within given normative structures and existing priorities work. Slavery, one could reply to the Stoics, is not something one can salvage by improving on the arrangement itself. The question then would be whether marriage presents the same type of problems as slavery does. To be sure, there are theories now available to us that would consider the marital relationship to be an irredeemable form of bondage. On the basis of attested forms of repression and abuse, these theories arrive at an a priori rejection of marriage, claiming that the very notion possesses an intrinsic structural flaw and that it cannot but lead to repression and failure. But insofar as the case of marriage is not that clear-cut, one could learn from the Stoics how to make this type of relationship a valuable expression of human beings' attempt to give meaning to their lives. The Stoic version of the marital bond is anything but cozy and "bourgeois"; it is as demanding as anything else that is required of a would-be philosopher and sets the highest possible goal. If we do not want to fall into the trap of denigrating functions such as childbearing—not to mention all the tasks that are traditionally ascribed to women, such as the rearing of children, storytelling, and care of the household—Musonius's approach of preserving the good potential of marital life might have its advantages, whereas the Stoic attitude toward slavery fails because there is nothing about it that can be redeemed.

* * *

To sum up, Musonius presents conjugal love as the highest form of *eros.* Procreation is central to marriage, but the latter's ultimate goal is the union of body and soul. If marriage is to embody not only a partnership of interest but also sympathy of mind, mutual affection, and the life of virtue among equals, men and women ought to be trained in philosophy. There is nothing to prevent this from happening, because men and women have in essence the same nature and the same potential for virtue. And although men's and women's daily tasks are different and distributed along conventional lines (according to degree of physical strength), Musonius does posit all human tasks as a common obligation. For both men and women, practical applications have priority over theory. As a result the tasks traditionally ascribed to women are as important as those of men.

Neither Plato nor Aristotle

The Early Stoics Zeno and Chrysippus started the Stoic tradition of responding to Plato's *Republic,* and by the time of Musonius Rufus, Stoicism could already look back on a series of such responses. We also know that some later Stoics did not approve of the more shocking aspects of their founding father Zeno's counterpart to Plato's *kallipolis* and tried to come up with reasons for not taking it seriously.[39] And neither does Epictetus approve of a reading of Plato's texts that would encourage promiscuity.[40] "Reading the *Republic*" is thus at the heart of the discussion of the value of relationships. Musonius, however, does represent a very definite direction within that tradition, as do Antipater and Hierocles. By offering a counterscenario, Musonius's views indirectly also help reveal what is problematic in Plato's account.

Both the affective dimension and the emphasis on reciprocity in relationships between men and women that are so predominant in Musonius's views are lacking in Plato's *Republic.* Plato pleads in favor of abolishing all family ties because he considers such ties to be the main source of factions and detrimental rivalries within the community.[41] All members of the previous generation are to be addressed as "mother" or "father," those of the same generation as "brother" or "sister," and those of the next generation as "son" or "daughter" (*Rep.* 461D), a claim Epictetus echoes in his description of the Cynic sage (*Diss.* 3.22.81–82). Mary Whitlock Blundell[42] draws a parallel between this claim and Hierocles' injunction to draw the concentric circles as close to the center as possible by calling cousins "brothers," and uncles and aunts "fathers and mothers" (Stob. 4.673.2–7 Hense = LS57G). But the crucial difference remains that for Hierocles and Musonius Rufus the family unit is the essential starting point of the larger community, whereas Plato proposes abolishing the ties between spouses and between parents and children and replacing them with surrogate community ties. For the later Stoics the spousal and parental relationships cannot be short-circuited in favor of the community at large.

In the process of mounting the case against traditional relationships among the members of the guardian class, Plato's Socrates uses the bon mot that "friends should hold everything in common," and he means it too. Other interpreters of book 5 have noticed that Socrates persistently takes up the man's point of view: it is men who hold women and children in common.[43] Only toward the very end of this exposition do we get something

39. Philodemus *De Stoicis* 9–12, 15; see Dorandi 1982. See also D.L. 7.34. For criticism of Chrysippus, see D.L. 7.187–89.

40. F15 = 53 Schweighäuser.

41. Geytenbeek 1963, 54–56. He emphasizes the parallels with Plato, though he does state that, unlike Musonius Rufus, Plato emphasizes the superiority of men over women. See also Festugière 1978. In his introduction to the passage "That daughters should receive the same education as sons" (4), Festugière (61–62) also draws parallels with Plato.

42. Whitlock Blundell 1990, 225–26.

43. For an excellent analysis and overview of the secondary literature, see Föllinger 1996, esp. 73–117, 256–87.

like a reciprocal statement, namely, "the natural community of men and women with each other."[44] In contrast, Musonius does not describe the choice of partners exclusively from the man's perspective and persistently argues for the reciprocal character of the spousal bond.

In Plato's account male guardians who perform well and are brave in battle are rewarded by being given women and more opportunities for mating. This is a remnant of the notion that women are war prizes. But what would the equivalent reward be for valiant women guardians, given that their reproductive cycles are strictly regulated? That the question sounds absurd in the context of book 5 is a sure indication that the reciprocity in Plato's regulations is severely restricted. As I have stated elsewhere, "Plato's 'feminism' for the ruler class entails moving women from the private sphere to the status of 'being held in common' in matters of sexuality, and hence still operates within the 'either/or' dichotomy of a secluded, lawful wife versus a 'public woman' or *hetaira*. The sexual identity of a truly free woman, however, and her freedom of action in the public realm do not have promiscuity as a necessary concomitant factor, nor should the project of philosophy's *Sitz im Leben* require of women that the ties with their children be severed."[45] Once one starts raising such issues, the strengths of the Stoic alternative to Plato's proposals become more apparent.

If one were to read Plato's works together and take a synoptic view of the different levels of philosophical initiation, as many ancients did, a male reader could move beyond the utilitarian outlook of the *Republic* and its regulation of mating. He could find a mirror for emotional affection and *eros* in the soul's ascents as described in the *Symposium* and the *Phaedrus*, which leave ample room for physically expressed tenderness even in the highest form of *eros* between two philosophical souls (*Phdr.* 255A–256A). But a woman reader would find herself walking into a wall. The *Phaedrus* does not include women in the model of affectionate soul union, a point stubbornly overlooked by modern interpreters but one that an ancient interpreter such as Plutarch knew he had to circumvent.[46] When in his *Laws* Plato does make room for the marital bond, we look in vain for Musonius's deep affection and community between the spouses, though Plato mentions once that a husband could be the close friend of his spouse (839B1).

44. 466D3–4; ἧπεφύκατον πρὸς ἀλλήλω κοινωνεῖν.

45. Reydams-Schils 2001, 43.

46. Compare the character Protogenes' speech against love for women in Plutarch's *Amatorius* (750C–751B) with the reply (766E ff.).

Lack of affection and lack of reciprocity are not the only problems with Plato's *kallipolis;* it also presents a skewed view of gender equality. In the evidence of Musonius's views, we noticed the connection between the quality of the bond in the marital relationship and the moral and philosophical potential of women. In contrast, the most striking feature of the *Republic* is how Plato applies the claim that men and women share the same nature with regard to virtue and philosophy, a claim that he may have inherited from Socrates.[47] Whereas one could expect the "one nature/one virtue" claim to yield a genuine and profound gender equality, as it does for Musonius, Plato actually uses it to seal the case of women's inferiority. Women are to be judged by the standards of "traditional" men, a point brought home by Plato's harping on physical prowess and valor in war as indications of manliness. It remains a baffling question why one would have to be a good soldier in order to be a philosopher, but that would be the topic of a different inquiry.

Plato's emphasis on manliness must have inspired the anecdote that is preserved in one of the fragments of Aristotle[48] and in Diogenes Laertius (3.46) and that reveals the ambivalence of Plato's insistence that men and women share the same nature. Here is another woman reading the *Republic* (and we have heard Epictetus complain before how that can lead women astray): Axiothea of Phlias. Her exposure to Plato's work inspired her to come to Athens and sit in on his lectures. But in order to do this, apparently she felt the need to cover up the fact that she was a woman. We may want to go further in breaking through gender roles than Musonius did, but if Axiothea had been a pupil of this Stoic, she presumably would not have felt the need to cross-dress and pretend to be a man.

Whereas Musonius admits that women may be physically weaker than men and does not posit bodily strength as sine qua non for philosophy, Plato claims that women are weaker than men *in every respect,* a claim he makes no less than four times,[49] even though he admits that many individual women may be better than individual men in many things (455D). Musonius grants both genders equal moral value and philosophical ability, and he does not rate traditional female tasks, such as spinning, lower than

47. See *Meno* 71E–73C, 74B ff.; Xen. *Symp.* 2.9; but note that in the Xenophon passage Socrates says women are weaker than men not only in physical strength but also in judgment: γνώμης δὲ καὶ ἰσχύος δεῖται [ἡ γυναικεία φύσις]. See also D.L. 6.12, who ascribes one-nature/one-virtue to Antisthenes as well.

48. Dorandi 1989. For Aristotle, see Νήρινθος F1, pp. 23–24 Ross.

49. *Rep.* 455C, 455D–E, 456A, 457A; see also *Tim.* 42A ff., 90E; *Lg.* 944D.

traditional male activities, such as outdoor work. Plato, on the other hand, does not want to dwell on the topic of women's traditional tasks and rejects these as irrelevant, presumably because they do not give scope for virtue. The tasks in which women traditionally are thought to excel do not really matter, he says, and maybe women do not really excel in these either (455C–D). The negative philosophical impact of a view such as Plato's also shows up in the pseudo-*Letters* of the Cynics: Crates allegedly told Hipparchia to give up trying to weave a cloak for him because they were supposed to have moved beyond such trivial household concerns (*Letter* 30, p. 81 Malherbe); she should "try to be of greater benefit to human life" instead, as Diogenes and he himself had taught her.[50] Is such a blunt dismissal of a task like weaving really an improvement on attempts to tie women down by praising their contributions to everyday life? For Plato, the "one nature/one virtue" claim leads to positing a norm according to which women as a group can only be second-best. Musonius sees men and women as true equals in their potential for embodying the philosophical life. He uses an analogy similar to Plato's, the training of horses and dogs, to enter into the one nature/one virtue claim, but his end result could not be more different.[51] He advances the one nature/one virtue claim to a much higher level than Plato did.

If women can be the equals of men, then Stoics can allow for the possibility of a soul-union between spouses. Thus, Musonius Rufus radically transforms Platonic *eros,* granting it to women too and redeeming the marital relationship from a mere utilitarian outlook. From a contemporary perspective, one may deem a complete union between lovers and spouses infeasible, even undesirable. But the point remains that Musonius does not exclude women from what *he considers* the highest form of *eros.* He vindicates for all women the right to love in principle and does not reserve this right for highly exceptional women, such as Alcestis or Hipparchia, Crates' remarkable life partner.[52]

But even in the case of a later Platonist such as Porphyry, who, contrary to Plato, does allow for a soul-union between a husband and wife, all is not

50. *Letter* 32, p. 83 in Malherbe tells her to "leave the wool-spinning, which is of little benefit, to other women."

51. According to Diogenes Laertius, 7.175, Cleanthes too wrote a treatise on the subject that men and women share the same virtue: Περὶ τοῦ ὅτι ἡ αὐτὴ ἀρετὴ [καὶ] ἀνδρὸς καὶ γυναικός.

52. This was Dugas's view in his interpretation of Plutarch's *Amatorius* (1894, 146). His analysis, however, labors under the distinction "normal"/homoerotic love; see also the entire section, 139–49.

well. Porphyry's rapport with his own wife, Marcella, as indicated in his letter to her, mentioned in the previous chapter, has obvious asymmetrical features. First, their bond is analogous to a teacher-pupil relationship (3.39–40, 3.44–46), with the important proviso (as the evidence now stands) that Marcella appears not to be a member of the inner philosophical circle and is not privy to any discussion of the first principles of being, which would constitute the highest form of knowledge. She is admitted into *his* life (2.21), on his terms; he is not interested in taking steps toward her. Second, Porphyry heavily emphasizes that he is doing her and her children a favor (ἐγὼ σέ), by accepting the burden and duty of taking care of the widow of a deceased friend. Third, she is, strikingly, his *sunoikos,* his "housemate" (1.3; see also 3.50, 4.65–66), a term Porphyry also uses for god's dwelling in the pure soul (20.326; see also 21.335–36), and which Plato had used to describe the presence of a divine demon in a human soul (*Tim.* 90C5). The analogy between their mode of cohabitation and human contact with the divine not only suggests that god is the true *sunoikos,* which ranks above any human partner, but could also imply that "his relationship with Marcella imitates the relationship between God and the soul" (33.515).[53] As Marcella's *sunoikos,* Porphyry would stand in for the divine mind and Marcella would rank lower, as the soul. Their relationship is certainly not one in which each is *sumbios* to the other, both sharing their lives in the full existential sense. *Symbiōsis* is the word for both the more traditional conception of marriage and the mode of life of Stoic spouses. The relationship between Porphyry and Marcella is not symmetrical, not reciprocal, and does not embrace all aspects of life.

Porphyry lectures to Marcella that her body is not her true self (passim and 32.484ff.), and he takes this claim far beyond any Stoic counterpart. Because it is not her womanhood that brought Porphyry to her, she ought to behave as if she had a man's *body* and reject "effeminate" aspects of her *soul* (33.511–14). This passage expresses the same ambivalence about women that we witness in Plato's *Republic:* Marcella is not automatically barred from the good life merely because she is a woman, but women are acceptable only insofar as they become like men and leave their womanhood behind. Porphyry denigrates physical contact (8.147–50, 10.177–83, with the use of καθαρῶς, "purely"), and we have already noticed that he has a low opinion of biological offspring. He consoles her for his absence and exhorts her to fortitude by claiming that she does not need his physical presence, that she can hold on to his precepts in her memory, that she al-

53. Wicker 1987, 81.

ways has the divine element in her own soul, and that whether he, Porphyry, is physically there or not, he is always present to her in soul anyway (8.136ff.).

The emphasis on the role of memory and the claim that the body is not one's true self are intriguing because both these points bear a similarity with Stoic modes of coping with loss and absence, and yet constitute a radical departure from the Stoic position. Admittedly, in an ancient cultural context, it might be liberating for a woman to be freed from the constraints of traditional marriage and from the dangerous cycle of reproduction (though Marcella could well be past the childbearing age). As Porphyry indicates, he freed her "from every master" (3.43–44), which could be meant to include the shackles of the body. Yet the Roman Stoics' claim that spouses share "even" the body now acquires new significance because it allows for a union that embraces more aspects of human existence. The conventional emphasis on the procreationist aspect of a marital union might also turn out to have a positive side: children do not become entirely irrelevant to the project of a meaningful life. The body is not to be discarded altogether. For the Roman Stoics, one's ability to handle absence does not come at the expense of devaluing physical presence. And as in the case of suicide, the fact that other people could live with our absence if they have the right philosophical perspective does not give us the right to impose our absence on them.

Admittedly, a black-and-white opposition between Stoics and Platonists would be facile and misguided. In this study, we have seen many points of continuity between Plato's—and others'— Socrates and the Stoics. As Pierre Hadot has rightly pointed out,[54] Porphyry's biography of Plotinus shows us the Platonist welcoming widows in his house and taking up the care of children entrusted to him (*Vita Plotini* 9). Platonists never abandoned the idea of the philosopher's responsibility to the community and to the political realm. Nor did they abandon the moral responsibility to imitate divine Providence and to bring the world we live in closer to perfection.[55] But what nevertheless remains distinctive about the Roman Stoics is their commitment to traditional modes of sociability and their philosophical valorization of the bond between spouses, and between parents and children.

Finally, let us turn briefly to Plato's most famous pupil, Aristotle. In Aristotle's case, there appear to be other similarities with the later Stoics,

54. P. Hadot 1989, 121–35. See also his introduction to Plotinus *Enn.* 3.5 [50] (1990, 26–29, 35–40), in which he points out that for Plotinus the physical beauty of women too, as well as of boys and men, can trigger the process of philosophical recollection. The texts, however, leave this only to be implied and are, in reality, quite moot. See also Reydams-Schils forthcoming-c.

55. For recent assessments of this question, see O'Meara 2003; Schniewind 2003.

and other divergences. Aristotle too holds that the family is the starting point for the polis-community, but his approach to the spousal rapport is notably more pragmatic and utilitarian. Spouses complement one another's efforts in carrying out the daily tasks. But because women are not equal to men,[56] and the strongest affective bond or friendship occurs between equals, for the sake of virtue, not pleasure or utility, the potential for companionship across gender lines remains limited.

In a passage from the *Nicomachean Ethics* in particular (1162a16–31), aspects of later Stoic treatments of marriage already appear: the comparison between animal behavior and marriage as a natural association, the importance of marriage for society (with respect to both its procreative function and companionship, κοινωνία βίου), the quality of the union between spouses, the virtue displayed by men and women, and the division of labor. But even though the Stoic approach is more similar in articulation to Aristotle's than to Plato's, the specific views that go with the headings are fundamentally different from Aristotle's too. Besides its procreative purpose, marriage according to Aristotle primarily has a partnership of responsibilities to offer. This partnership most often yields the two lower forms of friendship, those that are based on utility and pleasure. The occasional relationship may lead to sharing virtue, but not on the equal footing Musonius grants spouses in his model,[57] which posits virtue as the very foundation of marriage. Aristotle adheres to a strict division of labor among the sexes and does not espouse the one nature/one virtue claim.[58]

The comparison between later Stoics and Plato and Aristotle reveals how groundbreaking the views of Musonius Rufus in particular were. In his account of marriage we find the purest example of how the Stoic could transcend the distinction between philosophical ideal and so-called common morality.

Seneca, Epictetus, and Marcus Aurelius

A view of women like the one endorsed by Musonius Rufus, Antipater, and Hierocles could lead to two different claims that in practice are not always easy to distinguish: (1) the reductionist one, that virtue requires of a woman that she be a chaste and dedicated wife and mother; (2) the nonreductionist one, that marriage and parenthood are valid modes of the philosophical

56. See, e.g., *Pol.* 1259b1–2, 1260a10–15, 1260a21–24, 1277b; *Oik.* 1343b ff.; *Hist. Anim.* 608b; *Rhet.* 1361a.

57. *EN* 1158b.

58. See, e.g., *Pol.* 1260a21–24, with an explicit rejection of what he considers to be Socrates' view.

life. I interpret Musonius as primarily defending the second claim. But the reductionist claim, and the more traditional one, often accompanies the positive assessment of women in the work of Seneca. As far as Epictetus is concerned, he appears to be living and teaching in a man's world, and he shows limited interest in either of the above claims. In Marcus Aurelius's high-status social environment, we discover another complication in the distinction between official wife and concubine. Given the Roman Stoics' strong commitment to the practical application of philosophy, it is not surprising that their specific life situations in turn affect which problems they seek to solve and provide at least a partial explanation for distinctive nuances.

Seneca is markedly more mixed than Musonius Rufus, Hierocles, and Antipater in his assessment of women[59] and of the potential of marriage for achieving the life of virtue. As Chiara Torre recently has argued, Seneca is part of the Stoic movement to transform marriage into an integral part of the life of virtue (a point to which we shall return at the end of this chapter),[60] but in his realpolitik perspective, he is lucid about the disappointments married life can bring.[61] Seneca has a point when one reminds oneself, contra Musonius's idealizing prescriptions, that in spite of all precautions in the selection of a partner, things can still go wrong.

We have seen in Musonius's case that the assessment of marriage is intrinsically linked to the assessment of the moral value of women. Seneca agrees with Musonius that women have an equal potential for virtue: "But who has asserted that nature has dealt grudgingly with women's natures and has narrowly restricted their virtues? Believe me, they have just as much force, just as much capacity, if they like, for virtuous action; they are just as able to endure suffering and toil when they are accustomed to them" (*Cons. Marc.* 16.1). But equal potential for virtue, the point that Seneca defends in the above passage, does not automatically entail that women's nature is the same as men's.

Men are supposed to rule, and women ought to obey (*Const.* 1.1), Seneca states emphatically, thereby endorsing a much less innovative view of the rapport between the sexes than we find in Musonius. In other contexts as well women appear to be the "weaker vessels," and not merely in regard to

59. Contra Manning 1973.

60. See Torre 2000, ch. 1, "Seneca e il matrimonio," 19–76; with an analysis of *Ep.* 94, 95, 118; *Cons. Helv.* 16.2–7, 16.19; *Ben.* 1.9.3–4, 3.16.1–4, 4.14.1–2, 7.9.4–5. The marriage topos, however, is less pronounced in *Ep.* 95 than in 94, and 118 does not treat it explicitly either.

61. *Brev. Vit.* 3.2; *Ben.* 1.1.10, 4.33.2, 5.17.3–4; *Ep.* 119.6.

physical strength. According to Seneca, women are by nature more prone to lack of self-control, to moral weakness, and to the passions in general: they are more easily broken by excessive grief (*Cons. Marc.* 7.3); they get carried away by anger (*Clem.* 1.5.5); they are too soft in compassion (*Clem.* 2.5.1); they are incontinent in luxury and debauchery, and manipulative in trying to realize misguided ambitions.[62] In general Seneca qualifies lack of self-control as "effeminate" behavior.[63]

But Seneca does not limit himself to defining women's nature as merely a weaker version of men's. He also has a tendency to define a set of virtues that are specific to women's nature rather than men's. For a woman, the most important virtue is chastity and restraint, *pudicitia*.[64] A passage from the *De Matrimonio* attributed to Seneca (78–79 Haase) starts with the general claim that chastity is the anchor of all virtues, according to which *pudicitia* would not have to be limited to women (see also *Ben.* 1.11.4). And elsewhere Seneca, like Musonius, rejects double standards in sexual matters.[65] He does refrain, however, from explicitly prescribing *pudicitia* to men: a man, he claims, cannot both expect *pudicitia* of his wife and go around *corrupting other women* (i.e., ruin other women's *pudicitia; ipse alienarum corruptor uxorum, Ep.* 94.26). Seneca says nothing in this context about a man ruining his own *pudicitia* in the process. Men have several and public spheres of action, in politics, rhetoric, and war, as the *De Matrimonio* passage goes on to say, all of which give men scope for virtue. Men should strive for *gloria*. Women primarily have *pudicitia* to recommend them to the ancestors, to their family, and even to themselves. To be sure, women can be the equals of men (and in some cases surpass them in courage), but this is accomplished only through a woman's virtue that expresses itself in the sphere of the home and the family. Seneca also tends to complain that this virtue, which should be their "ornament," appears all too rarely among the women of his time.[66] Women do such shocking things as abandoning their "nature" (which includes being passive in sex, among other things) to rival men in debauchery (*Ep.* 95.20–21), whereas

62. This analysis is based on the excellent study of Mauch (1997, 29–66), with further references. See also *Cons. Helv.* 16.1–2, 16.5, 19.5: *imbecillitas; Cons. Marc.* 7.3, 11.1. Negative assessments of the later Stoic views of women tend to draw too heavily on the evidence of Seneca, at the expense of Musonius Rufus's views, as in Elorduy 1936, 194ff. See also Favez 1938.

63. Mauch 1997, 26–29.

64. See *Cons. Helv.* 16.3–5, 19.6–7; *De Matrimonio* 78–79 Haase.

65. *Ep.* 94.26, 95.37; Mauch 1997, 55–56.

66. *Ben.* 1.9.3–4, 3.16.1–4, 4.14.1–2, 7.9.4–5.

women who overcome the limitations of their sex and nature cross over to the category of heroic men.[67] In sum, it appears that for Seneca women not only are generally weaker than men but also have a different nature, though both natures have the potential for virtue.

Epictetus too, as we have seen, seems to be committed to a traditional view of masculinity, according to which a beard, for instance, is a sign bestowed by the gods so that the sexes may be differentiated.[68] Threatening a philosopher with cutting off his beard can be sufficient grounds for suicide. But Epictetus could in fact be perceived as not being entirely in line with Stoic teaching. In a delicious vignette in Lucian (*Demonax* 55), Epictetus lectures the Cynic Demonax that he ought to marry and have children. "I'd be happy to marry one of your daughters," is the reply he receives, the *pointe* being that (unlike Musonius, we could add) Epictetus has no daughters to bestow, given that he never married.

Epictetus appears uninvolved in social life because the Epictetus we know of in Arrian's records is heading a school in Nicopolis, far away from Rome, the center of sociopolitical activity. Though some of his visitors seem merely to have asked for advice as they passed through, most of his pupils would have been young men removed from their normal environments and usual activities and staying for a prolonged period of time. In this kind of setting traditional forms of sociability could actually constitute a threat: the attachments of his pupils to friends and relatives could pull them away before they learned all they could learn and were ready to face the "real world" again. From this concern, I would argue, follow some of the more Cynic-sounding traits in Epictetus's discourse. Epictetus himself is a philosopher in exile, and his pupils have to inhibit "normal" social modes of behavior if they want to make moral progress in his sanatorium for the soul.

Compared to a Seneca and a Marcus Aurelius, Musonius Rufus too, like Epictetus, appears to be relatively detached from Roman society, although he was more involved than many other philosophy teachers. Musonius expresses this distance in an idealization of a "pastoral" mode of existence, far from the hustle and bustle of city life. But if we take Musonius's relative detachment into account, it becomes all the more striking that there is so much more room for women in Musonius's world than in Epictetus's, even if we include in Epictetus's world the precious glimpse of the Roman official's little daughter (*Diss.* 1.11).

67. See the opening lines of *Cons. Marc.*; *Cons. Helv.* 15.1, 16.5: *quas conspecta virtus inter magnos viros posuit.*

68. See also Zanker 1995, 108ff.

Another type of woman besides daughter, sister, mother, or spouse makes a discreet but unmistakable appearance in the world of the Roman emperor Marcus Aurelius: the concubine, or what the French, with a wicked sense of humor, call the "second office" (*le deuxième bureau*). Marcus Aurelius mentions his adoptive brother Lucius Verus's concubine, Pantheia (8.37), with whom Lucius appears to have established a liaison before his marriage with Marcus's daughter, a relationship that continued throughout the years of that marriage. Marcus Aurelius distanced himself from such practices. He associates the time he spent at the house of his grandfather's concubine with sexual temptations that he managed to resist: "I preserved the flower of my youth and did not play a man's part before the proper season, but even deferred it until somewhat later" (1.17 Hard). He congratulates himself on not having succumbed to the charms of "Benedicta or Theodotus" (about whom nothing is known) and on having been cured of the passions of love that he did experience (see also 6.13, low opinion of sex).

The practice of taking a concubine after one's wife had died was more in line with an ideal of self-restraint, though hardly compatible with Musonius's stance on intimate relationships. We have an interesting testimony about Antoninus Pius, Marcus Aurelius's adoptive father, who was, as the first book of the *Meditations* reveals, an important role model for him. Antoninus Pius once wrote about his spouse to Fronto: "Indeed, I'd rather live with her in Gyara than in the Palatium without her."[69] Musonius's place of exile, Gyara, had come to be proverbial for harsh circumstances, so this is a marked testimony of affection. But we also know that after his spouse's death, Antoninus took a concubine, as seems to have been accepted practice.[70]

Unlike the image we get of the marital bond between Antoninus Pius and his spouse, the ancient historians' portrayals of Marcus Aurelius's spouse were not kind and mention many incidents of *impudicitia* and adultery on her part.[71] Marcus Aurelius himself, however, in a line of his *Meditations* (1.17), praises her for her obedience, affection, and simplicity. Be that as it may, Marcus Aurelius too is said to have taken a concubine after Faustina's death, namely, the daughter of one of his wife's procurators. He supposedly did this to avert pressures from a woman who had been

69. 1.128 Haines = 162.5 van den Hout.

70. *Corpus Inscriptionum Latinarum* 6.8972.

71. See *HA* 19, 23.7, 26.5, 29.

betrothed to him before his marriage with Faustina.[72] An imperial couple's social situation was clearly too complex for them to embody Musonius Rufus's ideal.

Seneca and Paulina

Another famous couple of the era seems to have done better. As we have seen in the first chapter, one of Seneca's letters (*Ep.* 104.2–5) is a very valuable testimony on his relationship with his wife, Paulina. That letter is governed in its entirety by the kind of counterpoint structure that would reflect a mediating self. It also embodies the very Stoic notion of ever-widening concentric circles: the first movement consists of Seneca's relationship with Paulina and his journey to improve his health; the second movement (7ff.) widens this perspective with reflections on the use of traveling in general and on the loss of dear ones; and the third movement (13–14), in a by now familiar paradox, makes us withdraw into studies and into ourselves, only to learn that there we have the fullest overview possible of space and time and can choose to spend time in the company of whichever role model we would prefer.

Seneca opens the letter by telling us about the powerful affection that Paulina and a friend have for him, and how he himself has benefited from "escaping the oppressive atmosphere of the city" (6). He both expounds on the idea that in general traveling will not improve one's condition, but that one has to change oneself (see also *Ep.* 28), and argues against considering the loss of a loved one the greatest loss (11). In the manner in which Seneca has arranged it, the letter displays the delicate equilibrium examined throughout this study, between affection for loved ones and not being devastated by loss; between being connected to one's external circumstances and being detached and independent at the same time. To escape from environmental conditions that are not conducive to one's bodily health is a different matter from seeking relief from one's inner turmoil in traveling, because one cannot escape oneself. To bear loss bravely is not the same as never having loved at all.

When Seneca, threatened by Nero, in the end does commit suicide, Tacitus describes the scene in terms that are indeed reminiscent of Socrates' death.[73] Like Socrates, Seneca is under orders to die. He rebukes his friends

72. See *HA* 29.10. Farquharson (1968, 2.480) doubts that this report is accurate and suggests it may have been confused with information about Antoninus Pius.

73. Döring 1979, 37–42; Griffin 1976, 376–91; Grimal 1979, 239; Maurach 1996, 44–54; Veyne 2003, 170–72. These scholars all underestimate the key difference between the two passages: the central presence of Seneca's spouse.

for their tears, reminds them of the precepts of wisdom, and delivers a long exposition. He uses the hemlock that he had kept in store, which "the Athenians reserved for those who were publicly condemned to death" (15.64). The all-important difference, however, between Tacitus's account and the *Phaedo* is that Paulina, unlike Xanthippe, stays with her husband and that her rapport with Seneca takes up most of this scene. The conversation between Seneca and his friends functions merely as a prelude; the long speech Seneca supposedly delivered receives only one line, as an afterthought. At the moment of Seneca's suicide, his wife actually surpasses his friends in fortitude.[74]

After he has finished talking to his friends, Seneca turns his full attention to Paulina. He embraces her and gives her a succinct *consolatio,* indicating how she is to combat her grief with virtue. In other words, he addresses a type of philosophical speech not only to his friends but also to his spouse. Unlike Seneca's friends, however, Paulina does not need an exhortation because she is already strong and courageous. Yet Seneca does not deprive her of consoling words about his pending death. Because of his love for her, he "softens a little" (*paulului mollitus*) in his resolve to die. But Paulina is ready to share his fate and die with him. Whereas Thrasea Paetus convinces his spouse to stay alive for the sake of their daughter (16.34)—an honorable motive the Stoics acknowledged—Seneca decides to honor Paulina's wish. Out of concern that harm may be done to her (*ne ad iniurias relinqueret*) and love (*amore*) for his one and only beloved (*unice dilectam*)—with Tacitus expressing what Seneca could not say of himself—he does not resist her sacrifice: "I showed you the delights of life, you prefer the honor of death; I shall not begrudge you to become exemplary [*exemplo*]. Let there be equal constancy for us both in such a brave death, but more brilliance in your end."[75] Here Paulina is presented as a heroine in her own right. She displays the same constancy and the same courage as Seneca, effectively demonstrating that virtue is the same for both men and women, but her death, Tacitus's Seneca goes even further, is more glorious than his because she dies of her own accord and has not been threatened with an execution.

Once both spouses have had their veins opened, Seneca is concerned that his suffering will break Paulina's resolve, and *hers his.* So that they will not have to see each other in pain, he asks her to retire to another room. He does not send her away or have her removed against her will but tries to per-

74. Mauch 1997, 67–74.

75. See Tac. *Ann.* 15.60–64; the quotation is from 63.

suade her by reasoning with her as an equal. The symmetry between Seneca and Paulina applies to their emotional struggles as well. Following Nero's orders, the people with her then recall her to life (with or without her knowledge, Tacitus hesitates)—the last few years of which she spends in faithful memory of Seneca.

Depending on one's tastes, one could be more or less moved by this scene, but there can be no question that it is as emblematic of philosophical aspirations as Seneca's imitation of Socrates. Of her own free will, Paulina resolves to die a heroic death. But in truth, is she free to choose? There is snag in the scenario, and there remains a darker strain beneath the surface. Dio Cassius (62.25) gives a quite different account, namely, that Seneca himself wanted Paulina to end her life together with his own and opened her veins. The two versions, taken together with Roman accounts about barbarian widows being cremated with their defunct husbands,[76] do remind us that even within the most positive accounts of women in Seneca's cultural context there still is a fine line between glory and oppression.

But if Seneca did not force the decision to die on Paulina, is it still not the case, as in Seneca's letter, that because she is unable to live without him, Paulina is too emotionally attached to Seneca? Such a mindset would be unacceptable to a Stoic. As Tacitus has it, however, her decision is not a sign of weakness but rather a truly heroic indication of virtue: she wants to commit suicide because she considers that ending her life is the morally right thing to do under the given circumstances. The later philosopher Montaigne (2.35) very perceptively argued that there is a symmetry of self-sacrifice in the rapport between the spouses: for Paulina's sake, Seneca gave up his desire to kill himself when he was suffering from ill health; Paulina now gives up her life because of Seneca. To us, Montaigne argues, it may seem that Paulina gets the raw end of the deal, but from a Stoic perspective, life and death are indifferents.[77] Not quite, one can reply to Montaigne: life still ranks among the preferred indifferents, death does not, and suicide requires justification. Who or what benefits from Paulina's sacrifice? And what exactly is honorable about her choice to die?

76. See pp. 385.29ff. of Bickel's edition of Seneca's *De Matrimonio*, but that passage from Jerome is not included in the Haase edition; see also Cic. *Tusc.* 5.78; Propertius 3.13.15–24; Valerius Maximus 2.6.14.

77. Harich 1994.

There are at least two aspects one can detect in the answer to this question. First, her suicide clearly has political implications insofar as it contributes to unmasking Nero as the brutal tyrant he in truth is. Nero himself is all too aware of this implication, and this is why he orders her revived. Second, Paulina's conduct is governed by the notion of an *univira,* a one-man woman: it suits a woman and is a testimony of her *pudicitia* to have been married only once and to have devoted herself completely to this one man in her life.[78] But here an undeniable lack of reciprocity creeps in again: we hear a great deal about widows devoting the remainder of their lives to their defunct husbands, but nothing about an analogous attitude on the part of Roman widowers. And the honor connected to being an *univira* is pushed too far, one could argue, in Seneca's praise of his aunt's marital fidelity (*Cons. Helv.* 19). In a shipwreck, we are told, she heroically risked her own life to bring the dead body of her husband to safety, so that it could be buried. Granted that burial is not a minor matter, is even a dead husband worth more than the life of his wife? A Stoic could conceivably have retorted to Seneca's praise of his aunt that she ought to have been more careful with her own life, given the network of social obligations in which she would still find herself enmeshed, even as a widow.

A woman like Paulina indeed has women role models for her virtuous action, which in some cases span several generations. But if, on the other side of the argument, Paulina's gesture is conditioned by the social code of a wife's honorable self-sacrifice, the distinction between freedom and social pressure again becomes blurred. It is indicative of this type of social pressure that, as discussed in the previous chapter, the philosopher Favorinus mentions breast-feeding to the mother of the young woman who has just given birth rather than to the young woman herself. He chooses to address the mother presumably not only because the young woman is asleep but also because her mother would be a very important influence on her behavior (Aulus Gellius 12.1). Similarly, Thrasea Paetus's spouse is emulating her mother's example when she offers to die with him. The very coinciding of philosophical norms with social exempla—that is, of people embodying the ideals—limits the possibilities of freedom for women, as it does for men, whose actions are also conditioned by what great men have done before them. But then too, freedom takes on a very particular configuration in the context of Stoic ethics and physics, in which the causal chain of divine reason and Providence are prominent. Taking all of the above into account, it should now come as

78. See also Sen. *De Matrimonio* 71–77 Haase.

less of a surprise that Dio Cassius could represent Seneca as having, at the very least, certain expectations about his wife's course of action.

Beyond the question of which of the two versions of Seneca's death is historically more accurate, Dio Cassius's or Tacitus's, apparently Tacitus could at least expect his audience to find his version plausible. And the affection is undeniably present in Tacitus's account of Seneca's final moments. Montaigne was not the only writer to have been influenced by Tacitus's rendering. Around 1405, when in *The City of Ladies* Christine de Pizan recounted Socrates' final moments, she too transformed the *Phaedo* account (2.21.1). Christine de Pizan turned Xanthippe into a wife fully devoted to her husband, deeply loving and venerating him and sympathizing with his philosophical ideals. Xanthippe is an active and spirited character, who, far from accepting Socrates' condemnation, tries to tear the cup of poison from his very lips. Socrates consoles her and takes great pains to explain to her why he consents to die. Though this irredeemably anachronistic and utopian account adds a distinctly un-Stoic flavor of pathos and emotional outburst to the scene, Xanthippe is a striking heroine in her own right, and the rapport between her and Socrates is center stage. In reading this passage, one has the curious impression that a Stoicized account was superimposed on Plato's version. That this turns out to be more than a hunch is confirmed by the sequel to this scene, its Roman twin (2.22.1): Christine's rendering of none other than Paulina and Seneca at the moment of the Roman philosopher's suicide. With the juxtaposition of these stories, Christine de Pizan, like Montaigne, appears to have understood Tacitus's depiction better than did many other interpreters. She realized the significance of Paulina's presence.

* * *

To understand how significant this Roman woman's presence at the scene of Seneca's suicide was and is, one has to grasp that later Stoics put a relationship such as the marital bond on an equal footing with friendship, and that they came to value highly the moral and philosophical potential of parenthood. Friendship and all types of relationships among rational human beings are so important for the Stoics because they consider reason to be intrinsically social. The relational mode of existence is not something humans merely share with animals, in terms of lower soul functions; it is something they have in common with the divine principle that structures all of reality. A Stoic gets to know herself properly and arrives at the proper relationship with herself only if, through the study of physics, she locates herself within this immanent ordered structure. The withdrawal into oneself, then, is a psychological process whereby one distances oneself from superficial, problematic, and conflictual forms of entanglement in everyday life only to arrive at the deepest engagement possible, not just with an anonymous humanity at large but with the people in one's immediate surroundings. At the start of this inquiry we found the mediating self talking to itself, but now we fully realize that it engages in such soliloquies not merely for the sake of itself but for the sake of community.

Bibliography

Abel, K. 1967. *Bauformen in Senecas Dialogen.* Bibliothek der klassischen Altertumswissenschaften, n.s., 2. Reihe, Bd. 18. Heidelberg: C. Winter.

Alesse, F. 2000. *La Stoa e la tradizione socratica.* Elenchos, vol. 30. Naples: Bibliopolis.

André, J.-M. 1966. *L'otium dans la vie morale et intellectuelle romaine des origines à l'époque augustéenne.* Paris: Presses Universitaires de France.

———. 1989. "Sénèque: 'De brevitate vitae,' 'De constantia sapientis,' 'De tranquillitate animi,' 'De otio.'" In *ANRW* 2.36.3.1724–78.

Annas, J. 1993. *The Morality of Happiness.* New York and Oxford: Oxford University Press.

———. 1995. "Reply to Cooper." *Philosophy and Phenomenological Research* 55.3:599–610.

———. 2002. "My Station and Its Duties: Ideals and the Social Embeddedness of Virtue." *Proceedings of the Aristotelian Society* 102.2:109–23.

———. Forthcoming. "Marcus Aurelius: Ethics and Its Background" [in Italian].

Armisen-Marchetti, M. 1996. "L'intériorisation de l'*otium* chez Sénèque." In *Les loisirs et l'héritage de la culture classique,* edited by J.-M. André, J. Dangel, and P. Demont, 411–24. Brussels: Revue d'Études Latines.

Asmis, E. 1989. "The Stoicism of Marcus Aurelius." In *ANRW* 2.36.3.2228–52.

———. 1996. "The Stoics on Women." In *Feminism and Ancient Philosophy,* edited by J. Ward, 68–92. New York and London: Routledge.

———. 2001. "Choice in Epictetus' Philosophy." In *Antiquity and Humanity: Essays on Ancient Religion and Philosophy Presented to Hans Dieter Betz,* edited by A. Yarbro Collins and M. M. Mitchell, 387–412. Tübingen: Mohr Siebeck.

Babut, D. 1963. "Les Stoïciens et l'amour." *Revue des études grecques* 76:55–63.

Baldry, H. C. 1959. "Zeno's Ideal State." *Journal of Hellenic Studies* 79:3–15.

Banateanu, A. 2001. *La théorie stoïcienne de l'amitié.* Vestigia 27, Pensée antique et médiévale. Fribourg Suisse: Éditions Universitaires Fribourg Suisse; Paris: Du Cerf.

Barnes, J. 1997. *Logic and the Imperial Stoa.* Leiden: Brill.

Benabou, M. 1987. "Pratique matrimoniale et représentation philosophique: Le crépuscule des stratégies." *Annales Économies Sociétés Civilisations* 6:1255–66.

Bodson, A. 1967. *La morale sociale des derniers Stoïciens: Sénèque, Épictète et Marc Aurèle.* Paris: Les Belles Lettres.

Bonhöffer, A. 1890. *Epictet und die Stoa.* Stuttgart: Enke.

———. 1894. *Die Ethik des Stoikers Epictet.* Stuttgart: Enke.

Bradley, K. 1986. "Wet-Nursing at Rome: A Study in Social Relations." In *The Family in Ancient Rome, New Perspectives,* edited by B. Rawson, 201–29. Ithaca: Cornell University Press.

———. 1991. *Discovering the Roman Family: Studies in Roman Social History.* New York and Oxford: Oxford University Press.

———. 1994. "The Nurse and the Child at Rome: Duty, Affect and Socialisation." *Thamyris* 1.2:137–56.

Brennan, T. 1996. "Epicurus on Sex, Marriage and Children." *Classical Philology* 91.4:346–52.

———. 1998. "The Old Stoic Theory of Emotions." In *The Emotions in Hellenistic Philosophy,* edited by J. Sihvola and T. Engberg-Pedersen, 21–70. Dordrecht and Boston: Kluwer.

———. 2000. "Reservation in Stoic Ethics." *Archiv für Geschichte der Philosophie* 82:149–77.

Broudéhoux, J.-P. 1970. *Mariage et famille chez Clément d'Alexandrie: Théologie Historique.* Paris: Beauchesne.

Brown, E. 2002. "Epicurus on the Value of Friendship (*Sententia Vaticana* 23)." *Classical Philology* 97:68–80.

———. Forthcoming. *Stoic Cosmopolitanism.*

Brown, P. 1987. "Late Antiquity." In *A History of Private Life, vol. 1,* From Pagan Rome to Byzantium, *edited by P. Veyne, 235–312. Cambridge: Harvard University Press.*

Brunschwig, J. 1986. "The Cradle Argument in Epicureanism and Stoicism." In *The Norms of Nature: Studies in Hellenistic Ethics,* edited by M. Schofield and G. Striker, 113–44. Cambridge: Cambridge University Press.

———. 1996. "La déconstruction du 'Connais-toi toi-même' dans l'*Alcibiade Majeur.*" *Recherches sur la philosophie et le langage* 18:61–84.

———. Forthcoming. "Sur deux notions de l'éthique stoïcienne: De la 'réserve' au 'renversement.'" In *Les Stoïciens,* edited by G. Romeyer-Dherbey and J.-B. Gourinat.

Brunt, P. A. 1974. "Marcus Aurelius in His *Meditations.*" *Journal of Roman Studies* 64:1–20.

———. 1975. "Stoicism and the Principate." *Proceedings of the British School at Rome* 43:7–35.

Citroni Marchetti, S. 1994. "Il *sapiens* in pericolo: Psicologia del rapporto con gli altri da Cicerone a Marco Aurelio." In *ANRW* 2.36.7.4546–98.

Claassen, J.-M. 1999. *Displaced Persons: The Literature of Exile from Cicero to Boethius.* Madison: University of Wisconsin Press.

Cooper, J. 1995. "Eudaimonism and the Appeal to Nature in the Morality of Happiness: Comments on Julia Annas, *The Morality of Happiness.*" *Philosophy and Phenomenological Research* 55.3:587–98.

———. 1996. "Eudaimonism, the Appeal to Nature, and 'Moral Duty' in Stoicism." In *Aristotle, Kant, and the Stoics,* edited by S. Engstrom and J. Whiting, 261–84. Cambridge and New York: Cambridge University Press.

Dean-Jones, L. 1994. *Women's Bodies in Classical Greek Science.* Oxford: Clarendon Press.

Deming, W. 1995. *Paul on Marriage and Celibacy: The Hellenistic Background of 1 Corinthians 7.* Society for New Testament Studies, Monograph Series, vol. 83. Cambridge: Cambridge University Press.

Dihle, A. 1982. *The Theory of Will in Classical Antiquity.* Berkeley and Los Angeles: University of California Press.

Dillon, J., and A. Terian. 1976–77. "Philo and the Stoic Doctrine of εὐπάθειαι: A Note on *Quaes. Gen.* 2.57." *Studia Philonica* 4:17–24.

Dixon, S. 1988. *The Roman Mother.* Norman: Oklahoma University Press.

Dobbin, R. F. 1991. "Προαίρεσις in Epictetus." *Ancient Philosophy* 11:111–35.

———. 1998. *Epictetus, Discourses, Book I: Translation, Introduction, Commentary.* Clarendon Later Ancient Philosophers. Oxford: Clarendon Press.

Dorandi, T. 1982. "Filodemo. *Gli Stoici* (*PHerc.* 155 E 339)." *Cronache ercolanesi* 12:91–133.

———. 1989. "Assiotea e Lastenia, due donne all'Accademia." *Atti e memorie dell' Accademia Toscana di Scienze e Lettere 'La Columbaria'* 40:53–66.

Döring, K. 1974. "Sokrates bei Epiktet." In *Studia Platonica: Festschrift für Hermann Gundert,* edited by K. Döring and W. Kullman, 195–226. Amsterdam: Grüner.

———. 1979. *Exemplum Socratis: Studien zur Sokratesnachwirkung in der kynisch-stoischen Popularphilosophie der frühen Kaiserzeit und im frühen Christentum.* Hermes Einzelschriften 42. Wiesbaden: F. Steiner.

Dugas, L. 1894. *L'amitié antique d'après les moeurs populaires et les théories des philosophes.* Paris: F. Alcan.

Dyck, A. R. 1996. *A Commentary on Cicero, "De Officiis."* Ann Arbor: University of Michigan Press.

Dzielska, M. 2001. "Among the 'Divine Women' of Late Antiquity." In *Studia Archaeologica: Liber Amicorum . . . Ostrowski,* 101–13. Cracow: Universitas Jagellonica.

Edwards, C. 1997. "Self-Scrutiny and Self-Transformation in Seneca's Letters." *Greece and Rome* 44.1:23–38.

Elorduy, E. 1936. *Die Sozialphilosophie der Stoa.* Philologus, suppl. vol. 28.3. Leipzig: Dieterich'sche.

Engberg-Pedersen, T. 1986. "Discovering the Good: *Oikeiōsis* and *Kathēkonta* in Stoic Ethics." In *The Norms of Nature: Studies in Hellenistic Ethics,* edited by M. Schofield and G. Striker, 145–83. Cambridge: Cambridge University Press.

———. 1990. *The Stoic Theory of Oikeiōsis: Moral Development and Social Interaction in Early Stoic Philosophy.* Aarhus: Aarhus University Press.

———. 1998. "Marcus Aurelius on Emotions." In *The Emotions in Hellenistic Philosophy,* edited by J. Sihvola and T. Engberg-Pedersen, 305–37. Dordrecht and Boston: Kluwer.

Engel, D. 2000. "The Gender Egalitarianism of Musonius Rufus." *Ancient Philosophy* 20:377–91.

Erskine, A. 1997. "Cicero and the Expression of Grief." In *The Passions in Roman Thought and Literature,* edited by S. Morton Braund and C. Gill, 36–47. Cambridge: Cambridge University Press.

Eyben, E. 1978. "De latere Stoa over het huwelijk." *Hermeneus* 50:15–32, 71–94, 337–59.

Farquharson, A. S. L. 1968. *The "Meditations" of the Emperor Marcus Antoninus.* Oxford: Clarendon Press.

———. 1989. *The "Meditations" of Marcus Aurelius Antoninus.* Oxford: Oxford University Press.

Favez, C. 1933. "Un féministe romain: Musonius Rufus." *Bulletin de la Société des Études de Lettres Lausanne* 20:1–8.

———. 1938. "Les opinions de Sénèque sur la femme." *Revue des études latines* 16:335–45.

Festugière, A. J. 1978. *Deux prédicateurs de l'antiquité: Télès et Musonius.* Bibliothèque des textes philosophiques. Paris: Vrin.

Fildes, V. A. 1986. *Breasts, Bottles and Babies: A History of Infant Feeding.* Edinburgh: Edinburgh University Press.

Fittschen, K. 1982. *Die Bildnistypen der Faustina Minor und die Fecunditas Augustae.* Abhandlungen der Akademie der Wissenschaften in Göttingen, philologisch-historische Klasse, 3rd ser., vol. 126. Göttingen: Vandenhoeck and Ruprecht.

Föllinger, S. 1996. *Differenz und Gleichheit: Das Geschlechterverhältnis in der Sicht griechischer Philosophen des 4. bis 1. Jahrhunderts v. Chr.* Hermes Einzelschriften, vol. 74. Stuttgart: Steiner.

Foucault, M. 1988a. *The History of Sexuality*. Vol. 3, *The Care of the Self*. Translated by R. Hurley. New York: Vintage.

———. 1988b. *Technologies of the Self*. Amherst: University of Massachusetts Press.

———. 2001. *L'herméneutique du sujet: Cours au Collège de France, 1981–1982*. Edited by F. Gros. Paris: Gallimard/Le Seuil.

Fraisse, J.-C. 1974. *Philia: La notion d'amitié dans la philosophie antique*. Paris: Vrin.

Frede, M. 1999. "On the Stoic Conception of the Good." In *Topics in Stoic Philosophy*, edited by K. Ierodiakonou, 71–94. Oxford: Clarendon Press.

Fuhrer, T., and K. Howald. 2000. "Wer nützt wem im stoischen Gemeinwesen? Zu Cicero *De finibus* 3.69." *Museum Helveticum* 57:81–87.

Gaiser, K. 1974. *Für und wider die Ehe*. Vol. 1, *Dialog mit der Antike*. Munich: Heimeran.

Gardner, C. 2000. "The Remnants of the Family: The Role of Women and Eugenics in *Republic* 5." *History of Philosophy Quarterly* 17.3:217–35.

Garnsey, P. 1991. "Child Rearing in Ancient Italy." In *The Family in Italy from Antiquity to the Present*, edited by D. I. Kertzer and R. P. Saller, 48–65. New Haven: Yale University Press.

Gersh, S. 1986. *Middle Platonism and Neoplatonism, the Latin Tradition*. 2 vols. Notre Dame: University of Notre Dame Press.

Geytenbeek, A. C. van. 1949. *Musonius Rufus en de Griekse diatribe*. Amsterdam: H. J. Paris.

———. 1963. *Musonius Rufus and Greek Diatribe*. Assen: Van Gorcum.

Giannantoni, G. 1990. *Socratis et Socraticorum Reliquiae*. 4 vols. Elenchos, vol. 18. Naples: Bibliopolis.

Gigon, O. 1947. *Sokrates: Sein Bild in Dichtung und Geschichte*. Bern: A. Francke.

———. 1956. *Kommentar zum zweiten Buch von Xenophons "Memorabilien."* Schweizerische Beiträge zur Altertumswissenschaft, vol. 7. Basel: F. Reinhardt.

Gill, C. 1983. "Did Chrysippus Understand Medea?" *Phronesis* 28:136–49.

———. 1988. "Personhood and Personality: The Four-*Personae* Theory in Cicero *De Officiis* I." *Oxford Studies in Ancient Philosophy* 6:169–99.

———. 1991. "Is There a Concept of Person in Greek Philosophy?" In *Companion to Ancient Thought*, vol. 2, *Psychology*, edited by S. Everson, 166–93. Cambridge: Cambridge University Press.

———. 1994. "Peace of Mind and Being Yourself: Panaetius to Plutarch." In *ANRW* 2.36.7.4599–640.

———. 1996. *Personality in Greek Epic, Tragedy, and Philosophy: The Self in Dialogue*. Oxford: Clarendon Press.

———. 2000. "Stoic Writers of the Imperial Era." In *The Cambridge History of Greek and Roman Political Thought*, edited by C. Rowe and M. Schofield, 579–611. Cambridge: Cambridge University Press.

———. Forthcoming. *The Structured Self in Hellenistic and Roman Thought*.

Golden, M. 1988. "Did the Ancients Care When Their Children Died?" *Greece and Rome* 35.2:152–63.

Görler, W. 1984. "Zum *Virtus*-Fragment des Lucilius (1326–1338 Marx) und zur Geschichte der stoischen Güterlehre." *Hermes* 112:445–68.

Gourevitch, D. 1984. *Le mal d'être femme: La femme et la médecine dans la Rome antique.* Paris: Les Belles Lettres.

Gourinat, J.-B. 2003. "Le Socrate d'Épictète." *Philosophie antique* 1:137–65.

Graver, M. 1999. "Philo of Alexandria and the Origins of the Stoic Προπάθειαι." *Phronesis* 44.4:300–325.

———. 2002. *Cicero on the Emotions: "Tusculan Disputations" 3 and 4.* Chicago: University of Chicago Press.

Griffin, M. 1976. *Seneca: A Philosopher in Politics.* Oxford: Clarendon Press.

———. 1986. "Philosophy, Cato, and Roman Suicide." *Greece and Rome* 33.1–2:64–77, 192–202.

———. 1989. "Philosophy, Politics, and Politicians at Rome." In *Philosophia Togata: Essays on Philosophy and Roman Society,* edited by J. Barnes and M. Griffin, 1–37. Oxford: Clarendon Press.

Grilli, A. 1953. *Il problema della vita contemplativa nel mondo greco-romano.* Milan and Rome: Bocca.

Grimal, P. 1979. *Sénèque, ou la conscience de l'Empire.* Paris: Les Belles Lettres.

———. 1989. "Sénèque et le Stoïcisme romain." In *ANRW* 2.36.3.1962–92.

Grisé, Y. 1982. *Le suicide dans la Rome antique.* Montreal: Bellarmin; Paris: Les Belles Lettres.

Grollios, C. 1956. *Seneca's "Ad Marciam": Tradition and Originality.* Athens: G. S. Christou.

Habinek, T. 1982. "Seneca's Circles: *Ep.* 12.6–9." *Classical Antiquity* 1:66–69.

Hadot, I. 1969. *Seneca und die griechisch-römische Tradition der Seelenleitung.* Quellen und Studien zur Geschichte der Philosophie, vol. 13. Berlin: de Gruyter.

———. 1996. *Simplicius, commentaire sur le "Manuel" d'Épictète: Introduction et édition du texte grec.* Philosophia Antiqua 66. Leiden: Brill, 1996.

Hadot, P. 1989. *Plotin, ou la simplicité du regard.* Paris: Études Augustiniennes.

———. 1990. *Plotin, "Traité" 50 (III, 5).* In *Les écrits de Plotin,* edited by P. Hadot. Paris: du Cerf.

———. 1993a. "Une clé des *Pensées* de Marc Aurèle: Les trois *topoi* philosophiques selon Épictète." In *Exercices spirituels et philosophie antique,* 135–72. Paris: Études Augustiniennes.

———. 1993b. "Exercices spirituels." In *Exercices spirituels et philosophie antique,* 13–58. Paris: Études Augustiniennes.

———. 1993c. "Socrate." In *Exercices spirituels et philosophie antique,* 75–116. Paris: Études Augustiniennes.

———. 1998. *The Inner Citadel: The Meditations of Marcus Aurelius.* Translated by M. Chase. Cambridge: Harvard University Press.

Hahm, D. 1999. "Plato, Carneades, and Cicero's Philus (Cicero, *Rep.* 3.8–31)." *Classical Quarterly* 49.1:167–83.

Halliwell, S. 1990. "Traditional Greek Conceptions of Character." In *Characterization and Individuality in Greek Literature,* edited by C. Pelling, 32–59. Oxford: Clarendon Press.

Harich, H. 1994. "Zu Seneca, *Ep.* 104, Tacitus, *Ann.* XV, 60, 2–64 und Montaigne, *Essay* II, 35." *Latomus* 53.2:354–65.

Heilmann, W. 1982. *Ethische Reflexion und römische Lebenswirklichkeit in Cicero's Schrift "De Officiis."* Palingenesia, vol. 17. Wiesbaden: F. Steiner.

Hemelrijk, E. 1999. *Matrona Docta: Educated Women in the Roman Elite from Cornelia to Julia Donna.* London and New York: Routledge.

Hendrickx, B. 1974. "Once Again: Marcus Aurelius, Emperor and Philosopher." *Historia* 23:254–56.

Holford-Strevens, L. 1988. *Aulus Gellius.* Chapel Hill: University of North Carolina Press.

———. 1997. "Favorinus: The Man of Paradoxes." In *Philosophia Togata II: Plato and Aristotle at Rome,* edited by J. Barnes and M. Griffin, 188–217. Oxford: Clarendon Press.

Horst-Theodor, J. 1968. *Trauer und Trost: Eine quellen-und strukturanalytische Untersuchung der philosophischen Trostschriften über den Tod.* Studia et Testimonia Antiqua, vol. 5. Munich: W. Fink.

Hoven, R. 1971. *Stoïcisme et Stoïciens face au problème de l'au-delà.* Paris: Les Belles Lettres.

Inwood, B. 1983. "Comments on Professor Görgemanns' Paper: The Two Forms of *Oikeiōsis* in Arius and the Stoa." In *On Stoic and Peripatetic Ethics: The Work of Arius Didymus,* edited by W. W. Fortenbaugh, 190–201. New Brunswick and London: Transaction Books.

———. 1984. "Hierocles: Theory and Argument in the Second Century AD." *Oxford Studies in Ancient Philosophy* 2:151–83.

———. 1985. *Ethics and Human Action in Early Stoicism.* Oxford: Clarendon Press.

———. 1993. "Seneca and Psychological Dualism." In *Passions and Perceptions: Studies in Hellenistic Philosophy of Mind, Proceedings of the Fifth Symposium Hellenisticum,* edited by J. Brunschwig and M. Nussbaum, 150–83. Cambridge: Cambridge University Press.

———. 1996. "L'*Oikeiōsis* sociale chez Épictète." In *Polyhistor: Studies in the History and Historiography of Ancient Philosophy,* edited by K. A. Algra, P. W. van der Horst and D. T. Runia, 243–64. Leiden: Brill.

———. 1997. "Why Do Fools Fall In Love?" In *Aristotle and After,* edited by R. Sorabji, 55–69. London: Institute of Classical Studies.

———. 2000. "The Will in Seneca the Younger." *Classical Philology* 95:44–60.

———. 2002. "God and Human Knowledge in Seneca's *Natural Questions.*" In *Traditions of Theology: Studies in Hellenistic Theology, Its Background and Aftermath,* edited by A. Laks and D. Frede, 119–57. Leiden: Brill.

———, ed. 2003. *The Cambridge Companion to the Stoics.* Cambridge: Cambridge University Press.

Inwood, B., and P. Donini. 1999. "Stoic Ethics." In *The Cambridge History of Hellenistic Philosophy,* edited by K. A. Algra, J. Barnes, J. Mansfeld, and M. Schofield, 675–738. Cambridge: Cambridge University Press.

Irwin, T. H. 1998. "Stoic Inhumanity." In *The Emotions in Hellenistic Philosophy,* edited by J. Sihvola and T. Engberg-Pedersen, 219–41. Dordrecht and Boston: Kluwer

Isnardi Parente, M. 1989. "Ierocle stoico: *Oikeiosis* e doveri sociali." In *ANRW* 2.36.3.2201–26.

Jagu, A. 1946. *Épictète et Platon: Essai sur les relations du Stoïcisme et du Platonisme à propos de la morale des Entretiens.* Paris: J. Vrin.

Kahn, C. 1988. "Discovering the Will: From Aristotle to Augustine." In *The Question of Eclecticism,* edited by J. Dillon and A. A. Long, 234–59. Berkeley and Los Angeles: University of California Press.

Kamtekar, R. 1998. "ΑΙΔΩΣ in Epictetus." *Classical Philology* 93:136–60.

Kassel, R. 1958. *Untersuchungen zur griechischen und römischen Konsolationsliteratur.* Zetemata, vol. 18. Munich: Beck.

Lana, I. 1996. "*Pingue otium et arbitrium sui temporis* . . . (Sénèque, *epist.* LXXIII, 10)." In *Les Loisirs et l'héritage de la culture classique,* edited by J. M. André, J. Dangel, and P. Demont, 425–33. Brussels: Revue d'Études Latines.

Laurand, V. 2003. "Souci de soi et mariage chez Musonius Rufus: Perspectives politiques de la κρᾶσις stoïcienne." In *Foucault et la philosophie antique,* edited by F. Gros and C. Lévy, 85–116. Paris: Kimé.

Lee, Chang-Uh. 2002. *Oikeiōsis: Stoische Ethik in naturphilosophischer Perspektive.* Freiburg and Munich: Karl Alber.

Lesky, A. 1968. "Homeros." In *RE* Supplementband 11, 687–846.

Lesky, E. 1951. *Die Zeugungs-und Vererbungslehren der Antike und ihr Nachwirken.* Akademie der Wissenschaften und der Literatur, Abhandlungen der geistes- und sozialwissenschaftlichen Klasse, Jahrgang 1950, no. 19. Wiesbaden: F. Steiner.

Lesses, G. 1993. "Austere Friends: The Stoics and Friendship." *Apeiron* 26:57–75.

Levick, B. 2002. "Women, Power, and Philosophy at Rome and Beyond." In *Philosophy and Power in the Graeco-Roman World,* edited by G. Clark and T. Rajak, 134–55. Oxford and New York: Oxford University Press.

Lévy, C. 1990. "Platon, Arcésilas, Carnéade: Réponse à J. Annas." *Revue de métaphysique et de morale* 95:293–306.

———. 2000. "Cicéron critique de l'éloquence stoïcienne." In *Papers on Rhetoric III,* edited by L. Montefusco Calboli, 127–44. Bologna: Clueb.

———. 2002. "À propos de *The Cambridge History of Hellenistic Philosophy.*" *Phronesis* 47.3:246–86.

———. 2003. "Sénèque et la circularité du temps." In *L'ancienneté chez les Anciens,* vol. 2, edited by B. Bakhouche, 491–509. Montpellier: Université Montpellier III.

Long, A. A. 1967. "Carneades and the Stoic *Telos.*" *Phronesis* 18:59–90.

———. 1983. "Greek Ethics after MacIntyre and the Stoic Community of Reason." *Ancient Philosophy* 3:184–97.

———. 1991. "Representation and the Self in Stoicism." In *Companions to Ancient Thought,* vol. 2, *Psychology,* edited by S. Everson et al., 102–20. Cambridge: Cambridge University Press.

———. 1995. "Cicero's Politics in *De Officiis.*" In *Justice and Generosity: Studies in Hellenistic Social and Political Philosophy, Proceedings of the Sixth Symposium Hellenisticum,* edited by A. Laks and M. Schofield, 213–40. Cambridge: Cambridge University Press.

———. 2000. "Epictetus as Socratic Mentor." *Proceedings of the Cambridge Philological Society* 46:79–98.

———. 2002. *Epictetus: A Stoic and Socratic Guide to Life.* Oxford: Clarendon Press.

Long, A. A., and D. N. Sedley. 1987. *The Hellenistic Philosophers.* 2 vols. Cambridge: Cambridge University Press.

Loraux, N. 1998. *Mothers in Mourning.* Translated by C. Pache. Myth and Poetics. Ithaca: Cornell University Press.

MacIntyre, A. 1977. "Epistemological Crises, Dramatic Narrative and the Philosophy of Science." *The Monist* 60.4:453–71.

Malherbe, A. J. 1977. *The Cynic Epistles: A Study Edition.* Society of Biblical Literature, Sources for Biblical Study, vol. 12. Missoula, MT: Scholars Press.

Manning, C. E. 1973. "Seneca and the Stoics on the Equality of the Sexes." *Mnemosyne* 26:170–77.

———. 1974. "The Consolatory Tradition and Seneca's Attitude to the Emotions." *Greece and Rome* 21:71–81.

———. 1981. *On Seneca's "Ad Marciam."* Mnemosyne, vol. 69. Leiden: Brill.

Martinazzoli, F. 1951. *La "successio" di Marco Aurelio: Struttura e spirito del primo libro dei "Pensieri."* ΜΟΥΣΙΚΑΙ ΔΙΑΛΕΚΤΙΚΟΙ. Bari: Adriatica Editrice.

Mauch, M. 1997. *Senecas Frauenbild in den philosophischen Schriften.* Studien zur klassischen Philologie, vol. 106. Frankfurt: Peter Lang.

Maurach, G. 1996. *Seneca, Leben und Werk.* Darmstadt: Wissenschaftliche Buchgesellschaft.

Mingay, J. 1972. "*Coniunctio inter homines hominum:* Cicero, *de Finibus* V 65 and Related Passages." In *Islamic Philosophy and the Classical Tradition,* edited by S. M. Stern, A. Hourani, and V. Brown, 261–75. Oxford: Cassirer.

Morford, M. 2002. *The Roman Philosophers from the Time of Cato the Censor to the Death of Marcus Aurelius.* London and New York: Routledge.

Natali, C. 1995. "*Oikonomia* in Hellenistic Political Thought." In *Justice and Generosity: Studies in Hellenistic Social and Political Philosophy, Proceedings of the Sixth Symposium Hellenisticum,* edited by A. Laks and M. Schofield, 95–128. Cambridge: Cambridge University Press.

Newman, R. 1989. "*Cotidie Meditare:* Theory and Practice of the *Meditatio* in Imperial Stoicism." In *ANRW* 2.36.3.1473–517.

Noyen, P. 1955. "Marcus Aurelius, the Greatest Practician of Stoicism." *L'Antiquité Classique* 24:372–83.

Nussbaum, M. 1986. *The Fragility of Goodness.* Cambridge: Cambridge University Press.

———. 1994. *The Therapy of Desire: Theory and Practice in Hellenistic Ethics.* Princeton: Princeton University Press.

———. 2002. "The Incomplete Feminism of Musonius Rufus, Platonist, Stoic, and Roman." In *The Sleep of Reason: Erotic Experience and Sexual Ethics in Ancient Greece and Rome,* edited by M. Nussbaum and J. Sihvola, 283–326. Chicago: University of Chicago Press.

Obbink, D. 1999. "The Stoic Sage in the Cosmic City." In *Topics in Stoic Philosophy,* edited by K. Ierodiakonou, 178–95. Oxford: Clarendon Press.

Obbink, D., and P. Vander Waerdt. 1991. "Diogenes of Babylon: The Stoic Sage in the City of Fools." *Greek, Roman and Byzantine Studies* 32:355–96.

O'Connor, D. K. 1999. "The Ambitions of Aristotle's Audience and the Activist Ideal of Happiness." In *Action and Contemplation: Studies in the Moral and Political Thought of Aristotle,* edited by R. C. Bartlett and S. D. Collins, 107–29. Albany: State University of New York Press.

Olson, H. 2000. "Socrates Talks to Himself in Plato's *Hippias Major.*" *Ancient Philosophy* 20:265–87.

O'Meara, D. 2003. *Platonopolis: Platonic Political Philosophy in Late Antiquity.* Oxford: Clarendon Press.

Opsomer, J. 1998. *In Search of the Truth: Academic Tendencies in Middle Platonism.* Verhandelingen van de Koninklijke Academie voor Wetenschappen, Letteren en Schone Kunsten van België, klasse der letteren, vol. 60.163. Brussels.

Pembroke, S. G. 1971. "*Oikeiōsis.*" In *Problems in Stoicism,* edited by A. A. Long, 114–49. London: University of London, Athlone Press.

Pépin, J. 1971. *Idées grecques sur l'homme et sur dieu.* Collection d'études anciennes. Paris: Les Belles Lettres.

Philippson, R. 1932. "Das 'erste Naturgemässe.'" *Philologus* 87:445–66.

Plessner, M. 1928. *Der* ΟΙΚΟΝΟΜΙΚΟΣ *des Neupythagoreers "Bryson" und sein Einfluss auf die islamische Wissenschaft.* Orient und Antike, vol. 5. Heidelberg: Carl Winter.

Pohlenz, M. 1948. *Die Stoa: Geschichte einer geistigen Bewegung.* Vol. 1. Göttingen: Vandenhoeck and Ruprecht.

Praechter, K. 1901. *Hierokles der Stoiker.* Leipzig: Dieterich'sche.

Rabbow, P. 1954. *Seelenführung: Methodik der Exerzitien in der Antike.* Munich: Kösel.

Rappe, S. 1995. "Socrates and Self-Knowledge." *Apeiron* 28:1–24.

Rawson, B. 2003. *Children and Childhood in Roman Italy.* Oxford and New York: Oxford University Press.

Reckford, K. J. 1998. "Reading the Sick Body: Decomposition and Morality in Persius' Third Satire." *Arethusa* 31.3:337–54.

Reydams-Schils, G. 1998. "Roman and Stoic: The Self as a Mediator." *Dionysius* 16:35–61.

———. 1999. *Demiurge and Providence: Stoic and Platonist Readings of Plato's "Timaeus."* Monothéismes et philosophie. Turnhout, Belgium: Brepols.

———. 2001. *An Anthology of Snakebites: On Women, Love, and Philosophy.* New York: Sevenbridges Press.

———. 2002. "Human Bonding and *Oikeiōsis* in Roman Stoicism." *Oxford Studies in Ancient Philosophy* 22.2:221–51.

———. 2003. "La vieillesse et les rapports humains dans le Stoïcisme romain." In *L'ancienneté chez les Anciens,* vol. 2, edited by B. Bakhouche, 481–89. Montpellier: Université Montpellier III.

———. Forthcoming-a. "Musonius Rufus, Porphyry, and Christians in Counterpoint on Marriage and the Good."

———. Forthcoming-b. "The Roman Stoics on Divine Thinking and Human Knowledge."

———. Forthcoming-c. "Virtue, Marriage, and Parenthood in Simplicius' *Commentary on Epictetus' 'Encheiridion.'*"

Richter, G. M. A. 1965. *The Portraits of the Greeks.* Vol. 1. London: Phaidon Press.

Rist, J. 1980. *Stoic Philosophy.* Cambridge: Cambridge University Press.

———. 1989. "Seneca and Stoic Orthodoxy." In *ANRW* 2.36.3.1993–2012.

Rutherford, R. B. 1989. *The "Meditations" of Marcus Aurelius: A Study.* Oxford: Clarendon Press.

Saller, R. P. 1994. *Patriarchy, Property and Death in the Roman Family.* Cambridge: Cambridge University Press.

Schniewind, A. 2003. *L'éthique du sage chez Plotin: Le paradigme du spoudaios.* Histoire des doctrines de l'antiquité classique. Paris: Vrin.

Schofield, M. 1991. *The Stoic Idea of the City.* Cambridge: Cambridge University Press.

———. 1995. "Two Stoic Approaches to Justice." In *Justice and Generosity: Studies in Hellenistic Social and Political Philosophy, Proceedings of the Sixth Symposium Hellenisticum,* edited by A. Laks and M. Schofield, 191–212. Cambridge: Cambridge University Press.

———. 1999. "Social and Political Thought." In *The Cambridge History of Hellenistic Philosophy,* edited by K. A. Algra, J. Barnes, J. Mansfeld, and M. Schofield, 739–70. Cambridge: Cambridge University Press.

———. 2000. "Plato and Practical Politics." In *The Cambridge History of Greek and Roman Political Thought,* edited by C. Rowe and M. Schofield, 293–302. Cambridge: Cambridge University Press.

Severy, B. 2000. "Family and State in the Early Imperial Monarchy: The *Senatus Consultum de Pisone Patre, Tabula Siarensis,* and *Tabula Hebana.*" *Classical Philology* 95:318–37.

Shaw, B. 2001. "Raising and Killing Children: Two Roman Myths." *Mnemosyne* 4.54.1:32–77.

Shelton, J.-A. 1995. "Persuasion and Paradigm in Seneca's *Consolatio Ad Marciam* 1–6." *Classica et Medievalia* 46:156–88.

Sorabji, R. 1999. "Soul and Self in Ancient Philosophy." In *From Soul to Self,* edited by M. J. C. Crabbe, 8–32. London and New York: Routledge.

———. 2000a. *Emotion and Peace of Mind: From Stoic Agitation to Christian Temptation.* Oxford: Oxford University Press.

———. 2000b. "Is the True Self an Individual in the Platonist Tradition?" In *Le commentaire entre tradition et innovation,* edited by M.-O. Goulet-Cazé, 293–99. Paris: Vrin.

Stanton, G. R. 1969. "Marcus Aurelius, Emperor and Philosopher." *Historia* 18:570–87.

Stelzenberger, J. 1933. *Die Beziehungen der frühchristlichen Sittenlehre zur Ethik der Stoa: Eine moralgeschichtliche Studie.* Munich: Hueber.

Stephens, W. 1996. "Epictetus on How the Stoic Sage Loves." *Oxford Studies in Ancient Philosophy* 14:193–210.

Stowell, M. C. 1999. "Stoic Therapy of Grief: A Prolegomenon to Seneca's *Ad Marciam, De Consolatione.*" PhD diss., Cornell University.

Striker, G. 1986. "Antipater, or the Art of Living." In *The Norms of Nature: Studies in Hellenistic Ethics,* edited by M. Schofield and G. Striker, 185–204. Cambridge: Cambridge University Press.

Tarán, L. 1981. *Speusippus of Athens: A Critical Study with a Collection of the Related Texts and Commentary.* Philosophia Antiqua, vol. 39. Leiden: Brill.

Taylor, C. 1989. *Sources of the Self: The Making of the Modern Identity.* Cambridge: Harvard University Press.

Thesleff, H. 1961. *An Introduction to the Pythagorean Writings of the Hellenistic Period.* Acta Academiae Aboensis, Humaniora, vol. 24.3. Abo: Abo Akademi.

———. 1965. *The Pythagorean Texts of the Hellenistic Period.* Acta Academiae Aboensis, Humaniora, vol. 30.1. Abo: Abo Akademi.

Torre, C. 2000. *Il matrimonio del sapiens, ricerche sul "De Matrimonio" di Seneca.* Genoa: Università di Genova.

Treggiari, S. 1991. *Roman Marriage: Iusti Coniuges from the Time of Cicero to the Time of Ulpian.* Oxford: Clarendon Press.

Valente, P. M. 1956. *L'éthique stoïcienne chez Cicéron.* Paris: Librairie Saint-Paul.

Vander Waerdt, P. 1991. "Politics and Philosophy in Stoicism." *Oxford Studies in Ancient Philosophy* 9:185–211.

———, ed. 1994. *The Socratic Movement.* Ithaca: Cornell University Press.

Veyne, P. 1987. "The Roman Empire." In *A History of Private Life,* vol. 1, *From Pagan Rome to Byzantium,* edited by P. Veyne, 5–234. Cambridge: Harvard University Press.

———. 2003. *Seneca: The Life of a Stoic.* Translated by D. Sullivan. New York and London: Routledge.

Voelke, A.-J. 1961. *Les Rapports avec autrui dans la philosophie grecque d'Aristote à Panétius.* Paris: Vrin.

———. 1973. *L'idée de volonté dans le Stoïcisme.* Bibliothèque de philosophie contemporaine. Paris: Presses Universitaires de France.

Walcot, P. 1987. "Plato's Mother and Other Terrible Women." *Greece and Rome* 34.1:12–31.

White, N. P. 1979. "The Basis of Stoic Ethics." *Harvard Studies in Classical Philology* 83:143–78.

———. 2002. *Individual and Conflict in Greek Ethics.* Oxford: Oxford University Press.

White, S. 1995. "Cicero and the Therapists." In *Cicero the Philosopher: Twelve Papers,* edited by J. G. F. Powell, 219–46. Oxford: Oxford University Press.

Whitlock Blundell, M. 1990. "Parental Nature and Stoic Οἰκείωσις." *Ancient Philosophy* 10:221–42.

Wicker, K. O. 1987. *Porphyry the Philosopher to Marcella.* Society of Biblical Literature, Texts and Translations, vol. 28, Graeco-Roman Religion, vol. 10. Atlanta: Scholars Press.

Wilhelm, F. 1915. "Die *Oeconomica* der Neupythagoreer Bryson, Kallikratidas, Periktione, Phintys." *Rheinisches Museum* 70:161–223.

Williams, B. 1993. *Shame and Necessity.* Berkeley and Los Angeles: University of California Press.

Wilson, M. 1997. "The Subjugation of Grief in Seneca's *Epistles.*" In *The Passions in Roman Thought and Literature,* edited by S. Morton Braund and C. Gill, 48–67. Cambridge: Cambridge University Press.

Wöhrle, G. 2002. "Wenn Frauen Platons *Staat* lesen; oder: Epiktet und Musonius konstruieren Geschlechterrollen." *Würzburger Jahrbücher für die Altertumswissenschaft,* n.s., 26:135–43.

Zanker, P. 1995. *The Mask of Socrates: The Image of the Intellectual in Antiquity.* Translated by A. Shapiro. Sather Classical Lectures, vol. 59. Berkeley and Los Angeles: University of California Press.

Zetzel, J. E. G. 1996. "Natural Law and Poetic Justice: A Carneadean Debate in Cicero and Virgil." *Classical Philology* 91.4:297–319.

Index of Cited Passages

General Index

Made in the USA
Coppell, TX
12 July 2021